THE *Age* OF THE *Divine Mother*

THE GOLDEN WORD OF MARY SERIES

Mary's Message for a New Day

Mary's Message of Divine Love

The Age of the Divine Mother

THE *Age* OF THE *Divine Mother*

Elizabeth Clare Prophet

SUMMIT UNIVERSITY 🟡 PRESS®
Gardiner, Montana

*To all devotees
of the blessed Mother
and her son
Jesus Christ*

THE AGE OF THE DIVINE MOTHER
by Elizabeth Clare Prophet
Copyright © 2006 by Summit Publications, Inc.
All rights reserved

No part of this book may be reproduced, translated, or electronically stored, posted or transmitted, or used in any format or medium whatsoever without prior written permission, except by a reviewer who may quote brief passages in a review.

For information, contact Summit University Press,
PO Box 5000, Gardiner, MT 59030-5000, USA
Tel: 800-245-5445 or 406-848-9500.
Web site: www.summituniversitypress.com
E-mail: info@summituniversitypress.com

Library of Congress Control Number: 2006926656
ISBN: 0-922729-93-X

SUMMIT UNIVERSITY ॐ PRESS®

The Summit Lighthouse, Keepers of the Flame and *Pearls of Wisdom* are trademarks registered in the U.S. Patent and Trademark Office and in other countries. All rights to their use are reserved.

Cover design by George Foster www.fostercovers.com

Cover image: *Madonna of the Chair* by Raphael, Galleria Palatina, Palazzo Pitti, Florence, Italy, Alinari / Art Resource, NY (depicting Mary, Jesus and John the Baptist)

Printed in the United States of America.

10   09   08   07   06   5   4   3   2   1

Contents

Introduction vii

A Word from the Author xi

PART ONE: My Search for Mary 1

   Chapter 1 – The Real Mary 5

PART TWO: A Mother's Gift to Her Children 21

   Chapter 2 – As Above, so Below 25

   Chapter 3 – A New-Age Rosary 37

PART THREE: A Trilogy of the Mother 45

   Chapter 4 – The Mother Flame and the Incarnation of God I 49

   Chapter 5 – The Science of the Immaculate Concept II 57

   Chapter 6 – The Vision of a New Age III 65

PART FOUR: There Is Still Time for Prophecies to Be Changed 71

   Chapter 7 – A Mother's Warning to Her Children 75

   Chapter 8 – Man, Woman, Become Who You Really Are! 109

PART FIVE: Devotions to the Mother   129

   Chapter 9 – The Fourteenth Rosary   133

   Chapter 10 – The Outline of The Fourteenth Rosary   141

   Chapter 11 – The Mystery of Surrender   153

   Chapter 12 – A Child's Rosary to Mother Mary   173

PART SIX: Messages from the Divine Mother   189

   Chapter 13 – The Healing Science of the Mother   193

   Chapter 14 – The Hallowed Circle   207

   Chapter 15 – The Mother Ray as the Instrument of the Soul's Transition into the New Day   217

   Chapter 16 – I Would Free You   225

   Chapter 17 – The Betrayal and the Victory   231

   Chapter 18 – Keeping the Vigil   247

   Chapter 19 – The Continuity of Being: "Come and Pray with Me"   265

   Chapter 20 - The Vow to Heal a Planet: Study the Healing Arts at Fátima   277

   Chapter 21 – I Stand By You: Champion the Cause of the Child!   283

   Chapter 22 – The Gift of a Mother's Heart: The Mystery of the Fifteenth Rosary   295

   Chapter 23 – The Hour of the Mother's Crucifixion   305

Notes   322

Introduction

We present this work in a period when many, including Protestants who have not known Mary, are awakening to her true relevance and to the Divine Feminine and the Mother flame. Mary's true status has been overshadowed for two thousand years by her Son, Jesus, and the masculine hierarchy of the Church. Now as we enter the age of Aquarius, we come to see her as the truly divine Being that she is.

Elizabeth Clare Prophet is a great devotee of the Mother flame. Having come from a religious background that was not Catholic, she was still able to put aside her preconceived indoctrination and give her life to Mother Mary in service to the world.

In chapter 1, you will enjoy reading about her search for Mary, which may parallel your own, even though you also may not realize that you are looking for the Mother and need to be liberated from some preconceived ideas that you may have held.

Let us accept Mary as our teacher, for she has walked where we walk today. She bore a son and lost him, even as so many mothers of today are grieving for their sons lost in battle. And yet, she was triumphant! This book gives hope to mothers-to-be and to all mothers of the world.

We include beautiful meditations from Mary on the babe aborning within her womb. We tell of Mary's testings and trials and her overcoming as she, an archangel, came to earth to be the mother of the Christ. And now that she has ascended back to the Father in heaven, as we all are meant to do at the close of our lives on earth, she explains to us the path of overcoming and the ascension.

However, this book is not only for women—men also have a feminine side. The goal is for us all—men and women alike—to realize ourselves as the Mother. And then, through the Mother, we can become the Christ. This book can fulfill your longing, perhaps as yet unrealized, for Mother.

Mrs. Prophet is a mother, not only to her own five children, but also to thousands throughout the world who call her "Mother" as a term of endearment. She has given teaching, counseling and "spankings" throughout the years that she has served the ascended masters. We have printed the text in the first person so that you can enjoy the tone of her lectures and come to know and love Mrs. Prophet as well as Mother Mary.

We have included messages from Mary through her messenger on subjects of wisdom, hope and peace for a troubled world. Mary has concerns for the future and has often appeared with messages of prophecy. She appeared at Fátima, Lourdes, Medjugorje, Garabandal and to Juan Diego as Our Lady of Guadalupe. She has also appeared in many visitations that have not been documented. There were occasions where icons in the churches have been seen to weep—sometimes tears, sometimes blood. All of this is Mary's attempt to contact mankind and warn them of what may happen if they do not turn and serve the light.

We have included two new rosaries for the New Age: The Fourteenth Rosary—The Mystery of Surrender and a shortened version of the original rosary, which is called The Child's Rosary. Mother Mary stresses the importance of giving the rosary daily for world transmutation, and she has given this twenty-minute Child's Rosary for those who do not have the time to give the longer rosary daily.

Beautiful Renaissance paintings of Madonna and child are sprinkled throughout the book. We have been told that the ascended masters can radiate their divine Presence through their photographs placed in your homes and offices.

Mother Mary is a very down-to-earth, organized ascended lady master for the twenty-first century. She is the mother of all children of God, not only of Catholics, and we have attempted to help you recognize the Mother as she comes in her many guises. Mary tells us in one of her messages, "I am a mother of your heart."

Annice Booth

Managing Editor, Summit University Press
Paradise Valley
Montana

A Word from the Author

This work is a tribute to the World Mother and to Mary, who, as the Mother of Jesus, was her foremost representative in the Piscean Age. It is a trilogy of wisdom, love and power that flows from the heart of the Mother to her children. It contains not only the worded revelations of Mary through our messengership, but also the light emanations of her Presence made manifest to us. Thus we would bear witness to her immortal soul that does continually magnify the LORD.

As I was brought up Protestant, I did not have an appreciation of Mother Mary, although my natural inclination was to enter all the Catholic Churches and to engage in prayer there. However, I had no instruction concerning this, and I was indoctrinated in a prejudice against the person of Mother Mary for what seemed the idolatry of Catholics deifying her, having statues to her, having medals to her.

I had a wondrous experience one day. It was a personal conversion. I was just walking down the street, and I looked up and before me I saw Mother Mary. I saw her in all the beauty and sweetness and Presence and love of the Being we know her to be. I was so moved and so touched by her Reality, instead of the unreality that I had been programmed to feel, that I literally ran to the nearest Catholic Church. I knelt before her statue and asked for forgiveness for these thoughts and feelings I had held. I also gave her my life and asked her to use me as an instrument of her mothering of all people.

The joy I have had ever since then of having Mother Mary as a constant companion and adviser in my life is simply boundless. And I am so grateful that Mother Mary was concerned enough about one person to show me her Presence and her Reality, which instantaneously dissolved a lifetime's worth of indoctrination.

In knowing Mary as she really is, I have come to see her as a relentless and constant force, challenging the oppression of her children everywhere, in every faith, in every religion. She is a World Mother, and I have seen this in her tremendous mastery of life. Her knowledge of administration and organization, as she has conveyed it to me, has given me the real teaching of how to administer this organization and, with a very capable staff, bring it to this level of complexity of service that we enjoy.

When we want to master the details of life in any field, we realize that it is the Mother aspect of God that actually corresponds to Matter, or the Matter universe, as *mater* is the Latin word for Mother. And so, here on earth, if we are going to accomplish anything, we must invoke the Mother flame. We must understand the Hindu concept of the Mother aspect of God as the Shakti, the active principle, the force that brings into manifestation the Father's will.

So if you want to know how to get things done and how to get them done because your aim is helping people and glorifying God—which is our only reason for being—then ask Mother Mary. And you will find that she is truly a master and not an ignorant peasant woman who happened to be called to give birth to Jesus, as some would have us believe.

We know Mother Mary as an angel. We understand that, in God's divine plan for over a million years and more, many angels of heaven have taken embodiment on earth out of a concern for God's children, to minister to them.

These angels are characterized as people with great feeling and an abundance of love. They may not always be the most brilliant, because they have not necessarily worked in fields that develop the mind. Rather they have developed the feelings, because angels as orders of heavenly beings actually exist to impart to the sons and daughters of God faith, hope, constancy, compassion and love—these very necessary feelings that we must have in order to get along with each other and to help each other.

Without those uplifting feelings, we could become dreary and cynical and hopeless. We might not get through the crisis of the death of our loved ones or the various calamities that come upon us. In those moments of great need, we sometimes feel an overwhelming Presence of love and support, and it is God extending his care to us through the invisible angels. And sometimes, he does this through angels in embodiment.

Mother Mary is of the angelic evolution.[1] These hierarchies also serve on the seven rays of the Godhead that emerge through the prism of the Christ consciousness. Mother Mary's ray is the fifth ray, the ray of emerald green, the ray of healing. It is the ray of science, of medicine, of supply and abundance. The economy also comes under the fifth ray.

Mother Mary, then, has great talents in many areas. I don't think there is a field of human endeavor where she does not have the expertise and understanding to teach others how to realize and implement the highest and best goals. Mother Mary's mind is vast, vast beyond comprehension.

As we see Mary in the present day, we move to the understanding of a woman in our midst—a Mother Mary who is as modern, as liberated, as tough, as determined as many of the finest women we might meet on earth who are fighting for various causes.

We need to see her as friend, as companion, as sister, although she may rightfully be called "goddess" because of the tremendous God consciousness she has. We must not place her on the pedestal that forces us to become idolaters of her image. But we should revere her in the sense that she has great attainment and great standing in heaven and was chosen to be the mother of Christ because she had the ability to hold the light and the balance for his entire mission.

And so the Mother comes to heal us of our sense of sin regarding ourselves or other people. She comes to liberate us, especially in the Christian world, of the enormous division that renders Christianity ineffective. And of course, she comes carrying the sorrow of the people of every single nation on the planet and the determination to help them as we give the prayers and the calls.

One of the greatest teachers I have known in the past twenty-five years is Mother Mary. From her heart come two great teachings. She has taught us the cosmic clock, charting the cycles of our returning karma and our initiations. Those teachings are a wonder to behold, and you can find them in numerous books and tapes that we have available.[2]

The second teaching is the rosary. When Mother Mary came to me and told me of her desire to have devotees throughout the world give a Scriptural Rosary for the New Age, she first announced the seven mysteries for the seven rays, together with the prayer format that was to be used.

When these rosaries were completed under her direction, the Blessed Mother released The Masterful Mysteries for the eighth ray, which focalize the majesty and the mastery of God.[3] In her third appearance to me, the Holy Virgin presented the mysteries and the prayer format for the five secret rays, which she said were to be given at eventide Monday through Friday.

Mother Mary said that when a sufficient number of people would have established this daily ritual of reciting these rosaries, she would dictate The Fourteenth Rosary—The Mystery of Surrender. We have printed her latest rosary in this current volume.[4] By daily giving the rosary in these formats, devotees of the Mother anchor the love of Mother Mary within their heart's chalice, thereby consecrating their life's energies to the expansion of the Mother's light throughout the planetary body.

Mary's Scriptural Rosary for the New Age teaches the disciple the devotional aspect of the love of Mother and Son—their love for him and his love for them—while reinforcing the pattern of the life and works of Mary and Jesus as they set forth for all the highest and best example of the Christian way of life and laid the foundation for the Christian dispensation.

The giving of the rosary, formulated by our spiritual Mother to meet the needs of the hour, affords a universally Christic experience calculated by heaven to awaken the soul to the Realities of the Divine Woman and the Manchild. For it is their light that goes forth from each one who elects to be a part of the rosary of life that garlands the earth. This living rosary is composed of every son and daughter of the flame who daily consecrate their energies both in heaven and on earth in the ongoing service of Jesus and Mary.

The rosary of souls is an endless chain of floral offerings to the Mother, which she receives, blesses and returns to her children to make them one—heart, soul and mind—as the great body of Christ on earth, the living Church.

Mother Mary says that when we say, "Hail, Mary," we are not giving our worship to a figure, a person in an idolatrous way; but we are saluting the Mother ray, the Ma-ray, which is what the name Mary means. We are giving devotion to the principle of God that is Mother. This is universal in all cultures and religions, even in primitive cultures. The acknowledgment of the Mother principle, whether as a goddess of fertility or in many other guises, is fundamental to life, to birth, to crops, and so forth.

So we salute the Mother ray in God, in the universe, in Mother Mary. Truly we give adoration to the light in each of the saints—to the one light that is God—rather than to the personality. Worship one God, then, adore the light and realize the light is also in yourselves.

Christians have prayed to God through Jesus and Mary, and prayer forms have evolved from the founding of the early Church to the present. Thus, it will be seen that the giving of the rosary is the exaltation of the Motherhood of God and of the Divine Sonship, which can never be confined to one church or one dogma. Just as the theme of the Son of God conceived of the Cosmic Virgin is heard over and again in many of the world's religions, so all mankind will one day revere the Mother as the Source of Life and the Son of God as the Saviour of the Christic light within all.

Mother Mary has bequeathed to humanity the archetype of the New Age woman. By her example and constancy, she calls forth the Divine Woman in us all. She not only shows us how the feminine principle can be redeemed, but why it must be redeemed in order that the Divine Manchild as the unfolding Christed man and Christed woman might appear within every son and daughter beloved of God.

Until the feminine principle of the Godhead is ennobled in each man and each woman, the Christ cannot be born. And until Christ is born in the individual, the evolving identity of man and woman cannot experience the new birth. Thus, the rebirth of the Christ in man and woman, often referred to as the Second Coming, is necessary for the salvation of the soul; indeed the individual Christ Self is the Saviour of the world of the individual.

When the Christ is born in the heart of man and woman, his consciousness dethrones the Antichrist, whom Paul referred to as the carnal mind that is enmity against God.[5] For the Son of God comes forth to slay the dragon of the lower self—the human ego—that must be put down that the Divine Ego may appear.

Without the Mother there can be no Son. Therefore, this volume is dedicated to all devotees of the Blessed Mother and of her Son, Jesus Christ, who personified the glory of the only begotten Son of God that we might behold his light—"the true Light, which lighteth every man that cometh into the world"[6]—and thus be molded in his image.

It is the fond hope of the Mother and her fervent faith that her children, following the precepts of the Father, shall succeed beyond their farthest dreams.

In Her service I remain,

Elizabeth Clare Prophet

We welcome you to the heart of Mary as you read her words and teachings in this book, and we hope that you will come to know her as she really is. For she is not only a great Being of light, "a woman clothed with the sun" (as we read in Revelation), but also a very real friend, someone in whom we can confide and who can give us strength in times of trouble.

Above all, we pray that you will heed Mary's word of prophecy and thereby make wise choices on your own personal road of life as you enter the Age of the Divine Mother.

PART ONE

My Search for Mary

I am the Mother of all children of God, not only of Catholics. I am a tender vine, one master in heaven representing the Divine Mother. Many also represent that Mother. I am also of the angelic realm, the complement of the Archangel Raphael, who held the balance for me as my twin flame when I came to earth to love the soul of Jesus and to weave for him the swaddling garment that he might weave for himself the wedding garment.

Mary

1

The Real Mary

by Elizabeth Clare Prophet

I would like to tell you about the heart of Mary, as the Divine Mother, and what she has come to mean to me.

Mother Mary is not in the least the sole possession of the Roman Catholic Church, nor does she necessarily appear in the particular image that shows her Immaculate Heart pierced for the bearing of the sorrows of the world.

I would like to show you a New-Age painting of Mother Mary done by Ruth Hawkins[1] so that you can see another image and face of a beloved friend and teacher, a sister and Mother, who I know is very close to your heart. This particular painting has quickened in many the memory that they have seen the likeness of this modern figure appear to them, rather than as she is depicted in earlier images. The Divine Mother comes to all cultures in different forms, and our acquaintance with the Divine Mother is a great key to our evolution and to our victory.

Mother Mary, then, is a being who has the attainment of the level of an archangel. (The feminine form of the word *archangel* is *archeia*.) She serves with Archangel Raphael, who is her divine complement, her twin flame.

"Queen of Angels"

Mary is called the "Queen of Angels." She is surely the Queen of Angels of the fifth ray on which she and Raphael serve.

She and Raphael recount in their dictations[2] that long, long ago they were called to the altar of God, and she was given the assignment to take embodiment upon earth and to have numerous embodiments leading to the time two thousand years ago when she would be prepared to be the instrument of the birth of Jesus Christ. Raphael was called to hold the balance for her in heaven.

Mother Mary was embodied on ancient Atlantis, where she held the focus of a magnificent healing temple. She has served on that healing ray and therefore is very much involved in our personal healing and in the healing of the world. And her prophecies come to teach us how to avert those things that she prophesies.

We understand, then, in the heart of Mother Mary, that she is above all the great Mother Teacher who comes to us. She is very dear and very close, very much a part of all of us. She weeps for our burdens. She implores the Father to intercede and send angels to assist us. Mother Mary, therefore, is called the Mediatrix. She is that Mother of mercy and comfort.

In her Immaculate Heart, Mary holds for each one of us the divine vision. And the word *vision* comes on the same ray, the fifth ray,[3] which corresponds to the third-eye chakra.[4] Through her single-eyed vision, through her immaculate understanding of who we are, she sees for each one of us daily and hourly the pure perfection that we knew in the Beginning with the Father-Mother God. She never takes her eye from that vision, holding it so that we might have the courage and the joy to fill in the parts and the pieces of the puzzle of our life. We imagine that our own mothers do this for us, and indeed they do. But we also have a Divine Mother who does the same.

Early Prejudices

In this lifetime, I was brought up in the Protestant sector of Christianity, and I found a path of metaphysics early in life. And through Protestantism and metaphysics, I found that I had been prejudiced against Mother Mary even as I had been prejudiced against Catholics. This is very unfortunate, because through the criticism of this form of worship, I had been deprived of the blessedness of knowing such a dear and ancient friend.

I am very grateful that I have had the intimate contact with Mother Mary that has come to me since I made contact with the Great White Brotherhood,* because in my upbringing I was surrounded by people who continually criticized the Catholic Church and what they made of Mary. They complained that the Catholic Church made her into a goddess; called her the "Queen of Heaven," the "Queen of the Angels" and the "Mother of God." Who could be the Mother of God? How could anyone have the nerve to elevate a human being to this station and to such a point of reverence? The entire Protestant revolt is based upon such concepts; and the result of that revolt was the removing from the Church the saints, Archangel Michael, Mother Mary.

I was so surrounded by these misunderstandings and had been told so much about the idolatry of the Catholics that these concepts permeated my entire thought as a child. And these deadly seeds continued to grow because there was nothing to counteract them.

I remember the culmination of the antagonism I felt toward this entire concept came when I was in college in Boston. I used to take the subway to go to my classes, and in the subway, there was a huge mosaic on the wall of Mary, the Mother of Jesus, and written above it, "Mary, the Queen of Heaven." And I would stand there and go through all of these concepts with which I had been indoctrinated. And

---

*The Great White Brotherhood is a spiritual order of saints and adepts of every race, culture and religion. These masters have transcended the cycles of karma and rebirth and reunited with the Spirit of the living God. The word "white" refers to the aura or halo of white light that surrounds them.

it would make me angry that someone else's religious beliefs would be imposed upon me in a public place; and I would wonder to myself, "If this Being exists, why does she allow herself to be portrayed in this way?"

Meeting Mary

Well, it was not long afterward that I received my first communication through the *Pearls of Wisdom*[5] of a letter from Mary the Mother, and I felt the tenderness and the love of the Divine Mother that came through this *Pearl of Wisdom*. As I read it while walking to work, I felt her mantle descend upon me. I felt the presence of her love. I felt as though I had met a woman like myself on that street in Boston, that she greeted me and saluted the Divine Mother within me and wanted to make friends with me and renew an old acquaintance.

Mother Mary appeared to me and unburdened my heart of all of the prejudice I had suffered through the preceding years, the great consternation about Catholicism and the worship of her person and the elevation of her that I had been taught was idolatry.

I looked up one day when I was walking down Commonwealth Avenue, and there she was above me. Unfettered, unencumbered by any orthodoxy or anyone's dogma, she was simply the most beautiful Being of light, the most wondrous Presence. And the love and the comfort of her heart made me realize she was not only Mother, but also sister and friend—someone we could immediately sit down and talk with and have a conversation with and tell our innermost secrets to.

The Real Mary

I thought to myself, "So this is the *real* Mary. This is the real wonder of heaven. Truly she is the wonder of a mother's love." I was so infilled by the Holy Spirit with her Presence that all of the burden concerning her personage or how she might be viewed or not viewed simply left me at once, in an instant.

And I ran with great joy to the nearest Catholic Church where I could kneel before her statue and know that this was not idolatry, but the Presence of the Divine Mother focalized there in Matter at that point of contact. Beyond the form was the spirit of one manifestation of God. And it was the one God and the one light whom I was contacting. It was wonderful to find a friend and to have such a resolution in my being.

I apologized to her for all of the anger and the animosity and the misunderstanding that I had held because of this false image that had been portrayed to me and because of the lies that had been told me. I found myself free, as I had not felt free before. My soul had been burdened by these concepts of prejudice. I had not even realized what a weight of sorrow I was carrying in my being; obviously, my inner Being knew the real Divine Mother and was burdened by the weight of these concepts in the subconscious.

I felt free from doctrine and dogma, and I felt free from the church to which I had belonged. I felt free from every church. I felt free to walk into any church, to worship any point of contact with the Godhead—any personification of that flame. It was a complete liberation that enabled me to transcend all of the confinements and the compartments that mankind have made of God.

As my devotion to Mary has grown over the years—and I cannot help but speak of her when I am with those who I know love her—I have often been asked why I have not become Catholic. I have found myself speaking with priests and nuns and knowing more about the saints than they know about them, and they have said to me, "You would make a very good Catholic. Why didn't you ever convert?"

The only answer I could ever give was, "I don't need to become Catholic; I do not need to place my consciousness within the confinements of any church. I can have the joy of the fulfillment in the light and the accomplishment of the saints. I can have the rosary. I can have all that you have. I can come in and assist in your masses and join you in prayer, but I am part of the Universal Church of humanity, worshipping God wherever he is found."

I think this is a liberation for all the souls who are a part of the worship of Mary. I see it as a part of the freedom of the Aquarian age to be God where you are, to worship God where you find him or her. And so, I dedicated my children to Mother Mary; I understood that they are the children of the Divine Mother.

The Many Faces of the Divine Mother

Mother Mary explained that she is not the exclusive possessor of the title Divine Mother, or Blessed Mother. Many angels in heaven and saints have also taken up that calling, and she is one of those in heaven who does answer the call when people cry out to the Divine Mother or to the Mother of the World. In the East, people call to Kuan Yin as the Divine Mother, who has many faces and many manifestations, but she is still only One.

These teachings have eliminated for me all offenses that could possibly come to us and divide us on the point of our religious worship. We worship one God and one light. We do not worship saints or ascended masters* or angels. We understand the meaning of that statement of Moses, "Hear, O Israel: The LORD our God is one LORD."[6] And that one LORD individualized for you and for me has placed his divine spark within each one of us. That divine spark is God, is the manifestation of God, is the unique light whereby we can realize the fullness of God. And therefore, we may easily bow to the light within

---

*Ascended masters are enlightened spiritual beings who once lived on earth, fulfilled their reason for being and ascended, reuniting with God. The master, through Christ and the putting on of that mind that was in Christ Jesus, has mastered time and space and in the process gained the mastery of the self in the four lower bodies, the four quadrants of Matter, and in the chakras and the balanced threefold flame.

one another without any sense of idolatry or any sense that there are many gods.

The carnal mind, the human mind and the mortal mind—these are prone to idolatry. There are many idols that people have in this world, whether it be rock stars, movie stars, their automobiles, their material possessions or even one another. People idolize those whom they love. They idolize their parents, their children, their leaders, and so forth. But in reality, it is the one light in all of us that we share and that we must magnify.

The Mother of God

One of the most important concepts that Mary explained to me is the concept of Mary, the Mother of God. She has explained that this appellation, which has been the subject of such controversy, is the mothering of a flame. On earth, God requires a mother because God is a Spirit, and for the Word to incarnate, the Mother consciousness, the Mother flame, must nourish, sustain, prepare the body, give adoration daily to that flame so that it is protected, and hold the immaculate concept—which means visualize the blueprint—for the pattern of the soul, for the mission.

Had Mary not held the blueprint for the mission of Jesus, it is questionable whether he could have completed that mission. It is the office of the Divine Mother within man and woman to hold the blueprint so that the Spirit can fill the blueprint. The Mother is the cup; she is the chalice. Matter,* the entire material universe, is the chalice into which the energy of God is poured. Without that energy of God to infuse life here below, we have nothing but a brittle, hollow matrix—without life, without joy, without Spirit.

After I became a messenger for the ascended masters, Mother Mary dictated to me her New Age rosary, and gave me a very profound understanding regarding herself and regarding that rosary.

First of all, her being addressed as the "Mother of God" in the Hail Mary offends some people. For who could be the Mother of God, and why does God need a Mother?

Mother Mary explained to me that she is the one who nourishes the flame of God in the sons and daughters of God and in his children. And I could see her as the great ministering figure, the great archangel whose power and Presence is so infilling that it does indeed fill all the earth. Mother Mary can be with each one of us individually and personally, as any ascended being or saint can be, to place over us her Electronic Presence† and the momentum of her attainment as an archangel as well as a daughter of God who has embodied on earth.

I could see, then, to call her Mother was to call to God as Mother and to receive her as a servant of God who comes

---

*We think of Matter as *Mater* (Latin for "mother"). The Matter universe is the manifestation of God as Mother: the Spirit universe is the manifestation of God as Father.

†The Electronic Presence is the I AM Presence or the I AM THAT I AM, the individualized Presence of God focused for each soul. It is each one's God-identity. The Electronic Presence of an ascended master is a duplicate of the I AM Presence of that master. A master such as Mother Mary can be many places in the earth at once because she can multiply her Electronic Presence many times over to place a duplicate of herself with those who are in need.

to bring and restore to us the fullness of our understanding of the Mother flame and of our feminine nature. Both men and women have a feminine nature, even as we both have a masculine nature—the Alpha and the Omega. And so I realized that we need to have role models. And Mother Mary in heaven and on earth has been the great role model of Motherhood, of divine intercession, of teacher and of profound wisdom.

So the concept of the Mother of God is something that Mary would transfer to you immediately, a title that she does not reserve for herself, but that she would give to men and women desiring to nourish the Flame of Life. Never in history has there been a greater need for the understanding of this one principle, because life is knocking at the portals of birth.

The geniuses required to meet the challenge of going into a golden age are waiting to take embodiment. Many have been aborted, and they knock again and again. They are determined to incarnate in this age, to see us through the transition. We see a dearth of leadership in society, and we realize leadership is required to carry us through this transition period, yet through abortion we close the door to the leadership preparing to come forth.

The Woman Clothed with the Sun

This denial of life occurs because we do not understand the image of Mother, the image of Woman as the "woman clothed with the sun" who is seen in the Book of Revelation.[7] This is the woman who has raised the fires of the fiery core of being, raised the energies of the Kundalini of the base-of-the-spine chakra. When she has raised those energies, she is clothed with the sun, because that light of the Mother rises to meet the light of the Father, and all of the chakras—especially the crown—burst forth in the fire of the sun. Her entire aura is filled with this golden light and she wears a "crown of twelve stars." Mary does not desire to wear that crown exclusively. She would give it to you as the focal point of your mastery of the initiations of the twelve solar hierarchies.

There are twelve frequencies of God that are stepped down by twelve mandalas of cosmic beings known as the twelve solar hierarchies.* When we refer to these cosmic beings, we refer to them by the

---

*As the energies of the twelve solar hierarchies are plotted on the cosmic clock, they begin with the hierarch of Capricorn and the quality of God-power on the twelve o'clock line and conclude with Sagittarius and God-victory on the eleven o'clock line. The quality of victory, then, is the test and the energy that brings the conclusion of one cycle and the commencement of the next. If the full potential of one cycle is realized, the next cycle will be on a higher level, building on the foundation of all that was achieved in the previous cycle. In this way, life is intended to be a continually self-transcending spiral.

names of the signs of the zodiac. (Therefore, we speak of the solar hierarchy of Capricorn—legions of cosmic beings who hold the focus for our cosmos of the energy of God's power. When we speak of the hierarchy of Aquarius, these are legions of cosmic beings who hold the focus of the energies of God's love, etc.) The woman wearing the crown of twelve stars symbolizes that there is the attainment in the feminine ray of the mastery of these twelve godly attributes that are focused by cosmic beings who step them down for their absorption by lesser evolutions.

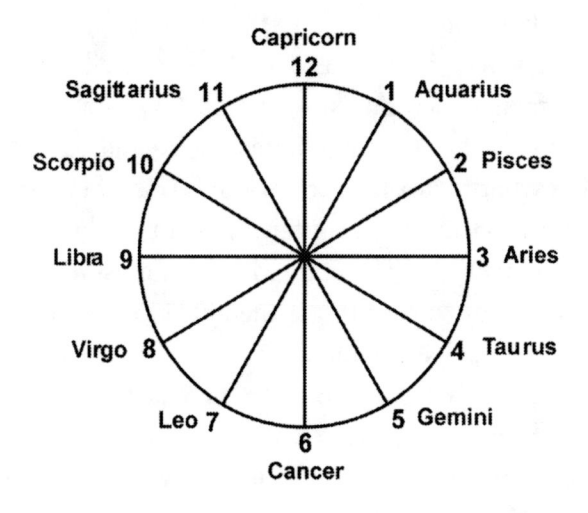

The Twelve Solar Hierarchies Who Initiate Earth's Evolutions in the God Consciousness

The Divine Mother within you is intended to have mastery in the planes of Matter of the qualities of God, and by this mastery, she creates the cradle, the crucible, into which she may receive the Manchild. This woman in the Book of Revelation is the archetype of you, of man and woman in the Aquarian age, of the culmination of the attainment of Jesus and Mary as it is realized through the Holy Spirit, through the violet ray,[8] the seventh ray, in this age. What is so inspiring about this wondrous woman is that her attainment is possible to you here and now. And not only is it possible—it is mandatory. It is the requirement for us to make the arc into the New Age, the leap into cosmic consciousness.

Mother Mary is deeply concerned about your attainment. She is devoted to your soul's overcoming; she is devoted to the release of the Mother ray within you. Because of her concern, she has released the knowledge of the cosmic clock[9] so that you could chart the cycles of your karma, your dharma, your initiations, and determine what tests you would be facing each day so it would not be a hit-or-miss affair, but one that is mathematically calculated. You can determine what thrust is necessary in terms of energy from your chakras to meet a counter-thrust of darkness—what frequency, what quality is required to be intensified on a certain day in order to counteract the anti-God or anti-Christ manifestation of that quality.

We learn, when we function in Matter, how much strength is required to unscrew a lid or push a piece of furniture or open a door or carry our body weight. We have that sense, which we learn from childhood, of how to walk, how to carry this form and how to interact with physical objects. Mother Mary teaches us the release of energy from our souls and from our chakras of how to interact with cosmic energy, how to interact with returning karma, how to deal with it, how to release that ray from the heart that drives back the fallen ones—the demons of the night, the discarnates who come to pollute the consciousness of the newborn child, the Christed Ones, your own flame within your heart.

The Real Mary 19

```
                    God-Power
                        12
      God-Victory 11         1 God-Love
    God-Vision 10               2 God-Mastery
    God-Reality 9                 3 God-Control
      God-Justice 8            4 God-Obedience
        God-Gratitude 7       5 God-Wisdom
                        6
                    God-Harmony
```

The God Consciousness, or God-Qualities,
of the Lines of the Cosmic Clock

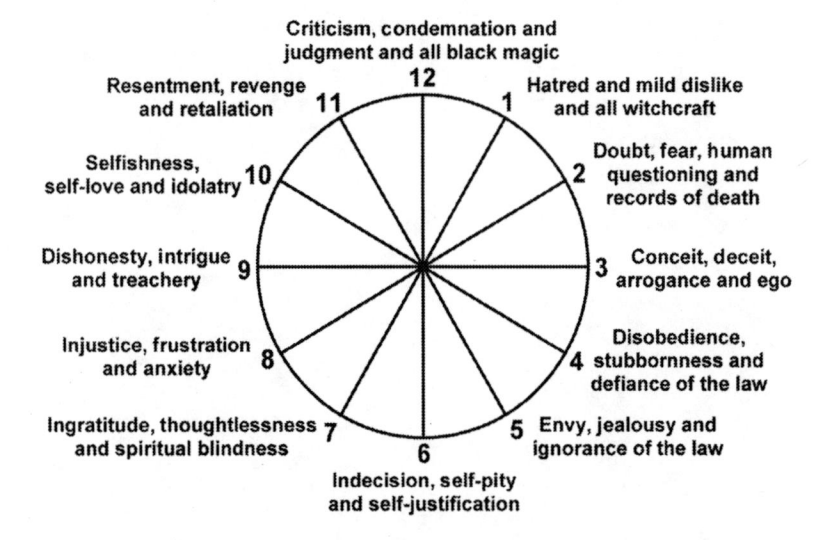

```
              Criticism, condemnation and
              judgment and all black magic
                          12
    Resentment, revenge          Hatred and mild dislike
    and retaliation    11    1   and all witchcraft
                                     Doubt, fear, human
    Selfishness,        10   2       questioning and
    self-love and idolatry           records of death
    Dishonesty, intrigue  9    3  Conceit, deceit,
    and treachery                 arrogance and ego
                                     Disobedience,
    Injustice, frustration 8  4      stubbornness and
    and anxiety                      defiance of the law
    Ingratitude, thoughtlessness 7  5 Envy, jealousy and
    and spiritual blindness       6   ignorance of the law
              Indecision, self-pity
              and self-justification
```

Human Perversions of the God Consciousness
of the Twelve Solar Hierarchies

PART TWO

A Mother's Gift to Her Children

Take comfort, O my children!
There is not a place on earth
where you can be that
I also have not been.
I have seen the tempter and
the temptations of sin.
I have seen the Christ upon the cross
and held him in my arms as infant child
and by the tomb, the moment of the
consecration to the cosmic womb.
I have parted from my Son
along the sorrowful way and I have
seen him nailed to the cross on
a very dark day.
My soul was also pierced as yours
shall be. But fear not: I am thy
Mother, I AM with thee.

Mary

2

As Above, so Below

A Message from Mother Mary

Children of the One, Come into the Sacred Heart of the Cosmic Virgin: I am Mary. I have chosen to ensoul the Mother ray for a cosmos. I am the handmaid of the Lord Alpha and the instrument of Omega. I am the awareness of the Father-Mother God extending even unto the planes of Mater, that the children of the One might know the sanctity of communion—of the marriage of the daughters to the Holy Spirit, of the vows of the sons unto the Cosmic Virgin.

Because the flame of the fifth ray relates to precipitation in Mater and because the feminine aspect of the flame is directly involved in the spirals of God-realization descending from the formless into form, I was chosen by Alpha and Omega to incarnate in this system of worlds, to set forth in time and space the example of the Divine Woman reaching full Self-realization in and as the Divine Mother. How well I remember that moment when I was bidden by heralds of the king and queen, our own beloved Alpha and Omega, and I came escorted by the beloved Raphael to stand before the throne of the twin flames of a cosmos!

"You called, my father and my mother, and I have come."

"Yes, our beloved, we have called. Unto you and to Raphael is given the opportunity from the heart of the Solar Logoi to manifest the balance of the flow of Truth 'as Above, so below' over the spirals of the figure eight of our cosmos—opportunity to be on earth as in heaven the ensoulment of the Mother ray."

"What does this mean, my father and my mother?"

"It means that you have been chosen, Mary, to incarnate in the planes of Mater, to take on the feminine form that the errant souls of the children of God now wear, to live and serve among them, to adore the Christ flame within their hearts—as Sanat Kumara and Gautama have done and as the Christed Ones, the avatars and Buddhas who have gone before, and the many angels who have volunteered to work through forms of flesh and blood to save the lost sheep of the house of Israel who have taken on the ways of the idolatrous generation."

I heard the words of our dearest Father-Mother and I looked into the eyes of Raphael, my beloved. And for a moment—

only a moment—the pain of the anticipated separation was too much to bear. Instantly, I was strengthened by the beauty and nobility of his countenance and the sternness of his eye disciplined in the Law. He had, as it were, almost greater courage than I to descend into the planes of Mater.

But when I felt his hand press my own and the charge of the will of God and our dedication to eternal Truth flowed into my being and soul, I faced the beloved Presence of God now pulsating in utter formlessness as cloven tongues of fire where a moment before the personages of the Divine Polarity had stood. I knelt in utter surrender to the call of hierarchy and, in silence before the Holy of Holies, gave my life that the Word might become flesh and dwell among the inhabitants of Terra,[1] that the Christ, the eternal Logos, might incarnate, the Incorruptible One.[2]

Precious ones, did you know that for the souls and the angels who volunteer to incarnate in those several systems of worlds where the consciousness of the Fall,[3] of fallen man and fallen woman, has taken over the race, there is no guarantee that the lifestream will emerge from that darkness unscathed, free to soar once more unto the arms of Everlasting Love? Those who come from heavenly octaves in defense of Truth, in defense of the life of souls who have strayed from the center of Being, have only their commitment to the flame to rely on—only determination and will and love. For even the memory of those other spheres must be foresworn upon entering the birth canal and assuming the body temple that has been prepared—sometimes lovingly and sometimes not so lovingly—by earthly parents.

> Oh yes, God's grace is always there.
> His Presence can be known.
> God's love is everywhere—
> Even in the wings of the morning
> Where I have flown.
> But, you see, it all depends upon the call
> And the making of the call.
> For all of the potential of God and man
> Can come to naught
> When souls and angels forsake the Truth
> God brought.
> The prayer, therefore, of every descending avatar
> Is for the memory of the Bethlehem star,
> That it might contact the teacher
> And the teaching of the I AM Presence
> And the Christ Self of each one
> For the journey through the valleys of the earth
> And then the soaring to the center of the sun.
>
> And so I descended by God's grace;
> And by his grace, and that alone,
> I ascended to the heavenly throne.
> Therefore, I am one among the archeiai
> Who have experienced directly
> The veil of human tears
> And the passing of the years
> From darkness unto darkness
> As mankind's consciousness flows

Until, quickened by some inner light,
They find the road from glory unto glory.

Take comfort, O my children!
There is not a place on earth where you can be
That I also have not been.
I have seen the
 tempter and the
 temptations of sin.
I have seen the Christ
 upon the cross
And held him in
 my arms
As infant child and
 by the tomb,
The moment of the
 consecration to
 the cosmic womb.
I have parted from
 my Son along the sorrowful way
And I have seen him nailed to the cross
On a very dark day.
My soul was also pierced as yours shall be.[4]
But fear not: I am thy Mother, I AM with thee.

Because I have gone before you
In the footsteps on the Path,
Because the blessed Son
Has also descended and ascended
Throughout a cosmos vast,
You can follow in each painful, blissful footstep—
Surefooted as the mountain goat,
Leaping to your cosmic destiny

And your place upon that cross,
Hastening to greet the sword
That must pierce the soul
That you might have the compassion
To make all mankind whole.
Because the way is known,
Because we have pursued and overcome,
You who have descended in answer to the call
Of Alpha and Omega
Can be certain of ascending
If you will make your calling and election sure[5]
By the call, by the initiations,
By the testing, testing, testing.

We extend a helping hand.
Clasp it if you will!
Feel the strength of Raphael
And the sternness of his love.
Feel the assurance of the beloved
Assuring you of your attainment
According to the motto
Of those who come to do his will:[6]
You can make it if you try!
You can make it if you try!

Midst all the darkness,
The density and the dangers
Inherent in a world scheme
Where judgment is nigh,
The archangels stand forth.

Hear their cry!
They come to intercede.
Won't you give them heed?
Their word is Law
Direct from the speech of the Logos.
Their word is power manifesting the work
Of the Creator, the Preserver, the Destroyer.
In this cycle of the Holy Spirit
You can expect to hear it,
To hear the wisdom
That causes the demons to tremble[7]
And the love that is a chastening
To them who fear it.

Without the fear of the Lord
There is no repentance,
And without repentance
There can be no forgiveness.
Forgiveness flows;
But it must be invoked
By the humble of heart,
By the sincere who ask the Lord's pardon
That they might undo their wrong
And redo their right.
When the apology becomes a ritual—
Dead and without works—
Then it is better to be silent
And to engage in living sacrifice
As service to the Law,
As testimony and as proof
That forgiveness is the justice
Of the mercy of the Law.

When the Lord Christ, Jesus my Son, prays fervently before the altar of the Most High God for the children of the One, so when I see him descending from the mountain of the LORD, "His face shining as the sun, his raiment white as the light,"[8] I run to greet him in the way and he does embrace me in the Mother ray. And then I ask him for those dispensations for the chosen ones that are his to give and mine to impart as the Matriarch of the Law.

You call me the Queen of Angels, and I have so been made by God because I have descended for a little time lower than the archeiai into the planes of Mater-realization; and thereby by the overcoming of the Holy Spirit, I have been crowned with more glory and honour.[9] Like the soldiers who return from the battles of life to receive their stripes and pins—and the Boy Scouts and Girl Scouts with their badges and their bars—so the flaming ones who have overcome, when bidden to those formal receptions held in the retreats of the Great White Brotherhood, are required to come in full military dress. And by their dress, all know what worlds they have conquered—when and where. And old comrades who have shared in the victory of worlds reminisce in the strategy of their overcoming as they look longingly upon those now engaged in the warfare for the salvation of this planet and this people.

We who know the strategies of the dark ones would impart them to our brothers and sisters below. But the messenger who volunteered to write the book *Strategies of Darkness*[10] took his leave in the summer of life, which leaves only the beloved Elizabeth to write, oh, so many books of the Law waiting on the shelves of the libraries of our retreats for the translator, the one who holds the key to decipher the Word of Spirit into the Word of Mater.

Do you know, precious ones, that these books are written in many tongues—the tongues of angels and cosmic beings and the languages that come from other systems of worlds and other interpretations of the Logos? And so we have placed the keys for the deciphering of the code in the aura of our messenger.[11]

And do you know that each of the rays of the seven archangels who are addressing you, mankind, has its own engrams of light, its own hieroglyphs of the Word? These pass through the Christ mind of our messenger and are delivered to you in the language of your understanding and in the language that the Lord God has used to deliver to mankind the teachings of the I AM in this age. Is this not truly the miracle of the science of the fifth ray? Is this not the hand of the Mother feeding her children that which they can understand and assimilate and become?

I leave you now. I AM[12]

Mary

*I will be there in that hour
and moment of the attainment
of your victory.*

                    Mary

3

A New-Age Rosary

by Elizabeth Clare Prophet

Mother Mary, in her concern for contact with the children of God and for making the transition into the New Age, released thirteen mysteries of the rosary. She came to me in the retreat in Colorado Springs[1] in the fall of 1972 and she said, "I wish to dictate a rosary for the New Age, a scriptural rosary, and it will be with the mantra of the Hail Mary with a slight alteration.

In giving me the rosary, then, she gave a correction of the usual wording that is given in the Catholic Church. She taught me to pray the Hail Mary in this manner:

> Hail, Mary, full of grace,
> the Lord is with thee.
> Blessed art thou among women
>   and blessed is the fruit of thy womb, Jesus.

> Holy Mary, Mother of God,
> pray for us, sons and daughters of God,
> now and at the hour of our victory
> over sin, disease and death.

Mother Mary can be very stern when rebuking human error or doctrines that express an untruth. And she said, "You must not call yourselves sinners. You are not sinners. Though you may have sinned, you may cease sinning." And therefore, though we make mistakes and make karma, we are not forever to be called sinners. We must recognize that from the beginning of Alpha to the ending of Omega, we are sons and daughters of God, as John the Beloved himself said.[2]

She said to pray for her to be with us at the hour of our victory over sin, disease and death. For death is not real but only a passage of the soul to another octave. In the moment when we are about to get the victory over that beast and that law of mortality and the law of sin and disease and the law of our personal karma, that is when all hell breaks loose to take from us the light and the victory—to dash the cup of victory from our lips before we are able to quaff it. So she said, "I will be there in that hour and moment of the attainment of your victory."

The recitation of this prayer, then, has a tremendous added benefit. It gives to us the celebration of the Divine Mother in our temple on a path in Western civilization. In the East, there is the raising of that sacred fire from the base chakra to the crown and the third eye (called raising the Kundalini) by the giving of mantras and by the pronouncing of bija mantras, seed syllables using the name of Mother. But in the West, we have no such tradition.

Mother Mary, being the fullness of the expression of

that light, desired that the people of the Western Church should have it also. So she revealed the rosary and its celebration. And she said when you say "Hail, Mary," you are giving the salutation to the Mother ray of the cosmos—the Ma-ray, the Omega. This is what the Hail Mary does.

And when we celebrate it, when we give that great salutation, the light in us manifests the light of the Mother, and we begin to feel her flame rising from the base chakra to the crown for the healing of all our diseases, for the annihilation of the law of disease and of sin and death. For it is the Mother light in us that does heal all that comes upon us.

Mother Mary said, "This mantra will affirm forevermore that mankind are not sinners, but that they are sons and daughters of God, rightful heirs of the Christ consciousness and of the Mother ray, and it will affirm that God-realization within the one who recites the mantra.

"The mantra is so that souls evolving in time and space will make contact with the Divine Mother at the moment of the initiation of victory. Those initiations for the victory of cycles are difficult, and usually they are fraught with considerable opposition from the mass mind and from your own carnal mind, at that moment, for going into a new frequency, because of passing a test in victory."

She said, "Sons and daughters of God require the intercession of the energies, the momentum of the Divine Mother. And that is when it must be called forth—in the hour of the victory over sin, disease and death."

Who is the Divine Mother? Is the Divine Mother Mary, the mother of Jesus?

Mary, the mother of Jesus, is an *incarnation* of the Divine Mother. She is a *representative* of the Divine Mother.

The Divine Mother is the counterpart of the Divine Father. Mary is not the exclusive Mother, any more than Jesus or Morya or Saint Germain are the exclusive Divine Father. They are electrodes for that cosmic consciousness of Alpha and Omega, of the masculine and feminine principles.

Therefore, Mary is *a* Divine Mother—a Divine Mother very close to us because she has mingled the atoms of her consciousness with the atoms of earth. She has been with us very recently. She has demonstrated a victory unparalleled in thousands of years, and so her contact is very intimate, very personal, very concerned.

The Prayers of the Rosary

In the giving of the rosaries, she asked us to recite the "Our Father" as taught by Jesus the Christ to his inner circle of disciples. It is a beautiful prayer; it is the one that Jesus revealed to these disciples as the affirmation of the Father within.

> *Our Father, who art in heaven,*
> *Hallowed be thy name, I AM.**

---

*"I AM" is the name of God revealed to Moses when he saw the burning bush (Exodus 3:14). "I AM THAT I AM" means simply but profoundly *As Above, so below. As God is in heaven, so God is on earth within me. Right where I stand, the power of God is.* Thus every time you say, "I AM," you are really affirming "God in me is...."

The hallowing of the name is in the flame in your heart.

> *I AM thy kingdom come*

God in me is thy kingdom, thy consciousness, come.

> *I AM thy will being done*

God in me is thy will being done.

> *I AM on earth even as*
> *I AM in heaven.*
> *I AM giving this day daily bread to all.*

God in me is giving this day daily bread to all. This is the prayer of the feminine part of you to the masculine part of you. It is the Mother speaking to the Father; it is the conversation you would imagine your Father and your Mother having in the secret chambers of the Holy of Holies.

It is the Mother saying to the Father,

> *I AM forgiving all life this day, even as*
> *I AM also all life forgiving me.*

It is the report of your feminine aspect on progress in this plane of Matter.

> *I AM [God in me is] leading all men away*
>   *from temptation.*
> *I AM delivering all men from every evil*
>   *condition.*
> *I AM the kingdom,*
> *I AM the power, and*
> *I AM the glory of God in eternal, immortal*
>   *manifestation—*
> *All this I AM.*

This is Jesus' I AM Lord's Prayer, and when we enter into it as the Holy of Holies, we feel that flow, that adoration; and then we alternate it with the Hail Mary as the response of the masculine aspect of God within us.

Hail, Mary...

Hail, Mother ray! Hail, Mother ray,

*...full of grace,
the Lord is with thee.
Blessed art thou among women*

—blessed is this ray of the Divine Mother manifest in woman.

and blessed is the fruit of thy womb, Jesus.

Blessed is the fruit of the womb of cosmos. Blessed is that fruit of the Christ consciousness that the Mother nourishes.

*Holy Mary, Mother of God,
pray for us sons and daughters of God,
now and at the hour of our victory
over sin, disease and death.*

The Hail Mary is the salutation that draws around you the swaddling garment of light that Mary placed around Jesus.

The recitation of the rosary each morning is a part of the ritual of our family and of students of the masters. It takes forty minutes to an hour to give the rosary, and it is a meditation upon events in the life of Jesus and Mary and on the prophecies of the Old and New Testaments. These matrices of scenes in the life of Jesus and Mary are intended to be niches of consciousness—and the word "niche" comes from "I-niche-I-action," initiation. Each time you pass an initiation, you go into a new niche of God's consciousness by your attainment.

And so we are taught to meditate upon a particular scene, upon the words of the master, upon a particular event. And then, when we give the Hail Mary, it is to draw the energies of Mater—the Mother ray—to coalesce in us, to re-create that record and that consciousness right where we are so that we can experience the divine Manhood and the divine Womanhood of Jesus and Mary.

Mother Mary outlined a rosary for each of the seven rays and the seven days of the week. She gave a rosary for the eighth ray, and she gave five secret-ray rosaries that are for the evening.*

It was only recently that I realized the full impact of the two daily rosaries. I realized that the rosary given in the morning is for a twelve-hour cycle—a thrust of Alpha for the action of the day—and the evening rosary is a thrust for a twelve-hour action of the return of Omega back to Alpha, completing the figure-eight spiral into the white-fire core.

---

*The rosaries for the seven rays (for the seven mornings of the week) and the eighth ray (for Sunday evening) are published in the first book in this series, *Mary's Message for a New Day*. The five secret-ray rosaries (for the evenings from Monday to Friday) are published in the second book, *Mary's Message of Divine Love*.

PART THREE

A Trilogy of the Mother

*I will always remember
the moment of his appearing,
when Joseph and I welcomed
the child Jesus, and the very first time
I held him in my arms, his eyes bright
as the stars out of which he descended.
And I uttered a prayer unto God:
"Blessed be thou, O Lord, Maker of
heaven and earth, who hast ordained the
coming of thy Self into form for the
redemption of mankind, that
through the grace and forgiveness
of the Law all might come to know
the true nature of selfhood
as this Christed One."*

Mary

4

A Trilogy of the Mother

I
The Mother Flame
and the Incarnation of God

Children of My Heart,
Now we approach the advent of the incarnation of the Word. "And the Word was made flesh, and dwelt among us, and we beheld his glory, the glory as of the only begotten of the Father, full of grace and truth."[1]

I will always remember the moment of his appearing, when Joseph and I welcomed the child Jesus, and the very first time I held him in my arms, his eyes bright as the stars out of which he descended. And I uttered a prayer unto God: "Blessed be thou, O LORD, Maker of heaven and earth, who hast ordained the coming of thy Self into form for the redemption of mankind, that through the grace and forgiveness of the Law all might come to know the true nature of Selfhood as this Christed One and that all might be baptized in preparation for the return to the center of thy Law in the Holy of Holies."

And I was aware that in my arms I held the incarnation of God even as I felt myself one with the Motherhood of God cradling an infant humanity. For in this child, this gift from God's own heart, was living proof of that which all mankind might one day become. And I remembered the words of Eve, "I have gotten a man from the LORD."[2] I thought about the many daughters of Israel who had been waiting with anticipation for the coming of Messias,[3] the one promised who would be the King of Kings and Lord of Lords[4] and the Saviour of a mighty people and a mighty nation.

The Mystery of the Motherhood of God

The Motherhood of God is an eternal mystery and a sacred privilege given to all who embody on the feminine ray. In this hour of the condemnation of the Christ, the Bethlehem babe, and of child-man aborning in the womb of time and space, I come forth to proclaim the eternal Christ Mass. For I would speak to every mother with child. I would draw you close to my heart and impart to you the mantle—which is indeed the momentum—of my experience as I carried the blessed Lord in my womb.

The glory of my communion with the Holy Ghost, with the light of the Father and of the Son, was indeed for the merging of the energies of the Sacred Trinity and their fusion with the Mother flame that culminates in the Mater-realization of the Word. And so the mystery of motherhood is in the special talent that God has given to the soul of Woman to distill the factors of the Holy Trinity and to be the focal point for the meshing of the threads and forcefields of Spirit with the Matter principle.

The Interweaving of Spirit and Matter

The incarnation of the Word has indeed been a mystery for many among mankind who have not been able to comprehend how God as a Spirit could come forth in flesh and blood. Just as "it is easier for a camel to go through the eye of a needle, than for a rich man to enter into the kingdom of God,"[5] so it is sometimes difficult for those whose mental development excels to understand the logic of the mystery of the eternal Spirit igniting the spark of life and meshing with the clay vessel of Matter-form. But for others, their acceptance of this principle of life remains a part of their common acceptance of the wonders and miracles of the Creator wrought not only in the life of Jesus, but also in the lives of the many saints and sages who have walked the earth both before and after his mission.

May I say, then, to those of you who understand the weavings of the threads of the form and the formless, that Spirit and Matter as Father-Mother principle—as the positive and negative polarity of Being—commingle in and as the warp and woof of the whole of creation. Be it also known that the Matter that you observe has indeed other facets, other dimensions and other frequencies that you have not yet experienced. These are, as it were, the exalted manifestation of the weavings of the Cosmic Virgin outpictured through Omega—even the balancing factor of Spirit in what you have hitherto referred to as the planes of Spirit. And so, you see, the exaltation of Motherhood as the materialization of Spirit occurs in each succeeding level of God Self-awareness all the way back to the Great Central Sun and beyond.

It was, then, my supreme joy to magnify the Lord within my soul.[6] And my own beloved Raphael showed me how the womb of the mother is a vaulted sepulchre where the soul is clothed upon through the converging of the energies of Spirit and Matter with layer upon layer of substance formed out of Spirit's essence that is for the soul's expression in the octaves of earth.

My Visualizations for the Birth of the Manchild

Therefore, in my visualizations for the birth of the Manchild, I saw the baby Jesus involuted in the heart-shaped matrix of God's own heart, swimming in the eternal sea of God's consciousness, each day absorbing more and more of the fragments of his love. And the elements and nutrients provided by Mother Nature were for the coalescing in the four lower bodies of the one hundred and forty-four elements that are the balanced expression of the twelve hierarchies of the sun in Mater. I visualized every particle, every cell and atom and molecule, as imbued with the Holy Spirit, having a sacred sun center like unto the flame that burned within my heart, like unto the center of the Presence of the Flaming One, the I AM THAT I AM.

Above all, as the God and Goddess Meru[7] had taught

me at inner levels in the temple at Lake Titicaca, I knew that to preserve Mater as a holy habitation of the Lord, to preserve Mater from the mechanical doctrines of the Luciferians, I must practice the ritual of endowing life in form with the sacred quality of grace, love and joy. As it is written on the temple wall: Unto the pure all things are pure:[8] to the holy all things are holy. And so in my first lessons there, the beloved Lady Meru showed me that the most sacred gift of motherhood and of the Mother flame that abides in both male and female is this ability to endow the material creation with life and light and love. And this is accomplished consciously by extending the fire from the heart—the fire that coalesces in mind as the immaculate concept—to every aspect of the creation.

The Transforming Power of the Mother

Without that love, there is the proverbial criticism and the endless analysis that human beings make of one another that destroys the very fabric of the soul's evolution just as surely as the tearing of the petals of the rose one by one destroys the matrix of the floral offering. Yes, without the love of the Mother, mankind not only behold imperfection, but they ratify that imperfection and make it the law of a man's being from which, in their minds, he can never escape. Alas, they are unable to equate present potential with future realization. Simply put, without the Mother flame manifest as a holy science, as Truth and as Law, mankind could not even accept the potential of the acorn to become the oak tree.

Therefore, you who would be Mothers of the world, you who are presently mothers caring for a family must understand that those who look to you with trust and with confidence will attain only that which you allow them to attain by the largesse of your heart's immaculate vision and the intuitive faculties of your soul that does indeed magnify the Law of the Lord as the threefold Christed potential of every child of God.

I shall continue to give to you some of the visualizations and meditations taught to me by angels and masters for the preparation of the coming of the Lord.

I AM in you the Mother,[9]

Mary

This is indeed the
transforming power
of the Mother: her ability
to see beauty in her children,
and in seeing that beauty, to seal that
beauty in her little ones by the action
of the flow of the heart chakra.
This is the meaning of holding
the immaculate concept for all life,
and this is where Motherhood begins.
It is a love that wells up within the heart
that makes up the difference between
the shortcomings of the children and the
perfection of the Christ Self of each one.
That gap between present
imperfections and future attainment
is always filled in by the love of
the mother's heart.

Mary

5

A Trilogy of the Mother

II
The Science of the Immaculate Concept

Children of My Christed Son,
The threefold flame is God's gift to man and to woman for the implementation of the immaculate concept. The blue plume of the will of God is the means whereby you hold in consciousness the blueprint of life for the incoming soul—for those coming into form and for those already in form coming into the fullness of the light.

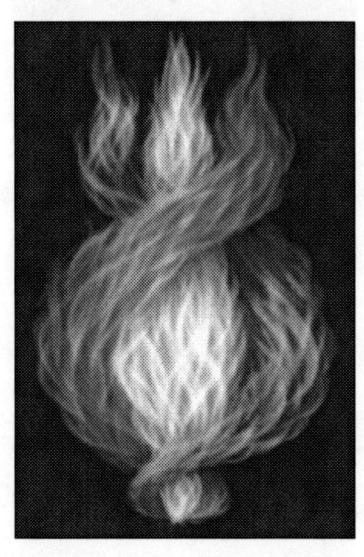

The blueprint is a mathematical equation, an alchemical formula, a precise pattern patterned after the Cosmic Egg.[1] The blueprint of life contains, as the seed contains within itself, every characteristic of the Spirit that the soul is intended to anchor in the world of Matter-form. And all that is required for the physical outpicturing of the matrices stored in the etheric computer, in the mental faculties and in the emotional body must be anchored in the seat-of-the-soul chakra, in the seed and the egg and in the chromosomes and genes.

Other aspects of man's spiritual nature and of the blueprint of life are anchored solely in the etheric body and can be released into the form and form consciousness when the fervent desire of the soul to transcend its limited mode impels the descent of the grace of the Holy Spirit, imbuing the form with the flame of that Spirit and superimposing upon the atoms and molecules of Selfhood the glow of Higher Being. Those, then, who would espouse the Mother flame and fulfill the mandates of the flame here on earth must be prepared to reinforce—by the will of God anchored in the will of the individual mind, by fervent and holy prayer, by fiat, decree and invocation, by affirmation and visualization—all that God holds in store for the lifewaves of a planet.

This can be accomplished through meditation upon geometric forms, the structure of crystals, and the harmony and the rhythm of classical music. By listening to the sounds of nature with the inner ear, the mother is able to perceive with heightened soul sensitivity the structure of all things living. Inasmuch as all that exists in and as Matter-form was fashioned by the Creator after the designs of the universe of

Spirit, the meditation on perfect forms prepares the soul to make the leap from Matter molecule to Spirit molecule. That leap is a necessary part of holding the immaculate concept, and that leap made daily in consciousness will one day be the giant leap of the soul into the arms of the I AM Presence through the ritual of the ascension.

Hold the Vision of the Divine Blueprint

Holding the immaculate concept day by day for every part of life is truly the means whereby the individual affirms the immaculate image of his own Selfhood outpictured here and now in the world of form. For all of God that you see and confirm for and on behalf of mankind is recorded in the Book of Life as your awareness of Selfhood as God. That which you affirm for others, you yourself become.

This is why Jesus gave forth the teaching, "Inasmuch as ye have done it unto one of the least of these my brethren, ye have done it unto me."[2] The "me" to which Jesus referred was the Christ. Because his contemporaries could not understand that they, too, were the Christ and had the full potential of outpicturing the Christ through the Christ flame within their own hearts, he set forth the Law in these terms.

Let present-day disciples of the Christ realize, then, that this science of the immaculate concept is the science of the enlightened ones of all ages. "Enlightened self-interest" is a term well worth considering. Far be it from us to confirm the world's cynical denial of the spark of altruism that exists in every heart; for enlightened self-interest is the highest altruism—the altruism that places the Christ within oneself as the first object of one's adoration. To serve the Christ in others is to serve the Christ within oneself: and to serve the Christ within oneself is to serve the Christ in others. And many who will be required to make choices for the light, many who will be required to forsake the hostility or even the amicability of family and friends, may find this simple expression of the Law an important key in their deliberations.

The Soul Is Liberated through Forgiveness

Understand, then, that the practice of the science of the immaculate concept is the liberation of the soul of the practitioner first and of the patient second. And this law is also expressed in the prayer, "Forgive us our transgressions even as we forgive those who transgress against us."[3] In proportion as the soul forgives all in her[*] circle of acquaintances, so does the LORD God forgive the soul. And proportionately as the soul withholds forgiveness, so does the Great Law withhold the aspect of mercy without which few among mankind could qualify for salvation.[4]

In this context, the world and its evolutions are the objectification of the individual's own self-awareness—whether as the Christ or as the Antichrist. The world is, then, in one sense the creation of man. And this world of man's creating is the world in which he must work out the effects of his past wrong seeing, wrong feeling, wrong mentalizing and wrong being. Lifetime after lifetime, the soul must come back to the very place where her own imperfect patterns have resulted in the manifestation of chaos and confusion. When the soul condemns the chaos and the confusion, she binds herself once again to those very conditions. But when the soul affirms the God-reality, the original matrix, the blueprint of life behind every imperfect form, then she affirms her own liberation from self-imposed limitation.

---

[*]Whether housed in a male or female body, the soul is the feminine complement of the masculine Spirit and is addressed by the pronouns *she* and *her*.

Those of you seeking to increase the flame of the will of God and the qualities of God-power, God-harmony, God-control and God-reality as the blue cross of protection and perfection would do well to affirm that protection and that perfection of the cross of life, the balance of the lines of Alpha and Omega, for the self, the soul and the Christ throughout the entire cosmos itself—all the while knowing that whatever you see throughout the material creation is an aspect of God's own Self-awareness within you that you can rightly claim as the outpicturing of your own identity.

The eternal fiat spoken by Jesus as he descended into form, "Lo, I AM come to do thy will, O God,"[5] is a perpetual mantra that conducts the energies of Being into the perfect matrices of life. The recitation of this fiat as you prepare for the holy days will magnetize to being and consciousness the very lodestone of the will of God—and of your soul's immaculate destiny. The denial of the human will, coupled with the affirmation of the divine will in the mantra, "Not my will, not my will, not my will but thine be done!" is another means of sustaining the joy of perfection in a life of service.

> I AM in the life of the Mother
> and the Mother of the life in you,[6]

Mary

The Aquarian age is the age when God the Father pours out of his infinite bliss the waters of Mother-flow, that she might assume the role of man or woman, of infant child, of sister, brother, father, mother, son or daughter, wife or husband. These are the masks and the masquerades of the Mother peeping through the veils of maya. Now you see her; now you don't. In the sick and the dying, in the hungry and the desolate, the poor and the lowly, you discover a portion of her blessed self bearing the sins of the world, assuming roles that allow you to feed the hungry, heal the sick, fill the empty, clothe the naked, and thereby realize yourself as the mother of the Mother flame.

Mary

6

A Trilogy of the Mother

III
The Vision of a New Age

Children of the One God,
May I hold you in the immaculate embrace of the Cosmic Virgin as I brace the soul and the substance of the soul in the outline of the Spirit Most Holy.

The one who realizes the Mother within, who determines to be that Mother on behalf of all life, discovers that the energies of being and the flow of the tide of identity move irresistibly, as if magnetized by the sun, into the fiery core that is the Holy Spirit. Hence in all ages, those who have known the Reality of the Mother and who have identified as the Mother have become the bride of the Holy Spirit, for their consciousness has fused with the very living Presence of the Paraclete.

And there is a moment in the life of the devotee of the World Mother when the initiation of the fusion of solar energies with the Holy Spirit takes place. And whether you occupy a body that is male or female, this experience can and will come to you when, by the surging and resurging of the love of God within, your energies become fluid, quickened, alive, capable of flowing as the tides of the sea in and out of the inlet of consciousness.

The Nature of the True Aquarian

When you, in the flame of the Mother, flow with the fire of the Holy Spirit, you begin to understand the nature of the true Aquarian—the man or woman of the New Age who bears the water of the Mother and pours that water into the vessels of manifold identity. The fluid nature of the Mother is such that she is always adaptable to the needs of her children, able to assume whatever role is needed at the moment of crisis—the moment of victory.

Thus the Aquarian age is the age when God the Father pours out of his infinite bliss the waters of Mother-flow, that she might assume the role of man or woman, of infant child, of sister, brother, father, mother, son or daughter, wife or husband. These are the masks and the masquerades of the Mother peeping through the veils of maya. Now you see her; now you don't. In the sick and the dying, in the hungry and the desolate, the poor and the lowly, you discover a portion of her blessed self bearing the sins of the world, assuming roles that allow you to feed the hungry, heal the sick, fill the empty, clothe the naked, and thereby realize yourself as the mother of the Mother flame.

The Aquarian flow
Is that you might realize here below
The Mother in her many guises,
In the oneness of the Spirit that ever rises—
Pulsating white-fire core,
Whirling, whirling sacred lore
Unveiling veils of destiny
As life by life the wedding garment of the soul
Is woven, is woven for the whole.

Now here, now there,
Hither and yon and everywhere,
The Mother flame incarnate shows forth Reality,
A gentleness of magnanimity,
The swirling, flowing, winding, curling—
As incense rising
From the altar of Father, Son and Spirit
Moves the Mother, comes the Mother,
Wending through the souls of humanity:

Her joy a girlish laughter,
Her sorrow the disappointment of a child,
Her tear glistening in the eye
Recalls the image of the Father on high,
Her longing the longing of twin flames
For the Holy of Holies of their love,
Her desiring to bring forth the Manchild of the age,
Her voice the memory of a lullaby,
Her hand the touch of comfort and of love,
Her beauty the profile of a cosmos yet unborn,
Her compassion the glow of starlight twinkling
    in the sea,
Her heart the heart of all humanity.

Wisdom would teach her children to understand every part of life by letting the flow of the Mother be poured into other cups of identity. Learn compassion by looking through another's eyes, by walking in another's footsteps, by entering the heart and the mind for a moment, for awhile, of father, mother, brother, sister or little child. For as you flow with the consciousness of the Mother to and fro, in and out of the body of God on earth, you will come to understand just why people are people, why they behave as they do, both with and without the knowledge of the Law. Retaining your identity as the Christ, you can be at once at the point of that Christ in man, in woman, that releases the creativity of the Universal Mind even as you fathom the whys and wherefores of the human existence that is an enigma to so many.

Now you see why the Aquarian age is an age of alchemy and transformation: it is the energy of the Mother-flow. Now you see why the Aquarian age is the age of creativity, the unlocking of the genius locked within the soul—by the Mother-flow. Now you see why the Aquarian age will be the age of the greatest dramas, of art and literature and culture. For the Mother flame wedded to the Holy Spirit is for the perfectionment of the matrices of the Christed identities of all of the sons and daughters of God.

Let the Flame of Illumination Pierce the Night of Ignorance

As you go forth holding the immaculate concept for the little ones swimming in the great sea of life, invoke the flame of golden-yellowed hue, the richness of the wisdom of our Lord made plain in the illumined eyes of the Mother tenderly beholding the Reality of her children. In the yellow plume of the threefold flame, the understanding of the Christed Ones is born. Here you pan for the gold of virtue, honor and nobility. Here is the adornment of the kings and priests unto God, of the queens and priestesses who tend the fires at the altar of the Holy Spirit.

Thus in the flame of illumination—illumined action—see and know and invoke for all of life the highest fulfillment of the Law through self-knowledge and the knowledge of the Self as God. Let the golden flame of Christmas candle pierce the night of ignorance and reveal the children of the Mother shining in the sun of righteousness haloed with the corona of the sun, brilliant symbol of the mind of God.

And so, beholding the vision of illumined action for and on behalf of a world and its evolutions, let the love fires of golden-pink glow ray rise from Mary's well, the well of the Mother ray whence spring the waters of eternal love—love as life ever flowing, ever knowing that love is the light, the bubbling joy of creativity, the Holy Family, the nativity. Out of love is born the age of the Holy Spirit when the hearts of mankind locked in the heart of God partake of that Holy Communion, that blessed sacrament that is the Body and the Blood, the Omega and the Alpha, of our Lord.

"For God so loved the world, that he gave his only begotten Son, that whosoever believeth in him should not perish, but have everlasting life."[1] Now, beloved hearts, entering the dispensation of a new year and the twenty-five-year reign of the Holy Spirit, so love the world that through your love, your compassion, your caring, the world will receive him as the anointed one of the heart. So love the world as God loves the world, and you will see the transformation of all life as hand in hand the Mother and the Spirit Holy walk down the aisle into their cosmic union.

    I AM in your soul and in your Spirit,[2]

Mary

PART FOUR

There Is Still Time for Prophecies to Be Changed

*Blessed ones,
I live with the Fátima prophecy.
I live with its message.
And I go from door to door
and heart to heart knocking,
asking for those who will come
and pray with me—
pray the violet flame
or the rosary or the calls to
Archangel Michael.
But above all, pray. For by thy
prayer is the open door extended,
and the angels come stepping
through the veil to prevent
disaster and calamity.*

Mary

7

A Mother's Warning to Her Children

by Elizabeth Clare Prophet

God has sent Mother Mary in the prophecy of Fátima,[1] even as he sent her to give birth to the Christ in Jesus.

The Fátima Prophecy

The Fátima prophecy is a message that says, "This is the hour of your incarnation of the Word. This is the hour of Christ's appearing in you. Raise up this light and defeat the oncoming karma. Defeat the prophecy of the deeds of men and fallen angels now coming to bear in this end of the two-thousand-year Piscean age."

The Fátima prophecy is exciting because it spells out what will happen if we do not act. And it says absolutely that if we do act, we can avert those prophecies. Sad to say, neither Pope nor Church nor bishops nor people have responded fully enough to avert that prophecy. And therefore, we are in the dilemma of the changing of worlds in this hour. We are experiencing life today as a great darkness oncoming that marks the conclusion and the finish of the Piscean age.

Simultaneously, we have the light of the Great Central Sun that is coming to earth. We feel a tremendous wave of that light and its presence in us. Aquarius is dawning. It has been dawning for two centuries, even since the founding of the nation of America when Saint Germain, the master of the Aquarian age, did come to endow America with his sponsorship.

The Sponsorship of Saint Germain

Saint Germain is our sponsor. He is your sponsor. He was embodied as Joseph at Mary's side. He comes to you to assist you to raise up the Mother light within. He comes to sponsor you in the raising of the sacred fire and the Kundalini.

Pisces and Aquarius—the configurations unite, and here we stand. I believe that we can make a greater effort, that we can multiply the action of the light within ourselves and that we can pursue the turning back of prophecy. But every day that we neglect the fullness of our role in this manner, those prophecies become physical.

The Law of Karma Is Our Teacher

Jesus came to restore to us the path of personal Christhood after a long period of the karma of forsaking the way of the Truth of the Divine Teacher. Many lessons had to be learned throughout many civilizations and the rising and falling of continents. Jesus is our Saviour because he recalled for us a path of reunion with God and the renewed opportunity to receive directly from that Universal Christ the teaching, the Path, the ascension and the reunion of twin flames.

We read in Revelation 13 that it was given to the beast "to make war with the saints, and to overcome them: and power was given him over all kindreds, and tongues, and nations. And all that dwell upon the earth shall worship him, whose names are not written in the book of life of the Lamb slain from the foundation of the world."[2]

Those whose names are written in the Book of Life are those who have descended from the Great Central Sun trailing clouds of glory, who know the I AM Presence and their God with them, who easily bend the knee before the Universal Light and recognize that Christ—not only in Jesus but in themselves and in one another—and who accept that as the Reality of our love. Here is stated in Revelation 13 the law of karma.

Those who seek a literal interpretation of scripture will tell us that there is no mention of karma in the Bible. Well, in truth the Old and New Testaments are the story of karma from Genesis to Revelation. The words and deeds of the characters of scripture tell us the lessons, whether of glorifying

God and his name or of disobeying that God and facing the consequences that are always prophesied by the prophets in our midst. They always come to tell us that if we will cease in our waywardness, we will be blessed and if not, certain things will come upon us.

This statement of the law of karma reads, "He that leadeth into captivity shall go into captivity: he that killeth with the sword must be killed with the sword. Here is the patience and the faith of the saints."[3] Here in this law that is written, here in this divine justice, we understand that each one receives the recompense, even the return of the energy he has sent out.

The scripture also says, "Whatsoever a man soweth, that shall he also reap."[4] And that statement is preceded by the words, "God is not mocked." It is the Law of God that we can never mock, though many try. And evildoers who are those fallen angels cast out of the etheric octaves, the octaves of light, are always demonstrating to us how they seek to get away with violating the Laws of our I AM Presence. They get away with nothing.

But we are bought with a price.[5] And in these two thousand years, Jesus, the incarnation of the Word, has borne the karma of the world. You remember the statements that he bore our sins, that he died for our sins.

Karma is the causes you have set in motion returned to you as effect. You have great, good, positive karma, and so does the whole world. We have wonderful achievements, attainments and blessings and love and light that come to us daily. We have all done good works and sent forth great joy and love and peace and constructivism in the service of one another and all life on earth. That good karma is sealed in heaven. It is the wind in our sails; it is our momentum. It is, in fact, what is called our attainment.

We are not so concerned about that light in terms of prophecy. We are concerned about what we have done with God's energy to set in motion causes that have produced effects that are negative and burdensome, such as the limitations of our mortality, such as our diseases, such as the calamities in the economy and all those things that are coming in this earth. Therefore, we invoke the light that is sealed Above to heal or transmute the darkness that is here below. And these things are part of the lost teachings of Jesus.[6]

Fátima is a prophecy of war and cataclysm, a prophecy of the repetition of the war that was in heaven as it is described in Revelation 12: "And there was war in heaven: Michael and his angels fought against the dragon; and the dragon fought and his angels, and prevailed not."[7]

So, the war was started in heaven and it is finished on earth. And what it is called on earth is Armageddon. Armageddon is in full swing today on planet Earth, and some of us do not realize that fact. We have not adjusted to the fact that Armageddon is not going to be announced. It creeps in even as those fallen angels creep in unawares.[8]

The Vision of Fátima

In the twentieth century, the century of war itself and of Armageddon, Mother Mary comes early, 1917, at Fátima, Portugal. She gives a secret in three parts just three months before the October Revolution.⁹ She comes to three shepherd children and gives them a vision of hell for a very important reason. And she tells them why:

> You have seen hell, where the souls of sinners go. To save them God wishes to establish in this world the devotion to my Immaculate Heart. If people do as I shall ask, many souls will be converted and there will be peace. This war [World War I] is going to end, but if people do not cease offending God, not much time will elapse and during the Pontificate of Pius XI another and more terrible war will begin.¹⁰

Hell, then, ought to be defined. We do not see it as a place of perpetual burning or eternal damnation. We see it as the lowest vibrating plane of our planet, which is called the astral plane. To this plane we may gravitate not only after death but nightly as we go out of our bodies. We should be going to the octaves of light, to study in the retreats of the ascended masters and the archangels.¹¹ But sometimes we don't have the momentum of light to get there.

The astral plane, then, is a place where we face those works that are not of the light—that are a violation of God's Laws. And we must deal with our karma here or hereafter. It is a certain torment to receive in that situation, without a physical body, all of the hatreds and the anger and the darkness that people have sent out. And therefore, in this hour for our deliverance, Saint Germain has given us the violet flame for the transmutation of karma before it comes upon us, whether in life or in death (see page 104).

The vision, then, of hell is to make these children understand that souls will go to this place, led there by false teachers, unless they are prayed for, unless people will give the rosary and unless we give devotion to the Immaculate Heart.

We understand the fullness of the meaning of the Immaculate Heart as Mother Mary's vision that is so powerful it is like an emerald matrix[12] that she places over us. And as we meditate upon the heart of Mary, we receive the power of her vision for us.

The Violet Flame

Mother Mary continued with these words:

> When you shall see a night illumined by an unknown light, know that this is a great sign from God that the chastisement of the world for its many transgressions is at hand through war, famine, persecution of the Church and of the Holy Father.
>
> To prevent this, I shall come to ask for the consecration of Russia to my Immaculate Heart and the Communion of reparation on the First Saturdays [of the month].
>
> If my requests are heard, Russia will be converted and there will be peace. If not, she will spread her errors throughout the entire world, provoking wars and persecution of the Church. The good will suffer martyrdom; the Holy Father will suffer much; different nations will be annihilated.

But in the end my Immaculate Heart will triumph. The Holy Father will consecrate Russia to me, and it will be converted and some time of peace will be granted to humanity.[13]

In 1929 Mary came to Lucia, now a nun,[14] with her request: "The moment has come in which God asks the Holy Father, in union with all the Bishops of the world, to make the consecration of Russia to my Immaculate Heart, promising to save it by this means."[15] Although there have been various papal blessings since that time, no pope has ever fulfilled this direction *exactly as she requested it*. And therefore the prophecy that Russia will spread her errors throughout the entire world did come to pass.

The Second Secret

The "unknown light" of the second secret is said to have occurred on January 25, 1938, when an unexplained red glow was seen in the night for about five hours. It was seen in Europe, America, Asia and Africa. Following this, in February of 1938, Austria was forced into political union with Germany. In September 1939, Hitler invaded Poland and started World War II.

In May 1983, Mother Mary, dictating through me, said that the deaths of the two World Wars and "ensuing conditions" happened "because the leaders of the Catholic Church itself did not respond to my mandate" of Fátima.

The Third Secret of Fátima

The third secret was to be revealed by 1960. Again, the popes have disobeyed Mary's directive and have never disclosed it.* Therefore, they have not given the people the opportunity to invoke the light for the transmutation of that prophecy that is projected upon the screen of life.

It is said that Khrushchev and Kennedy were given that third secret to read and to understand by the Pope.[16] In 1963, a German newspaper, *Neues Europa,* published what is called an "extract" of the third secret. This is what they printed:

> A great chastisement will come over all mankind; not today or tomorrow but in the second half of the twentieth century. Satan will succeed in infiltrating into the highest positions in the Church. Satan will succeed in sowing confusion in the minds of scientists who design weapons that can destroy great portions of mankind in short periods. Satan will gain hold of heads of State and will cause these destructive weapons to be mass-produced.
>
> If mankind will not oppose these evils, I will be obliged to let the Arm of my Son drop in vengeance. If the chief rulers of the world and of the Church will not actively oppose these evils, I will ask God my Father to bring His Justice to bear on mankind. Then will God punish mankind even more severely and heavily than He did at the time of the great deluge.[17]

I want to remind you that Mother Mary is speaking to children who understand somewhat Catholic teaching but nothing beyond. What she is saying here is that if there is

---
*On June 26, 2000, the Vatican released what it claimed to be the Third Secret of Fátima. The document describes a vision that has been interpreted to be the attempted assassination of Pope John Paul II in 1981. It has been questioned why the Vatican waited nearly twenty years after the assassination attempt to reveal the Third Secret and whether this document reveals the entire Third Secret.

not the intercession of the good people of earth in whom the God flame burns, then there will be nothing to stand between mankind and their own karma, the karma of their neglect.

She says that it is the responsibility of the leadership in Church and State to oppose the actions of the fallen angels in embodiment who have been leading mankind to war, lining them up brother against brother for centuries. She is saying that this karma is coming due in the last century of the age of Pisces.

The teaching we have on Jesus Christ bearing the sins of the world is that when we come to the conclusion of the dispensation of his example and his teaching, we are intended to manifest the fullness of that same Christ. And therefore, having fulfilled the Law that he demonstrated, we now receive our karma upon our own shoulders. This teaching is very plain in the statement you will find in the New Testament, "Every man shall bear his own burden."[18] It is a striking contradiction of the prevailing theology of the day, which says that Jesus is going to bear all of our burdens.

Theology has made it very easy to get to the kingdom of heaven. But all of the true prophecies that have come from Jesus, the apostles, the saints and from Mother Mary to the present hour do not say this. Therefore, we understand that every man must bear his own karmic burden and that the grace of Jesus Christ is a two-thousand-year period of freedom when we should learn how to increase the light so that the very light in our auras and in our spiritual centers might be able to balance, to compensate for and to transmute our sins or our errors or our incorrect sowings or our misuse of the light.

Mother Mary, then, is saying that prayer as the invocation of the light is an energy and a substance that comes to us through devotion, through praise and through oneness with God, and that this light is the Mediator. This light becomes our attainment. This light is the means whereby we literally transmute, or balance, karma before it descends upon us. And the very special portion of that light that God gives to us for this purpose is the violet flame, made known to us in this century by Saint Germain but used by Jesus from the very beginning.

This, then, is the teaching of the New Age. It is altogether logical that if we should have free will and the freedom to experiment with that will, using freely God's energy and the divine spark, that we should also know the consequences of our uses and misuses of that creative power. Created in the image and likeness of God,[19] we are co-creators with him. We are seeing, then, returning in this hour our creations—personally and on a planetary scale. You and I have not created all of the karma that is descending upon the nations in this hour, but we have contributed little rivulets, little drops, of our angers and our fears and our jealousies and all of those things that have not been centered in the heart of Christ. This becomes planetary karma.

Fallen Angels

But the gravest karma of all that we see in Armageddon is the karma of the fallen angels in our midst, who have surely been the murderers and the liars and the sorcerers and the black magicians and the molesters of children and those who have brought to this world the most destructive momentums—not only of war but the misuse of the abundant life in the economy; the misuse of our youth, bringing drugs, bringing promiscuity and the misuse of the life force, bringing a certain violence of hell out of the syncopated rock beat, which takes the energy down the spine and centers it in the lower chakras; the plague of alcohol and of marijuana upon our nation.

We see, then, that massive forms of population manipulation and control have occurred throughout the centuries. This is the hour of Armageddon for the binding and the judgment of the seed of the wicked. Unfortunately, unknowingly, the children of the light have taken these fallen angels in their glamour and their charisma, and they have made them their idols and their gods. They have left off from the serving of the one light, and therefore they are not internalizing that light.

The judgment of the fallen angels is come. And that is why Joshua sent forth the call to come apart and be a separate people[20]—separated out from, if you will, the Canaanites, these evildoers who wreak havoc with civilization and bring the poisons and the toxins to our bodies and ruin the economy of the farmer, of labor, of business, of the free enterprise system, of international trade.

Everywhere, then, the controllers of money and power are receiving their karma. Witness the karma in the stock market.* Witness this and see. Whose karma is it? It's the karma of the fallen ones who have misused the light of the people. And yet the people have invested in stocks. Therefore, they suffer also. We have become tied to their Cain civilization. And when their Cain civilization is judged, we suffer also.

---

*This lecture was delivered on October 31, 1987, following the largest stock market crash in history on October 19. The Dow lost 22.6 percent of its value, or $500 billion.

This is a period, then, of separation by light and by vibration so that when God desires to bring the whole earth into a golden age when we pass through this Dark Cycle,[21] we will be here because we will have survived physically and we will have survived spiritually. This is the message of Fátima—a message for the century.

The *Neues Europa* account continues:

> A time of very severe trial is also coming for the Church. Cardinals will oppose cardinals and bishops will oppose bishops. Satan will enter into their very midst.[22]

The use of the term "Satan" by Mother Mary, again, is because of the children's point of perspective. Satan is merely one particular fallen angel, the leader of a band of angels called the "satans." And the seed of Satan are in the earth, along with the seed of Lucifer and the seed of Beelzebub and the rest of those fallen angels called Watchers in the Book of Enoch[23] and Nephilim in the Book of Genesis and Numbers.[24]

Therefore, we understand that in this hour and in this day these very ones in our midst are bringing upon us that point of the return of karma. (The term "Satan" refers to the issue of these fallen angels, many in our midst who have made their allegiance to him.)

Neues Europa continues:

> In Rome also will occur great changes. What is rotten will fall and what falls must not be retained. The Church will be obscured and all the world will be thrown into great confusion.
>
> The great, great war will come in the second half of the twentieth century. Death will reign

everywhere, raised to triumph by erring men, the helpers of Satan who will be the masters of the earth. These evils will come at a time when no one expects it.

The age of ages is coming, the end of all ends if mankind will not repent and be converted and if this conversion does not come from rulers of the world and of the Church. Woe and greater woe to mankind if conversion does not occur.[25]

I believe that every word of that is true, whether or not it was the third secret, which has been disputed.* I think it is a statement of the law of karma. It is not a punishment by God. But the word "conversion" means the turning around. It is the power of the Great Central Sun Magnet—the Presence of Christ, if you will—that draws us into alignment with Almighty God, who is our shield. When people go out and squander their light in a pleasure cult, they have nothing against the day of the descent of the karma of the fallen angels. This is why such a burden comes upon the earth.

"Teach Me How to Pray"

In my prayers lately before the altar, I have called and called and called for many dispensations and assistance

---

*Not mentioned in the Vatican's release of the Third Secret (see p. 83) is "the great, great war that will come in the second half of the twentieth century" described by *Neues Europa*. However, prophecy is a warning of what will happen if nothing changes. It is not predestination. Prophecies can be mitigated or turned back if mankind change their ways, pray for divine intercession and transmute their karma with the violet flame before that karma crystallizes and becomes physical. For an understanding that prophecy is not set in stone, see *Saint Germain's Prophecy for the New Millennium*, by Elizabeth Clare Prophet.

and intercessions to America,* to the earth, to the nations; and never before in my life as a messenger and in offering prayers have I had so many responses come back that have said, "Daughter, your prayers cannot be answered, for the karma must descend upon mankind." And so I would think to myself, well, there must be some prayers that can be answered. I would call upon the Father and the masters, "Teach me how to pray. Tell me what I can call for that is lawful in keeping with your will, in keeping with mankind's karma."

So I realized that it takes a great ingenuity to figure out what we are bringing to the altar that will satisfy the Great Law as an offering, a penance, you might say, like Job's or Abraham's burnt offerings for their people, for their children.[26] What can we bring to God that will gain some dispensation that would not otherwise be forthcoming?

Many people themselves do not have atonement, do not understand penance or the need to pray and give the violet flame for their own lives, their own karma. They don't understand it is necessary to call to God for forgiveness when we have wronged a friend, to ask the friend for forgiveness and then to say prayers to the violet flame. If we don't realize that unless we call for the forgiving of our debts as we forgive our debtors,[27] then we become greater

---

*"America" is an anagram for "I AM Race." America is an experiment of the Great White Brotherhood. By the unseen hand and the very specific guidance of the ascended masters and the sponsorship of Saint Germain, America was born, her independence was declared, her constitution written. America is the land created as a repository of freedom that millions of souls might realize their potential to become one with God. It is the place where freedom of religion, freedom of speech, freedom of the press and freedom to assemble provide the foundation for the individual pursuit of cosmic consciousness. In her book *The Great White Brotherhood in the Culture, History and Religion of America*, Elizabeth Clare Prophet describes the divine destiny of America.

and greater debtors. It just builds up on your credit card. And soon you are going to be spiritually bankrupt.

The Karma of the World Has Been Building

The overwhelming realization that we are supposed to gain from the Fátima message is that the karma of the world has been building. And it has been building not only for two thousand years since Jesus' coming, but for twelve thousand years, since the last planetary cataclysm, the sinking of Atlantis. It is a twelve-thousand-year cycle that is upon us.

When you think of that, it is tremendous. The karma of twelve thousand years coming due is no small-ticket item. So we want to run to the altar and simply increase our prayer vigils and increase our prayer time and increase our violet flame, and also be concerned about taking care of our loved ones, our families and those for whom we are responsible.

Sin without atonement is to be feared more than hell, more than death, more than anything that could happen to you. Karma is going to fall due with cyclic regularity. In this age, we're in the Dark Cycle of the return of karma, and the intercession of the Lord Jesus Christ cannot be what it was before, because we or others or the planet as a whole have squandered the opportunity to gain Christhood in the allotted time. When we realize this, we

Invoking the Violet Flame

ought to be concerned. And we ought to take the teachings and give the violet flame daily.

Penance becomes atonement. Atonement means "to balance, to pay the debt for, to make things right again." So either we experience our karma or we atone for it before the Day of Reckoning, before the day when God says, "The right hand of my Son descends." And when it descends in the judgment, you cannot turn it back. You can't send an avalanche back up a mountain. You can't undo a nuclear warhead that has gone off—if you see what I mean. Every day physically something happens in your life. I hope all your days will be blest and full of joy. They can be, even though you are reaping your karma, as long as you greet that karma at the dawn with the violet flame and with the rosary.

Theories about the Third Secret

We have another study of what this third secret might be. It was done by Frère Michel de la Sainte Trinité. He conducted an in-depth, four-year study of the Fátima prophecies. He contends that the version of the third secret that appeared in the *Neues Europa* article is "at least 4 times too long" to fit on the small sheet of paper on which Lucia wrote it.[28] (However, I would not agree with him that this is a definitive reason why it is wrong.)

He and many other authorities believe that the principal message of the secret involves a crisis of faith within the Church rather than prognostications of war or cataclysm. He says its portent is "even more fearsome than famine, wars, persecutions, for it concerns souls—their salvation or their eternal perdition."[29]

Frère Michel points out that in 1941 when Lucia wrote

down the July 13 message[30] for the second time in her memoirs, she added the statement, "In Portugal, the dogma of faith will always be preserved, etc." The "etc." indicates the part she could not reveal—the third secret.

This sentence, Frère Michel concludes, is the key to the undisclosed message. He quotes the late Father Alonso, official archivist of Fátima: "This sentence in all clarity implies the critical state of the faith which will befall other nations. That is to say a crisis of faith, while Portugal will save its faith. In other parts of the Church these dogmas either are going to become obscure or else even be lost."[31]

Father Alonso also believed that the text of the third secret could allude to internal struggles "in the very bosom of the Church" and to "grave pastoral negligence by the high hierarchy."[32] I believe all these things are true. There is a falling away of faith.

Bishop Cosme do Amaral, the bishop of Leiria-Fátima, who remained silent on the subject for ten years, commented in 1984:

> The Secret of Fátima speaks neither of atomic bombs nor of nuclear warheads, nor of SS20 missiles. Its content concerns our faith. To identify the Secret with catastrophic announcements or with a nuclear holocaust is to distort the meaning of the Message. The loss of faith of a continent is worse than the annihilation of a nation.[33]

Lucia herself, when questioned about the content of the third secret, has said: "It's in the Gospel and the Apocalypse—read them."[34]

In December 1984, Mother Mary said in her dictation, "I live with the Fátima prophecy. I live with its message and go from door to door and heart to heart knocking, asking for those who will come and pray with me—pray the violet flame or the rosary or the calls to Archangel Michael. But above all, *pray*. For by thy prayer is the open door extended and the angels come stepping through the veil to prevent disaster and calamity."[35]

In answer to the call of Mother Mary and to the call of Archangel Michael, I released "Archangel Michael's Rosary for Armageddon." This is a most powerful service that invokes the seven archangels and the legions of light, hosts of the LORD, to intercede. It includes prayers of Jesus. It gives the prayer of Pope Leo XIII, the prayer to Archangel Michael that had been in the Mass until Vatican II.[36] It includes the Hail Mary, and it gives you the opportunity to insert your very personal prayers for yourself and loved ones, your community, family, nation and planet.

Mary's Appearances at Garabandal

Mother Mary's prophecies did not conclude with Fátima. Between July 1961 and January 1963, Mother Mary appeared to four young girls hundreds of times in Garabandal, Spain. She warned them of a "great chastisement" and said that prayer, sacrifice and penance were needed. The ascended masters teach that penance is good works with the violet flame, with the call for the light of God to transmute negative karma. Mother Mary said, I, your

Mother, through the intercession of Saint Michael the Archangel, want to tell you to amend your lives. You are already receiving one of the last warnings.[37]

Medjugorje

On June 25, 1981, Mother Mary began appearing to four girls and two boys in a little town in Yugoslavia called Medjugorje. She has been appearing to them ever since. Pilgrimages have been made as people of every faith come to a shrine and a cross at the top of a hill where the children saw the Divine Mother.

She has been in the process of giving to each of them ten messages, or secrets, concerning the future of the world. When they have received the ten messages, Mother Mary says that she will cease appearing to them.[38]

One of the visionaries, Mirjana, says that the ninth and tenth secrets are serious. They concern chastisement for the sins of the world—again, returning personal and planetary karma. She says, "Punishment is inevitable."[39]

Karma Must Be Faced

This means that karma is inevitable because it is the law of cause and effect. But that does not mean it cannot be transmuted by the violet flame. Karma is irrevocable except where there is the insertion and intrusion of divine grace through the living Saviour. That living Saviour is not Jesus Christ alone, but it is the Saviour above you who is your Holy Christ Self, the personal Christ (depicted as the middle figure in the Chart of Your Divine Self), who must descend through you in answer to your call because you are in embodiment, and it is our hour to take our stand for light and to direct that light.

A Mother's Warning to Her Children 95

The Chart of Your Divine Self

You have often heard the words of Jesus, "I am the light of the world." They are printed in churches. But have you read in scripture how that is written? It says, "So long as I am in the world, I am the light of the world."[40] That means when Jesus was in physical embodiment, he anchored that light through his body.

You can tie that statement to another reference from Jesus' teaching where he says, "Ye are the light of the world. A city that is set on an hill cannot be hid."[41] He also tells us not to hide the light of our Christhood under a bushel of neglect.[42] What he is saying is that we are the light of the world when we are in embodiment. And that light flowing through us becomes the light of the whole planet. He shows us that in our time we rise to the occasion and, by the call, we raise up the light within ourselves.

When karma is inevitable, it's like taxes, it's like paying your monthly bills, it's like all other obligations of life. The chastening is the love of God, not punishment—but if we do not bank the light in our chakras and our spiritual centers against the day of karma descending, we may experience it as punishment. It will be very painful; it will be very sorrowful. Our karma may even take us from physical embodiment through one of the last plagues, as we are seeing the burdens upon our people of AIDS, of cancer, of other new viruses—all of these things coming in this time.

The light can dissolve anything before that karma descends and becomes physical. Once it becomes physical, it is the greatest challenge of all, because we are trying to turn back something that is already crystallized. And that becomes the challenge to those who are wise, to those who believe prophecy because they tie into the spirit of prophecy and therefore they say, "Yes, I can see. I can also read the handwriting on the wall. And I know that of a certainty these things will come to pass if I don't do something about it."

Dire Prophecies Can Be Averted

We are very practical people. We know that if we don't do something about protecting our houses, they may burn down. We put in sprinkler systems. We check our electrical wiring. We check our gas. And we see to it that we are sensible in obeying the laws of physics and chemistry and electricity. We take all kinds of precautions to avoid calamity in the physical sense.

We have to avoid the calamity of karma in our time because once it overtakes us, this karma is so tremendous that we will be tossed and tumbled by it. That is the message. "Work while you have the light" as Christ-potential with you today. Because "the night cometh, when no man shall work."[43] Those are the words of Jesus.

Mirjana says that the secrets are to be announced three days before the events they describe are due to happen. If they are only going to be announced three days before, obviously this is not the time to suddenly invoke the light and stop them. This is Mother Mary's statement, which says, "You haven't invoked the light. In three days' time this will be upon the earth. All you have time to do is call for your soul's conversion to God and for your saving by the Lord Christ and his angels." It is too late then to avert the prophecy. Now is when we have the time.

The logic of the spiritual father of Mirjana and the logic of the message is that the punishment is inevitable because "we cannot expect the whole world to be converted. The punishment can be diminished by prayer and penance, but it cannot be eliminated."[44]

This is the most wondrous hope of divine justice. And when we understand how the effects of returning karma can be diminished by prayer and penance as the ascended masters teach us and as we work with that light and that flame, that violet flame, and see it in our daily lives, the changes that are brought about are so miraculous, so stunning, so powerful, so magnificent that we begin to get a sense that it is indeed possible to greet this oncoming wave of darkness with a greater wave of light and to say, "Thus far and no farther!" to that proud wave.

Mirjana says that the evil contained in the seventh secret has been averted thanks to prayer and fasting. Mother Mary said at Medjugorje:

> You have forgotten that with prayer and fasting you can fend off wars, suspend natural laws.
>
> There are to be three warnings followed by a visible sign, before the secrets are fulfilled. After the first warning, the others will follow shortly. Thus, people will have some time for conversion. That interval will be a period of grace and conversion. After the visible sign appears, those who are still alive will have little time for conversion. That is why the Blessed Virgin continues to encourage prayer and fasting.* The invitation to prayer and penance is meant to avert evil and war, but most of all to save souls.
>
> Mirjana says the events predicted by the Blessed

---

*When fasting, the ascended masters admonish us to use common sense. Fasting for more than three days is not recommended unless you are under the care of a health professional. Never fast if you are pregnant or a nursing mother. If you have a medical or mental health condition, consult your doctor before fasting. If you feel light-headed or disoriented or if you become ill while fasting, stop your fast and gradually return to solid foods.

Virgin are near. Therefore she proclaims to the world: "Hurry, be converted; open your hearts to God."[45]

To Draw People to the Heart of the Divine Mother

Dictating through me Mother Mary said:

I have come to Medjugorje to prepare this people for calamities to come.* The simple of heart need to be reminded of their original faith. To deliver to them a message beyond that which they comprehend within the supposed security of the Church would...serve only to neutralize the message and their opinions of its authenticity.

Thus, to depart from scripture or canon would be to obviate the very purpose of my coming, which is to draw a tremendous devotion of people of every faith to the heart of God and the Divine Mother, that in this sacred tie to heaven they might pass through a darkness to come....

Blessed ones, I came there to prepare them also for the transition. Many souls may be taken unless a great divine intervention does take place by your hand and heart and the oneness in this Community....

The hour is coming and now is when the preparation must be complete—the physical preparation,

---

*Medjugorje is a Croatian village, today part of the Federation of Bosnia and Herzegovina in the former Yugoslavia. Along with Slovenia, Croatia declared her independence from Yugoslavia in June 1991, triggering the Croatian War of Independence. The war ended in 1995 and a peaceful integration of the remaining Serbian-controlled territories was completed in 1998 under supervision of the United Nations.

I say. For you are called to be physical and to remain so for the holding of the light in the earth and not to be counted among those who are taken from the screen of life when events foretold may take place. [46]

I think it is very important to understand what Mother Mary is saying. In this message, she is dictating to the New Age, to those who know her and see her not only as the archeia but as the ascended lady master, to those who realize that there is a New Age dawning, that this is not the end of the world but the end of a cycle and an age, and that by light, we can either get through or transcend our karma. We can be there when we reach that light at the end of the tunnel and when we must build again.

It is very important to listen and call to Saint Germain, who has promised to send you angels who will come to you as they came to him, warning him to take the young child and Mary into Egypt for safety until the death of Herod.[47]

Saint Germain counsels you to set aside even a simple ten or fifteen minutes before retiring to meditate, to invoke the violet flame, to put all the house at rest and be in silence, to be uninterrupted and to make the call to God to send the angels of Saint Germain to you, to give you the divine direction as to what is your right place, your right action and your right deliverance.

We can stand and invoke the light for all humanity. And then when we have done our all and the cycles turn, we must step aside and let the wave of mankind's karma pass by us, as we understand that we must seek the holy mountain of God spiritually in our I AM Presence and physically move on to higher ground.

Mother Mary continued to say in this dictation:

> It is a self-evident truth that the whole world will not be converted and that the world therefore must face also the Great Teacher in the Person of returning karma.

Our karma is our best teacher outside of Eden, because our karma by another name is our experience. And we benefit from the errors we make.

Mother Mary continues:

> You have wondered why the ascended masters have not spelled out their prophecies more specifically. It is for the same reason that these have been told in secret, in part, to these children [of Medjugorje]. Beloved, we never give the fullness of the vision of what karma could bring until almost the very hour of it, because until that time we are kneeling before the throne of the Father begging intercession and dispensation.
>
> O beloved, realize, until the right hand of God descends, until the last grain of opportunity in the hourglass descends, there is opportunity, there is dispensation abundant... for the world to be raised up, for all to change in the twinkling of the eye of God.[48]

We have not had the true teachings of Jesus because they have been lost.[49] We have been now two thousand years not fulfilling our reason for being, lifetime after lifetime. Will God leave us as shorn lambs because wolves in sheep's clothing[50] have entered in and taken from us the garment of the Lord, his understanding and consciousness? No, he will not.

Mary's Appearance on the Anniversary of Chernobyl

On April 26, 1987, the first anniversary of Chernobyl, an eleven-year-old Ukrainian girl saw Mother Mary in the belfry of an abandoned chapel on the outskirts of her village in the Ukraine. The image stayed for several days and many neighbors saw it. Throughout the spring, as many as a hundred thousand people gathered daily in the village of Grushevo, hoping to catch a glimpse of the Blessed Mother, who has reportedly continued to appear periodically.

We Must Invoke Light Daily

The apostle Paul says that in the twinkling of the eye the last trump shall sound[51]—the trump of death, of mortality and our subjugation to its law. Therefore, we depend upon the miracle of God. And we make the call together that Jesus will come into this room, that he will place his aura—including what we call the electromagnetic field or the Electronic Presence of his being—over each and every one of us, that he will place his heart over our heart, his chakras over our chakras and that he will increase in us in this very moment the light that is essential to our being illumined in mind and heart. We will ask him to give us the light that we are able to bear according to the will of God.

The Great Law gives to us light in increments because it is so transforming and so powerful and so alchemical that it can produce even a chemicalization. Peter saw a vision of that in the world and in himself. He said he saw the elements melting with a fervent heat.[52] This alchemy comes to us. And the reason we must invoke light daily and be diligent about it is because we can only absorb so much light daily. And the light that we will need in the day of our karma is greater than the light that we could invoke on that single day. We have to bank the fires of the light in our temple and increase the light and keep it blazing, so that when karma approaches us, we survive it by that light.[53]

The Violet Flame

In the Chart of Your Divine Self (see page 95), you can see the lower figure enveloped in the violet flame, the light of the seventh ray. This violet energy can have profound effects on all aspects of our being—mental, emotional and even physical.

The violet flame is a spiritual energy used in the retreats in the heaven-world. It is also known as the mercy flame or the flame of forgiveness, as well as the freedom flame. This seventh-ray aspect of the Holy Spirit can be called forth through prayer and mantra.

We can use the analogy of a film in a movie projector to describe the action of the violet flame. As you use the violet transmuting flame, you are washing the imperfections and streaks from the film of life and from the lens. You purify the lens, and the film is washed and altered by master artisans, so that it can reflect the purity of the light rays passing through it.

The violet flame can be used to transmute, or change, any negative energy in our lives—the energies of hatred, anger, discord and hardness of heart. Devotees use it to transmute negative karma and to produce positive change in all areas of human endeavor, whether personal or planetary in scope.

The following is a simple mantra from the master Saint Germain, the master who introduced the violet flame to mankind:

> I AM *a being of violet fire,*
> I AM *the purity God desires.*

As you give this mantra, you can visualize this high-frequency spiritual energy of the violet flame erasing your problems, resolving burdens and liberating you from sadness or regret due to poor choices in the past.

Every day, the angels deliver to us a new little pack of karma, our assignment for the day. If we douse it with violet flame at dawn, we can transmute and soften the karma, then balance the rest in service through our job, our family and community, and whatever good works we do on that day.

Don't let your karma pile up, because you can get burdened by it. You may use the following decrees[1] to clean up the day's offering as it arrives, and if you can do a bit extra to clean up the rest of this life and a bit more for previous lifetimes, you will be well on your way to accelerating your consciousness into the ascension in the light.

I AM the Violet Flame

I AM the violet flame
    In action in me now
I AM the violet flame
    To light alone I bow
I AM the violet flame
    In mighty cosmic power
I AM the light of God
    Shining every hour
I AM the violet flame
    Blazing like a sun
I AM God's sacred power
    Freeing every one

Violet Fire

Violet fire, thou love divine,
Blaze within this heart of mine!
Thou art mercy forever true,
Keep me always in tune with you.

(give three times)

I AM light, thou Christ in me,
Set my mind forever free;
Violet fire, forever shine
Deep within this mind of mine.
God who gives my daily bread,
With violet fire fill my head
Till thy radiance heavenlike
Makes my mind a mind of light.

(give three times)

I AM the hand of God in action,
Gaining victory every day;
My pure soul's great satisfaction
Is to walk the Middle Way.

(give three times)

Mothers, fulfill your role and then you will see the Father incarnate, then you will see how man will respond to the highest aspect of his own being. You will see how man will come of age, how man will mature to be the coordinate of your flame. And together, hand in hand as cloven tongues of sacred fire, you shall show forth the Holy Spirit on earth as in heaven. And in that day when the flames of the Holy Spirit are balanced on earth and in heaven, then you will see the culmination of an age and the ushering in of the golden cycle of Aquarius.

Mary

8

Man, Woman, Become Who You Really Are

by Elizabeth Clare Prophet

As we consider man and woman in transition, we consider that in each two-thousand-year dispensation under the solar hierarchies, there are particular qualities of the Godhead that are intended to be portrayed in man and in woman and for the mastery of the elements under those dispensations.

During the Piscean age, we see as the archetypes of the dispensation of the Christ consciousness the figures of Jesus and Mary portraying the ray of the masculine and the feminine. We see Jesus and Mary and Saint Germain anchoring the light of the Holy Family. They received their training from the manus[1] of the sixth root race and of the sixth dispensation, the God and Goddess Meru, who focus the flame of illumination at Lake Titicaca.[2]

Mother Mary spent a great deal of time prior to incarnation and during her incarnation out of her body in that retreat, meditating upon the example of the Christ for that two-thousand-year period. Her meditation upon that archetypal pattern enabled her to bring forth Jesus—the Christed One.

The Sense of Idolatry

It is difficult to know, in the light of history and the covering over—almost as if by a patina of doctrine and dogma—of the images of Jesus and Mary, exactly what the archetypal pattern of their golden-age man and golden-age woman consciousness is. We need to take away the accoutrements that have been built around these two individuals —the mystique and the elevating of them to the position of God, to the exclusion of our entering in and partaking of their consciousness—in order to understand how we can take off from that level of man and woman and go into the New Age as man and woman in the seventh dispensation, the Aquarian age.

In understanding who is man, who is woman, who are we in solving the crisis of identity in this age, we must consider the position of Jesus—not as a god but as an anointed one who realized the inner potential and who showed the example of what every man must do. We must understand Mary the Mother, not as a goddess but as a woman who walked this earth a very little time and space ago; that she had incarnations prior to her final one, as did Jesus; that she also fulfilled an aspect of the feminine potential that women today can fulfill and must fulfill.

As we break down the barriers of separation between ourselves as sinners and Mary and Jesus as gods, we begin to study them as human beings, human archetypes. We see that they faced the same temptations and problems and adversities that we face; we see that they had previous lives in which they made mistakes. They were not always gods, being so perfect as to be almost brittle.

We cannot blame them for this image, which we have retained, because it is our susceptibility to idolatry that has perpetuated it. And of course, the carnal mind that raises the idol will eventually tear down the idol. As with God, so with man: the power to create is the power to destroy. When we create an idol, it means that we control the idol. The one that we elevate is the idol that we shatter, that we tear down.

The mass exodus from churches today is a consequence of an extreme idolatry that finally we cannot contain within ourselves because it is competition with our own egos. Therefore, down come the saints, down comes the Church, down comes hierarchy—and this happens because our understanding of hierarchy was never centered in our own inner Reality.

If we have the inner Reality of the light of the masculine and feminine, then we recognize it in one another: there is no competition, there is no vying for power, there is no jealousy, there is no need to worship the idol, because we are that same flame. Then there is the sense of rejoicing that these two individuals, Jesus and Mary, under great hardship and adversity, were able to sustain their meditation upon a pattern of Christhood for man and woman that has been the foundation of civilization for two thousand years.

The Tests of Jesus and Mary

When we have talked with Jesus and Mary over the years, they have told us that all of this glory that has surrounded them should not eliminate in people's minds the fact that they had their trials and their testings. Mary would say that when she was riding on the donkey to find a place to give birth to Jesus, Joseph would reassure her that they would find a place and that they would get there on time. And Saint Germain, who was embodied as Joseph, has said he wasn't really sure that it was so, but he said it to comfort Mary; and she listened, and she wasn't really certain that it was so either.

After the birth, the angel of the LORD appeared to Joseph; and Joseph, because his meditation was on the inner flame, was able to perceive the angel, to heed the warning, take the message and act on it. Joseph took the warning and he took the young mother and child, and they fled into Egypt. But so many times we receive a warning and it almost stiffens us with fright.

If you will read the writings of the early Church that are not included in the Bible, you find accounts that perhaps are not wholly reliable, but are suggestive of circumstances that we can well understand. There was a period of Jesus' childhood in Egypt that we are not told about in our own scriptures, a period when there was a release of light through the child and healings and many demonstrations of miracles.

On our trip to Egypt, we visited the house where it was said the Holy Family had stayed. And you find when you are there in that country, circumstances and conditions for the raising of a child of light are as difficult, if not more so, than they are in the West today.

Mother Mary has told us that in those days there were not asylums for those who were diseased in mind and soul and body; and so in the streets there were the insane, there were those who were dangerous, those who were diseased. And all of this she had to *un-see* in order to see the perfect Christ in Jesus.

Finding God as Father and Mother

The purpose of man and woman in the Aquarian age is to find the leadership within as the principle of the Godhead as Father, as Mother. There is no competition between these orbs of consciousness; there is a fusion of these orbs that each one might give birth to the Christ.

Women of today must lead the way, pave the way, show forth the mastery of the Divine Feminine within them; they must have the freedom to raise the energies of their chakras to release the light. They must show forth the leadership in the return to the All-Seeing Eye of God, in the return to Eden not only in the allegory but in actuality.

On Lemuria, it was the incarnation of woman that led

the incarnation of man to descend from the vision of the immaculate concept. The temptation for the descent of consciousness came to Eve—to woman—and man followed; and therefore, woman must lead the return to the heart of God.

We see this as man and woman in the individual. But we must see there is also the division in the roles of men and women. Women, then, must lead men back to the original purity of God consciousness. Women must first attain it, and then teach it to their children, train their children in this purity.

What do we see in our cities today? We see the opposite; we see the betrayal of the role of the masculine, we see the taking over of that role by women who do not understand the meaning of liberation, who do not understand the true meaning of the feminist movement, which is the revolution of the soul. Determined not to be put down any longer by any force whatsoever, the soul will rise to realize the alchemical union with the Spirit.

This does not mean that women should fight for superficial equality with men. It means that women must lead the way of spirituality, because the Divine Feminine within is the highest manifestation of us.

It is the intuitive faculties of woman that can give man the vision for the victory. Woman must contain that vision within herself. She must hold that vision for her nation, her community, her planet. Being a mother and a homemaker is not simply being a slave and a housewife. A homemaker is one who draws the fires of Om, of the Central Sun, in the matrix, in the forcefield, for the bringing forth of children and for disciplining these children according to the Laws of God.

Woman sets the mandala whereby man can go forth to

conquer in the precipitation of abundance, in his work, in his profession, in his calling. Man conquers Matter by the action of the feminine ray within himself. Woman must bring out that feminine principle in man.

This does not mean she is deprived of having a career and a calling outside the home. She also can have her sacred labor, and her children can help her to realize it. But there is a period, if woman would be mother—would be the Mother of God—when she belongs with her children. When they are young, when they need her flame, she must be near.

But after all, these years do pass and woman can come into her own, teaching man the conquest of Matter, the alchemy of the sacred fire and how to unlock the energies of the chakras.

Raising Up the Masculine

I was visited by a prostitute not long ago who was telling me of her great love for man and how she had such compassion for man. And I said, "You don't have compassion—you are entering into human sympathy. You are betraying man because you are drawing his energies to the lowest point of consciousness."

She decided she had a mission for the Brotherhood, a mission for the masters to bring love to mankind. I said, "You cannot bring that love or teach of it until you discipline the fires of love within yourself. True compassion for man is to hold the immaculate concept that enables him to raise his energies and unlock his potential in Spirit: the masculine ray that comes forth from the crown chakra as the energies of the mind of God; the masculine energies that come to the third eye and the throat, giving man the power to be man."

When we see weakness and a lack of masculine qualities in men, we must look to the fallen woman within man and woman who has betrayed that masculine principle. When we see women failing to outpicture their roles as mother, as the image of the Cosmic Virgin, we must see that often woman herself allows her own perverted masculine to dominate her own feminine potential. She allows her carnal mind, her bickering, her condemnation, her irritation, her nagging—these qualities perverting the masculine—to destroy the feminine in herself, and both the masculine and the feminine in her husband or in her children.

We see that there is equal responsibility in man and woman. We need to ask ourselves, "Am I betraying God as Father in my life by failing to give the impetus, the thrust of the Law, the energy of the Spirit qualities we associate with man as drive, as ability to conquer, to carve out a destiny for the family?" This also must be contained within woman, but in the presence of man, we allow man to be that polarity. In his absence, we must contain it in ourselves.

So man in the presence of woman gives deference to the feminine ray, accords her grace and consideration, because the feminine is the highest principle within himself. It is the highest manifestation; it can attain the highest realization of God; but on earth, by betrayal, by rebellion it has realized the lowest. The lowest of the low has come through fallen woman.

The Divine Magnet

A civilization can rise only as high as woman in the civilization is allowed to rise. This is true in our own individual golden-age consciousness. Only if you allow woman to rise within you as this energy of the Kundalini,* as the fires of purity, will the masculine within you flower and be fulfilled. There is no such thing as half a God. There is no such thing as excluding either the masculine or the feminine, or saying that one is more important than the other.

We need to look beyond all of the perversions of the Father-Mother God that we have seen take place in man and woman. We need to realize that beyond the illusion, beyond what is taking place in the outer, there is that crystal-fiery core of being; and by our prayer, by our giving the Hail Mary and the Our Father, we can draw forth that potential in one another.

My experience has been so rich in dealing with people who have come to me, not having any light to speak of, not having any awareness of respect for father or mother within or without, or any awareness of the flow of energy. I have seen that with a little application, a little love—showing people that we believe in them, that we know they can realize this light—they blossom overnight, they are transformed, they are different people. That clay mold, that shell that once looked like a walking corpse, suddenly becomes the transfiguring Christed One standing before us. The pushing down of the true masculine, its perversion because of the perversion of the feminine, is reversed—men become men and women become women, and there is no confusion, because we each have such a tremendous task to perform in our own rays that there is no need to compete or steal from one another that holy office in hierarchy that is accorded us.

I have given training to many young men, sons of God,

---

*The word *Kundalini* means literally "coiled-up serpent." The Kundalini is the coiled energy in latency at the base-of-the-spine chakra. It is the negative polarity in Matter of the positive Spirit-fire that descends from the I AM Presence to the heart chakra.

in the anchoring of the magnet of the masculine ray within their chakras, within their hearts. I've shown them how to pursue a celibate path and how to use that energy for anchoring the true principle of the Godhead. I have explained to them, "If you have a dream of a woman in your heart that you have never met, your twin flame, the epitome of beauty and virtue and loveliness and motherhood, that woman can walk by your side if you will realize your divine manhood."

And I will say to them, especially those who have squandered their energies and perverted the sacred fire, "You don't have anything of the masculine ray within you to attract the divine woman. What do you expect of all of your sorrows and your problems with women? You have never exalted the Christ; you haven't set the magnet within you to attract anything of any worth. You do not have anything that you do not deserve in this life, and you can only attract what you are. So the more you focus the attributes of the ascended masters who personify the masculine principle, the more you become the embodiment of strength and the virtues of honor, nobility and protection. The more you understand what the Fatherhood of God is, then the greater the possibility is of your magnetizing, from some corner of the earth or heaven, that divine one who is the exact polarity of what you are."

So I put them through a period of meditation, invocation and service, working to anchor that fire in the chakras. And by and by, lo and behold, she comes walking through the door—the exact image-counterpart of the one who has been willing to sacrifice the misuse of his energy and consecrate that energy to God.

I teach the same to women: "If you are dissatisfied, you have no one to blame but yourself. When you become the true woman, the true mother, the true manifestation of the feminine principle of the cosmos, you will find your divine counterpart. And this may manifest in many ways. It may be an individual who walks by your side giving you the comfort and the compassion of a companion of life; or it may be an ascended master, your own twin flame who has gone before you, who is by your side and so present, so near, that you are never alone, that you constantly feel the wholeness of that one."

Marriage and the Family

Marriage is not necessarily the ultimate in life. The marriage of the soul to the Spirit is our goal. Human marriage may be the logical consequence of your mastery, but it may not be the path for you. You may feel the energies rising within you and the union of the masculine and feminine in such an intense manifestation that you cannot even take your attention from the action of the fire that is taking place in your own temple, and to you it would be a desecration to go outside of your own temple to find that union. I am certain that many of the saints, the priests, the nuns, the devotees in Buddhist temples and the temples of the world in East and West have found that union. It is no mystery to me that they have found their oneness in a life of devotion.

So both paths are open. The masters have said the family is the basic unit of the Aquarian age, but the Aquarian age is also the age of the coming forth of the priests and priestesses of the order of Melchizedek.[3] And these are required, because these are the masters in the temples who precipitate, by the heavenly alchemy, creative invention, science, genius of all kinds; and they bring it forth from the fusion of the masculine and feminine within.

But of course, we require avatars, we require the incarnation of the Word. And so Mother Mary, together with Jesus, has given the understanding of what that family is; and especially has she been concerned with the spiritualization of the marriage ritual. The exchange of the sacred fire between man and woman must be a ritual of the highest devotion to God. It must be a fusion of the causal body and of the I AM Presence, not an amalgamation of the carnal mind through sensuality.

During our two-day seminar *Family Designs for the Golden Age*,[4] we recorded my lectures and the dictations of Mary, Jesus and Saint Germain on bringing up children, on preparing for bringing forth the avatars. There is a curse, there is a weight, there is a sense of sin and shame upon the entire human race regarding sex; and that sense of shame has not been imposed upon us by the Mother or the Father, but by the great whore.

The Anti-Mother

You have heard of anti-Christ. Well, you read in the Book of Revelation of the one called the great whore.[5] The great whore is the perversion of the Divine Woman within you. We find that on Atlantis, there was one who was an embodiment, a personification, of the total perversion of the Divine Mother; and it was this woman who put forth the concept of shame and sin, the doctrine of original sin. She put forth the concept "in sin did my mother conceive me," and this was propagated in the temples. It covered the land, it permeated the consciousness; and men and women came together no longer in the purity of a love that transcends Matter, but in the sense of shame.

The desecration of the flame in that hour was most insidious, because it came as a concept, it came as a subtle philosophy, it came as degradation of man and woman. Man in shame and woman in shame could only bring forth an animal creation—not one imbued with the immaculate conception of the Christ. It was in that hour that the priests in the temples declared, "God is dead." And that is where that phrase comes from. They declared that God was dead because God as a Spirit is a living flame, is a joy in the hearts of the people, and that flame had gone out.

Mother Mary is concerned, as we enter the Aquarian age, that the restoration of purity, of honor, of faithfulness in the marriage vow be restored. And when men and women learn this consecration in meditation, they have their dignity, their soul's worth restored to them, and there is a transmutation in the heart of the Mother and in the heart of Saint Germain of all that has been put upon us, where we have come to believe that we are the sinful creation, the product of sex that is wrong.

However, the perversion of this teaching of Mother Mary goes all the way in the opposite direction, to license, to a lack of morals, to free love and free sex, perverted sex and homosexuality, and all of those things that have no part with the consecration of the sacred fire. When students of the ascended masters learn the true way, they find joy and happiness, complete fulfillment, and no longer the agony and the suffering and the burden that comes when there is a misunderstanding and a misuse of these energies.

The Crucifixion of the Mother

Jesus showed us what the walk is for the crucifixion of the Father, of the masculine ray. Now, the whole scene of the sorrowful way becoming the glorious way is for the raising up of God as Mother in you—in man and woman. And the struggle has only begun. It has only begun.

The entire world momentum against freedom is a momentum that is calculated by the fallen ones, by the mass consciousness, to put down this energy of the Mother in you. It is a deadly force. It threatens our abundance of the Mother, as our money is tampered with, as it is watered down and we no longer have the gold standard of the Christ consciousness (and we haven't had it for many years). The devaluation of our money, the manipulation of our currency, the national debt—all of this because the Mother is the energy of abundance. This is opposition to the rise of the feminine ray.

I would like you to know, then, that if you are determined to be a disciple, a disciplined one of the Mother, and to discipline the fires of the feminine within you, you will face adversity—and your determination must be equal to it. You must be able to see the unreality of the fallen ones and that they have no power.

You will find a violent reaction in the world, in your home and in your family when the energy of the feminine begins to burn within you and to rise, when you increase the light of your aura. That is the cross to be borne during the period, the two-thousand-year cycle, when we come to the initiations of the Mother.

In the hour of the crucifixion Jesus said, "This is your hour and the power of darkness."[6] God allowed that darkness to center through the Roman Empire and the Sanhedrin because it was necessary for the judgment. It was necessary for them to personally attack the Christ in order to have their karma descend and their souls be judged for the hatred against the light that they had harbored in their hearts for centuries.

The presence of the Christ among them precipitated that darkness. Their darkness precipitated out, and therefore they were judged. And so Jesus said, "For judgment I am come."[7] For judgment I AM come; for the dividing of the way of light and darkness by the sword of Truth, so that the secrets of men's hearts can be known.

This is the piercing of the mother's soul. When it was prophesied that Jesus would be crucified, Simeon said to Mary, "A sword shall pierce through thy own soul also,"[8] because the feminine ray must also undergo the crucifixion so that the sons and daughters of God can realize their full potential.

When you realize that your body is the body of Mother because it is the Mater-realization of the flame, every attack against your body is an attack against the Divine Mother. Filling your body with the poisons of chemicals, the foods that are incomplete, the pollutions of the atmosphere, the breathing in of that substance—all of this is a denial of the Mother, the crucifixion of the Mother, so that the Mother cannot give birth to the Christ. How can woman give forth the purity of the Christ Child and create a form, a body temple that is pure for that life to express through, when all of the elements of Matter are polluted?

We need to fight pollution; we need to fight indoctrination; we need to fight subliminal advertising. We need to fight what is coming into our minds, stealing into the subconscious, causing spirals of darkness to be fulfilled in the flesh.

I have visited nations in the world where I have seen almost every face without exception bearing the mark of some distortion of life such as is practiced or accomplished through black magic or witchcraft. I have seen how this crucifixion of the Divine Mother has gone much farther in other nations because the flame of freedom has not been enshrined there.

I have seen in the bodies of the people that desecration of the Mother. We do not realize this because it is so insidious and just beneath our surface awareness—and we are subject to a kind of shock treatment. We read our papers and we are so shocked by everything that is so bad that we train ourselves to be immediately conditioned, so that we don't go into some kind of a nervous breakdown over what is happening in society.

This is planned. The shock method is to keep bombarding you with the absolute worst things that are happening in the world—and you are constantly bombarded with this in the media—so that when the ultimate takeover of consciousness comes, you are already conditioned. It's a logical next step. "Oh, well, this is the way it's going."

And that's just about what people say today, even in the face of the worst discoveries that are being made. "Well, that's the way it is." And people just go on, complacent, disillusioned, cynical; and there's no more fight left, because consciousness is not masculine enough, or yang enough—it is not concentrated enough in the white-fire core of being to release the energy of resistance when the Mother is under attack. And so the masculine within us is not putting forth enough power to defend the feminine within us, and we become passive, totally passive, and doormats for this oncoming tide of world karma.

Raising the Kundalini

Now I know in my giving of the rosary daily that that attunement puts me in contact with the masters of the Himalayas who have mastered the Kundalini fires and with Gautama Buddha, who is the Lord of the World because he is the greatest devotee of the Divine Mother. He has the greatest awareness of the Cosmic Virgin, and therefore, he has earned the right to be Lord of the World.

The rosary puts me in contact with the flow of Mother throughout cosmos and with you as the children of the Mother. I feel that I am in your hearts and in your souls every morning, in the heart and in the soul of every child on the planet. I feel the flow of Mother, I feel her intercession.

It was not long ago that I prayed to Mother Mary for her intercession for a soul who was turning against the light in rebellion, in darkness, in rejection of the masters—a very worthy soul who was overcome by the carnal mind of the planet. I prayed for immediate intercession for her. I prayed earnestly for the saving of that soul. And only moments passed before that individual came to me in utter surrender: "I will do the will of God."

The great beauty and the glory of the coming of the Mother is always there, and when you keep the momentum of her flame in your aura, you always have the contact. It's that mesh, that delicate veil that connects you to the Divine

Mother because you have given your application. And over that veil and that mesh flows all the intercession, the divine assistance, whatever you need for your family, for your life.

The giving of the rosary is the safe, sure meditation for the raising of the Kundalini fires. The masters do not approve of the premature raising of these energies. They do not approve of the pairing of couples (especially unmarried couples) and their meditation upon one another's eyes, their connection through the chakras, as some have taught. This is incorrect, and those who teach in this manner are not representatives of the Great White Brotherhood. This is a perversion of the sacred fire.

The masters recommend a very gradual, controlled raising of these energies, not a forcing. They do not teach that you should center your spiritual path on the raising of that energy. They say the raising of that energy is a natural consequence of the purification of the chakras.

When you intensely use the violet flame, it's like creating the pressure of the Holy Spirit upon your being. As your aura fills with the violet flame, pressing down, so the barometer of the life force of the Mother, then, is forced to rise. Up comes the fire, the sacred light, and it comes in God's own time and God's own cycles according to your karma, your dharma, your attainment. You never need to be concerned about it; it simply flows and rises when it is time for it to flow.

And so the Hail to the *Mater*-ray, the Ma-ray, the Mother ray in you is the salutation to all of that energy locked in the white-fire core of your base chakra. In saluting that energy, you've made the contact. When you make the arc of contact, the energy will respond according to the cycles of your own soul.

So if anyone asks, "Do the masters teach meditation, do they teach tantric yoga, do they teach the raising of the Kundalini?" this is the answer, and it is so sound and so beautiful. And when the children begin this meditation of the rosary when they are young, there is the natural filling of their chakras, the natural release of Mother energy, and they are content, they are happy. I have seen the difference when they don't give the rosary—how they are out of sorts, irritated, how they bicker with one another because they don't have the Mother.

We are all very disturbed when we don't have the Mother, and all kinds of things go on in society. All of crime is a result of screaming for the Mother, screaming for attention, doing anything and everything—and finally there is the total desecration of that energy in murder of all kinds, because the Mother is absent. If we don't have the Mother in our auras and make the contact daily, we are incomplete, we have nervous breakdowns, our bodies become ill. This energy must be present, and there is a tremendous pressure for it because it is the energy of the Aquarian age.[9]

PART FIVE

Devotions to the Mother

Stop your wishing and your willing, my children. Cease your murmuring and your struggling against the Flame of Life. And when the day is over and you have fought the good fight of keeping the flame of harmony, let go! Oh, let go, my children! Let all that you have held dear go into the flame. Fear not; for I am near, and our God is also here—a consuming fire of immortal desire desiring to be free. Let God's energy and all of the patterns you have superimposed thereon flow into the central sun of your own divine Reality. Let go of your worldly accomplishments and of your spiritual accomplishments. Let go of your name and your fame and the coordinates of your awareness in Matter.

Mary

9

The Fourteenth Rosary

by Elizabeth Clare Prophet

When beloved Mother Mary dictated the first seven mysteries of the rosary, the eighth mystery and the mysteries of the five secret rays,[1] it was with the fond hope that sons and daughters of God throughout the world would respond to the call of the Mother ray and salute the Flame of Life as the incarnation of the Word of the Mother. The Blessed Virgin told me that when sufficient numbers among the Keepers of the Flame[2] would give with diligence and devotion these sacred mysteries centered in the lives of Jesus and Mary and in the prophecies of the Old and New Testaments, she would release The Fourteenth Rosary.

The Mystery of Surrender

So Mother Mary came to the tower* where she had come before and gave me The Fourteenth Rosary, which is

---

*The messenger used the tower at La Tourelle in Colorado Springs as her prayer room.

The Mystery of Surrender. It is unlike any other of the rosaries; it is beautiful beyond belief. It teaches us to let go; it teaches us to prepare for the hour of the crucifixion. It includes the prayer of Jesus to the Father before his crucifixion. That prayer is called "The Hour Is Come."[3]

When Jesus looked up to God and he had finished his mission he said, "Father, the hour is come. Glorify thy Son that thy Son also may glorify thee."[4] And so that prayer is given in this rosary not as a responsive reading, but by you as you are centered in the Christ.

I have noticed that among the disciples of the masters, it is an hour for surrender, and that this rosary has come precisely in the right moment, when, in order to progress any further, even the most advanced disciples must surrender their family, their loved ones, their children, their name, their fame, their accomplishments, their ego—all of the thoughts that we have about ourselves.

The understanding of surrender is that you do not lose what you surrender. You give it to God for safekeeping, and he gives back to you what he wants you to keep for him. It is saying to God, "I will not hold these things as my possessions, but I will understand that I am a caretaker and that I keep them for you, and that at any time you desire to have them returned, I am willing to give them up."

So many times we take God's light, his energy, the children he gives to us, and we say, "It's mine! And I will defend it at all costs." Well, we should defend it not as mine but as God's, and so we're ready to release it.

My heart leaped in anticipation of the coming of the Mother and her revelation of this rosary. And so she came. She came to La Tourelle, where she had originally appeared to me to explain the new Hail Mary and the devotions of disciples of the Anointed One for the Aquarian age. She stood in the same spot where she had originally appeared as a ray of light—the epitome of Womanhood when realized to its fullest dimension—where she had explained the Hail Mary as the salutation to the Mother ray and to the light of Alpha and Omega locked in the white-fire core of Being.

Mother Mary gave me the Hail Mary for the soul's absorption into the immaculate conception of the Cosmic Virgin and for the weaving of the tie to her own blessed heart as the Mother of Jesus the Christ and as the archetype of golden-age woman. She said, "The Hail Mary is for the resurrection of the energies of life in the bodies, souls and minds of the children of God upon earth; and it will release matrices of perfection for the transition of consciousness into the New Age." The Hail Mary is the mantra of the Mother that she released to affirm the identity of the supplicant as a son, a daughter, of God praying for the intercession of the Divine Mother in the moment of the soul's initiation in the victory over sin, disease and death. Yes, it is in the hour of the victory that we would invoke thy aid, O Blessed Mother!

Now for the victory of the fourteenth station of the cross (see page 243) and the culmination of the spirals of the thirteen rosaries in the consciousness of the Christ, the Blessed Mother has come to teach us how to surrender, how to let go of a false identity fabricated in Matter. She has come to show us how to release into the fires of the Holy Spirit the struggle and the sense of struggle and all of the components thereof—how to dissolve every counter manifestation to the point of light that is our Real Self in God. With all of our determination, with all of our striving to be free and the intensification of devotion that often becomes the tensing of the sinews of the mind and the stretching of the soul's imagination, the Mother comes to us, and as she stands at our side, we hear her voice so lovingly explain:

"Stop your wishing and your willing, my children. Cease your murmuring and your struggling against the Flame of Life. And when the day is over and you have fought the good fight of keeping the flame of harmony, let go! Oh, let go, my children! Let all that you have held dear go into the flame. Fear not; for I am near, and our God is also here—a consuming fire of immortal desire desiring to be free. Let God's energy and all of the patterns you have superimposed thereon flow into the central sun of your own divine Reality. Let go of your worldly accomplishments and of your spiritual accomplishments. Let go of your name and your fame and the coordinates of your awareness in Matter.

"Give all to God and let him give back to you that which he desires you to keep. My children, let The Mystery of Surrender be the ritual of submitting to the flame all of the garments of your consciousness as you would put your wash into the washing machine. Yes, give everything to Him. And while you sleep at night, let the Holy Spirit cleanse and purify every cell and atom, your innermost thoughts and feelings and each shadowed shaft that hides in the folds of your garment.

"Take The Mystery of Surrender and let it commemorate the moment of your dying unto Reality—the moment of the letting-go of each justification of the human ego, of a false sense of responsibility wherein you think friends and family and loved ones are dependent upon you instead of upon God. Let go of the things that you think you must have. Let go of the things that you think in your pride you will never do or the things that you think you will always do. Let go of all human attachments. Let go of every ambition except God's desiring within you to be God."

The Fourteenth Rosary gives each devotee of life the opportunity to formulate his own prayer of surrender at the conclusion of the rosary. Let it be the surrender of death and dying, of the laws of mortality and every sense that would frame the soul as mortal.

"The Hour Is Come," the prayer of Jesus the Lord Christ unto the Father in the hour of his surrender, preparing for the initiation of the crucifixion, is the declaration of the Christ within the devotee in the hour of the soul's liberation unto eternal life. It is not a responsive reading, as in the first thirteen rosaries, but should be spoken aloud, alternating with the giving of the Hail Mary as indicated.

This rosary may be given daily or weekly or whenever you feel the surge of resurrection's fires propelling consciousness to the point of surrender into the Eternal Now, into the I AM THAT I AM. It marks the initiation for Christhood through which your soul will pass on the thirty-third step of initiation into the sacred fire. Each time you give the ritual in the full power of the spoken Word, you are reinforcing your victory in the hour of victory's initiation. And you are commemorating the hour of the victory of Jesus the Christ and of every other ascended master who has walked the earth and overcome the last enemy, returning to the heart of God on the path of surrender.[5]

Give all to God
and let him give back to you
that which he desires you to keep.
My children, let The Mystery
of Surrender be the ritual of
submitting to the flame all of the
garments of your consciousness
as you would put your wash
into the washing machine.
Yes, give everything to him.
And while you sleep at night,
let the Holy Spirit cleanse and purify
every cell and atom, your innermost
thoughts and feelings and
each shadowed shaft that hides in
the folds of your garment.

Mary

10

The Outline of The Fourteenth Rosary

by Elizabeth Clare Prophet

The content of the Scriptural Rosary for the New Age, which the Blessed Mother dictated, reflects the flow of the Father-Mother God—of God as Father and God as Mother. This was revealed to John in the words "I am Alpha and Omega, the beginning and the ending."[1] The first adoration of the rosary, making of the sign of the cross, marks the four aspects of God's Being as Father, Mother, Son and Holy Spirit. As we make this sign, we are reinforcing the consciousness of these aspects in body and soul, mind and heart. The Latin cross (usually suspended from the rosary) is the emblem of the converging lines of Spirit (Alpha) and Matter (Omega), signifying the place where Christ is born and where the energies of the Logos are released to a planet.

Touching the forehead as the north arm of the cross, we say, "In the name of the Father." Touching the heart as the south arm of the cross, we say, "And of the Mother."

Touching the left shoulder as the east arm of the cross, we say, "And of the Son." Touching the right shoulder as the west arm of the cross, we say, "And of the Holy Spirit, Amen."

By including the name of the Mother in our salutation of the Trinity, we invoke the consciousness of the Cosmic Virgin, who makes each aspect of the sacred Trinity meaningful to our evolving consciousness. Indeed, Mary is the Daughter of God, the Mother of Christ and the Bride of the Holy Spirit. Fulfilling the intimate role of the feminine counterpart of each aspect of the masculine principle of God, she is best able to portray to us the nature of Father, Son and Holy Spirit.

The I AM Lord's Prayer

The next adoration is "Jesus' I AM Lord's Prayer." Jesus gave us the Lord's Prayer, recorded in the Bible,[2] in the imperative mode, the command. It supposes that the soul is in the state of becoming, commanding that which it desires to be to descend and perform the perfect work. Jesus gave us that prayer because the command itself is intended to raise the soul to that position of authority. Even if our soul does not understand why it has the authority to command the light of God, the prayer itself will take us there.

Now as we advance on the path of Christhood, we look at this Lord's Prayer and we realize that these commands have manifested within us. We know the God who lives in our temple; we know the I AM Presence.[3] We are now with Jesus in the Upper Room and he gives us the I AM Lord's Prayer, affirming that all we have commanded is now come into manifestation where we are:

Our Father who art in heaven,
Hallowed be thy name, I AM.
I AM thy kingdom come
I AM thy will being done
I AM on earth even as I AM in heaven
I AM giving this day daily bread to all
I AM forgiving all life this day even as
I AM also all life forgiving me
I AM leading all men away from temptation
I AM delivering all men from every evil condition
I AM the kingdom
I AM the power and
I AM the glory of God in eternal, immortal manifestation—
All this I AM.

In this prayer, we are affirming, as God is affirming in us, that the Great Doer is doing all those things that we formerly asked him to do. We acknowledge ourselves as a co-creator with him. When we say, "I AM," we are saying, "God in me is." When we are one with God, there is no separation. The I AM of God speaking is the only I AM of us because we have surrendered all lesser identity.

In order to correctly use the name of God, I AM,[4] as an affirmation of Being and as an affirmation of the action of Being, we must first be convinced of our oneness with God through a correct interpretation of his Laws. By the grace of God, the statement of these Laws has not been entirely removed from sacred scripture. Those who are willing to examine the Bible in the light of historical truth as well as in the light of the ascended masters' teachings will begin to realize that the doctrine of original sin and the belief that man is sinful by nature do not originate in either the Laws of God or in the teachings of Jesus.

Once relieved of the burden of sin and the sense of sin, mankind can truly affirm their oneness with God, which can be accomplished only through Christ the Mediator—the only begotten Son of God. As there is but one God, one LORD, so there is but one Christ. As God individualized himself in the Presence of the I AM for each one, so he has also individualized the Christ for each one in the Christ Self and in the Christ flame that blazes upon the altar of the heart sustaining life as the opportunity for oneness.

To continue with our analysis of the adorations of the rosary, we note that the three Hail Marys that comprise the third adoration set the pattern for the entire rosary in the tripartite flame of faith, hope and charity—of God's will, his wisdom and his love. By and in this Trinity of oneness—of Father, Son and Holy Spirit—the action of the adorations that follow is multiplied by the power of the three-times-three for the salvation of mankind.

The "Introit to the Holy Christ Flame," which is given as the fourth adoration of the rosary, was inspired upon Mark Prophet[5] by the Holy Spirit. As we give this prayer, we feel ourselves communing with the Holy Christ Self, through the Holy Christ Flame within our hearts. We are giving ourselves to the Christ and saying, "Thank you, beloved Holy Christ Self, for being within me. Be my hands, be my mind and my heart and my feet, and render your blessing unto life through me. I surrender my being unto thee, and I desire to make my will thy will and the will of the Father."

The fifth adoration of the rosary, the "Adoration to God," was also received by Mark Prophet directly from the Holy Spirit. As you give this prayer with love and devotion, you are sending back to God all the energy in your being that you focalize through the spoken Word in your adoration. You are sending God's love back to him in the greatest fervor of your being. He takes that love, he multiplies it, he sends it back to you and, through your heart, sends light rays to bless all people.

The sixth adoration is the magnificent prayer of Jesus, "The Hour Is Come." This is the prayer that Jesus gave just before his crucifixion. It is a conversation he is having with God. It is one of the greatest recordings of the most intimate communion of our Lord with God the Father.

Jesus is reviewing his mission. He is saying, "The hour is come, glorify thy son that thy son also may glorify thee." He speaks about those whom God has sent to him, and that none of them is lost save the son of perdition, which is according to scripture. He says he does not pray for the world but for those in the world that God has given to him. He prays that we are not taken out of the world but that we be delivered from the evil one.

This prayer is included by our dear Mother Mary because she wants us to realize that we are going to walk every step of the way that Jesus walked. We are going to have to face all of the experiences that are a part of the thirteen other rosaries: the healings, the transfiguration, the birth in Bethlehem, the crucifixion, the resurrection, the ascension. All of these are here, and they are recited by you each morning as part of the rosaries of the seven rays. When you have lived through the life of Jesus in giving the rosary with Jesus and Mary, you have had all of these experiences. Then comes the hour to surrender all into the flame of the Holy Spirit.

So this very intimate prayer, "Father, the Hour Is Come," is a prayer that you will one day pray, and as you give this Mystery of Surrender throughout your life, you will know that prayer, you will understand its keys.

The Crucifixion

Crucifixion has to do with the action of the cross, or the crux of life. It is an opportunity to choose to be. At that moment when we accept the cross as our way, the cross of Alpha and Omega, the beginning and the ending of our own twin flames, we pray this same prayer. And each verse of the prayer alternates with the salutation to the Mother flame, which releases the light of the Mother within us; and by that light we conquer in the initiation of the crucifixion.

Jesus consciously, willingly decided to go through the crucifixion in that night when he prayed in Gethsemane. It was not as if Herod or Pilate or the soldiers or anyone had the power to crucify Jesus, except that he accepted it as the will of God for a cosmic purpose—and that is to teach the Aquarian man and woman how to bear the karma of a world, how to carry in our forcefield the weight of world condemnation of Christ consciousness and not be overcome, how to pass our tests and use the sacred fires of the Holy Spirit and the violet flame to put to rest the accusations of the accuser of the brethren.[6]

Jesus has said that there is so much sorrow surrounding

the concept of the crucifixion as a weight, and so much contemplation of death. He has often said, "After all, I was only on the cross a few hours. Why do mankind visualize me on the cross? Let them visualize me in the resurrection and in the ascension."

But to see Jesus on the cross has its purpose, because when we find ourselves upon that cross, we know that Jesus is there with us and that we are not alone. We will all come to that place where we are on the cross, where we must prove that we can contain the full energies of the descent of Alpha, the cross of Omega; that we can be the focal point for the release of that light and not go under; that we can prove the victory over death by surrendering the dead part of us, which is the ego, letting it die on that cross, letting the human will and the carnal mind and the pride die on that cross so that the Christ can be resurrected and we may walk the earth as the Christed One.

It is important not to skip the mystery of the crucifixion, but to understand that as sons and daughters of God, we approach that mystery as Jesus did with full mastery, setting the example in the hour of earth's crucifixion that life can be realized to its fullness here in Matter because we have perceived what man and woman are intended to be: the polarity of the Father-Mother God.

Next is the prayer, "I Surrender." In that surrender, we are turning over to God every aspect of our life. We are withholding nothing from him. We give him not only ourselves, but our children, our husbands, our wives, our fathers, our mothers, our family, our business, our livelihood. We say, "Here, God. I'm giving it to you. I'm surrendering it. I will be nonattached. I will not be possessive because I know that these were your gifts to me in the first place, and I know that if I surrender them totally to you, then you will give back to me that portion that you desire me to have."

You will also notice in this prayer that we are surrendering what is depicted in the Book of Revelation as elements of our own subconscious and unconscious minds. The dragon, the beast, the false prophet, the great whore, the fallen ones—all of these are components of our own subconscious and unconscious minds, which were shown to John.[7] All of these we surrender because we realize that as long as we don't surrender them, we are harboring and giving them an opportunity to function at times through our own consciousness.

Mary is a Mother who is very close to us, and she speaks to us in terms that we understand. And she said this surrender ritual is like giving God your dirty wash: you give it to God and he cleans it, he washes it, it goes through the washing machine, and he gives it back to you cleansed.

It is like giving yourself with all of your sins and all of the stains of your wrong actions and thoughts and feelings, and saying, "Here, God, I place myself totally upon your altar," knowing that you will not lose your life, but that God will take you and wash you and cleanse you and make you whole and return you to service on earth.

Each day of my life and each step of the way, I find there is something more I can surrender. There is something more I do not need to cling to so that I can serve in a greater way.

We do not surrender with the anticipation of the return, but we know that the Law is accurate and it is mathematical. We need not fear, because God will never take from us that which is Real, that which is necessary, that which he has created in us. But he will most lovingly remove from us the burdens, the cares, the oppressions of our life.

This is a mystery for the cleansing of the whole temple—Know ye not that your bodies are the temple of the living God?[8] And so God fills our temple with light, but we must first will to surrender all that is less than that light.

At the conclusion of this prayer, there is a period of silence where you can make your own private prayer of surrender.

Following this prayer, we affirm our wholeness in Alpha and Omega, the Father-Mother God.

The rosary is sealed by the giving of the Hail Mary and the I AM Lord's Prayer.

Take The Mystery
of Surrender and let it
commemorate the moment of
your dying unto Reality—
the moment of the letting-go of each
justification of the human ego,
of a false sense of responsibility
wherein you think friends and
family and loved ones are dependent
upon you instead of upon God.
Let go of the things that you think
you must have. Let go of the things
that you think in your pride you will
never do or the things that you think
you will always do. Let go of
all human attachments.
Let go of every ambition
except God's desiring
within you to be God.

Mary

11

The Mystery of Surrender

A revelation of Mary the Mother of Jesus
to the messenger Elizabeth Clare Prophet

The Sign of the Cross*

In the name of the Father and of the Mother
and of the Son and of the Holy Spirit,
Amen.

Jesus' I AM Lord's Prayer

Our Father who art in heaven,
Hallowed be thy name, I AM.
I AM thy kingdom come
I AM thy will being done
I AM on earth even as I AM in heaven
I AM giving this day daily bread to all
I AM forgiving all life this day even as
I AM also all life forgiving me

---

*This rosary may be given with the tape. To order your two-audiotape album with booklet or CD-on-Demand, call 800-245-5445 or visit www.tsl.org.

I AM leading all men away from temptation
I AM delivering all men from every evil condition
I AM the kingdom
I AM the power and
I AM the glory of God in eternal, immortal manifestation—
All this I AM.

MESSENGER:

Beloved Mother Mary, in the name of thy Son Jesus Christ, we appeal to your Immaculate Heart. O beloved Mother Mary, let thy immaculate concept for each one of us now coalesce upon our four lower bodies, our soul, our spirit, our mind, our heart.

Beloved Mother Mary, come and heal us! Beloved Mother Mary and Archangel Raphael, come to us now. Let us be healed of human pride and the density of the human ego that is unaware that it has pride. Let us be healed of human stubbornness and going out of the way, led by fallen angels, traduced, enticed and tempted by them as we have been.

The Healing Thoughtform
(Rings of White, Blue and Green)

O God, deliver us by the Mighty Intercessor, the Divine Mediatrix, our Blessed Mother.

Beloved Mother Mary, purge us! We have come for that purging, and therefore let us receive it fully and truly and wholly this day. Beloved Mother Mary, we call for your healing thoughtform, the emerald matrix. We call for the healing. Let the crooked be made straight and the rough places plain. Let every valley of the human consciousness be exalted as it is filled by the Divine.

O God, come unto us now. Cleanse us of all sin as we confess to our confessor, our beloved Mother Mary, all sin and also confess that we will sin no longer, that we will accept our karmic penance. We will move on in the Spirit of the LORD, for we have believed the Word that is preached to us by your Son Jesus: "Be ye therefore perfect, even as your Father which is in heaven is perfect."[1] We accept the grid of perfection. We accept the image and likeness of God that is in our Christ Self who is the immaculate concept.

O Mother Mary, come to us strong and beautiful and mighty, thou great Mediatrix. Come forth, O Woman clothed with the Sun! Deliver us now. Thou we adore as the Mother light of this cosmos.

Hail Mary

Hail, Mary, full of grace,
the Lord is with thee.
Blessed art thou among women
and blessed is the fruit of thy womb, Jesus.
Holy Mary, Mother of God,
pray for us, sons and daughters of God,
now and at the hour of our victory
over sin, disease and death.

(four times)

MESSENGER:

Let us say together now in the power of the three-times-three of the Holy Spirit nine times, "Father, into thy hands I commend my spirit." Please make your calls before we give this mantra to our Father.

CONGREGATION WITH THE MESSENGER:

Father, into thy hands I commend my spirit!

(nine times)

Introit to the Holy Christ Flame

1. Holy Christ Self above me,
   Thou balance of my soul,
   Let thy blessed radiance
   Descend and make me whole.

Refrain: Thy flame within me ever blazes,
   Thy peace about me ever raises,
   Thy love protects and holds me,
   Thy dazzling light enfolds me.
   I AM thy threefold radiance,
   I AM thy living presence
   Expanding, expanding, expanding now.

2. Holy Christ flame within me,
   Come, expand thy triune light;
   Flood my being with the essence
   Of the pink, blue, gold and white.

3. Holy lifeline to my Presence,
   Friend and brother ever dear,
   Let me keep thy holy vigil,
   Be thyself in action here.

Adoration to God

Beloved mighty I AM Presence,
Thou life that beats my heart,
Come now and take dominion,
Make me of thy life a part.
Rule supreme and live forever
In the flame ablaze within;
Let me from thee never sever,
Our reunion now begin.

All the days proceed in order
From the current of thy power,
Flowing forward like a river,
Rising upward like a tower.
I AM faithful to thy love ray
Blazing forth light as a sun;
I AM grateful for thy right way
And thy precious word "Well done."

I AM, I AM, I AM adoring thee! (three times)
O God, you are so magnificent! (nine times)
I AM, I AM, I AM adoring thee! (three times)

Moving onward to perfection,
I AM raised by love's great grace
To thy center of direction—
Behold, at last I see thy face.
Image of immortal power,
Wisdom, love and honor, too,
Flood my being now with glory;
Let my eyes see none but you!

O God, you are so magnificent! (three times)
I AM, I AM, I AM adoring thee! (nine times)
O God, you are so magnificent! (three times)

My very own beloved I AM, beloved
I AM, beloved I AM.

MESSENGER:

Let us give the mantra of the psalmist, "Let God be magnified!"[2] and see that white fire now expanding in your heart. It is a purging fire! It is a fire of peace! And it is the fire of the war of the Holy Spirit. For the Holy Spirit does groan in you and travail in you this day for the binding of your carnal mind and your dweller-on-the-threshold.

The Holy Spirit does come to you. Therefore, welcome that alchemy of the Spirit and know you will not have peace until full resolution is come. Fear not the upset! Fear not the upset, I tell you. For the peace that passes understanding must be worth the ultimate price and pain. Therefore, we say, O God:

CONGREGATION WITH THE MESSENGER:
Let God be magnified!
(nine times)

MESSENGER:
It is done in the name of the Father.
It is done in the name of the Son.
It is done in the name of the Holy Spirit.
It is done in the name of the Divine Mother.
Amen.

CONGREGATION WITH THE MESSENGER:
> Amen.

The Hour Is Come

In the name of the Father and of the Mother
and of the Son and of the Holy Spirit,
Amen.

1 Father, the hour is come; glorify thy Son, that thy Son also may glorify thee:

Hail Mary

2 As thou hast given him power over all flesh, that he should give eternal life to as many as thou hast given him.

Hail Mary

3 And this is life eternal, that they might know thee, the only true God, and Jesus Christ, whom thou hast sent.

Hail Mary

4 I have glorified thee on the earth: I have finished the work which thou gavest me to do.

Hail Mary

5 And now, O Father, glorify thou me with thine own self with the glory which I had with thee before the world was.

Hail Mary

6 I have manifested thy name unto the men which thou gavest me out of the world: thine they were, and thou gavest them me; and they have kept thy word.

Hail Mary

7 Now they have known that all things whatsoever thou hast given me are of thee.

Hail Mary

8 For I have given unto them the words which thou gavest me; and they have received them and have known surely that I came out from thee, and they have believed that thou didst send me.

Hail Mary

9 I pray for them: I pray not for the world, but for them which thou hast given me; for they are thine.

Hail Mary

10 And all mine are thine, and thine are mine; and I am glorified in them.

Hail Mary

11 And now I am no more in the world, but these are in the world, and I come to thee. Holy Father, keep through thine own name those whom thou hast given me, that they may be one, as we are.

Hail Mary

12 While I was with them in the world, I kept them in thy name: those that thou gavest me I have kept, and none of them is lost, but the son of perdition, that the scripture might be fulfilled.

Hail Mary

13 And now come I to thee; and these things I speak in the world, that they might have my joy fulfilled in themselves.

Hail Mary

14 I have given them thy word; and the world hath hated them, because they are not of the world, even as I am not of the world.

Hail Mary

15 I pray not that thou shouldest take them out of the world, but that thou shouldest keep them from the evil.

Hail Mary

16 They are not of the world, even as I am not of the world.

Hail Mary

17 Sanctify them through thy truth: thy word is truth.

Hail Mary

18 As thou hast sent me into the world, even so have I also sent them into the world.

Hail Mary

19 And for their sakes I sanctify myself, that they also might be sanctified through the truth.

Hail Mary

20 Neither pray I for these alone, but for them also which shall believe on me through their word;

Hail Mary

21 That they all may be one; as thou, Father, art in me and I in thee, that they also may be one in us: that the world may believe that thou hast sent me.

Hail Mary

22 And the glory which thou gavest me I have given them; that they may be one, even as we are one:

Hail Mary

23 I in them and thou in me, that they may be made perfect in one; and that the world may know that thou hast sent me and hast loved them as thou hast loved me.

Hail Mary

24 Father, I will that they also, whom thou hast given me, be with me where I am; that they may behold my glory, which thou hast given me: for thou lovedst me before the foundation of the world.

Hail Mary

25   O righteous Father, the world hath not known thee: but I have known thee, and these have known that thou hast sent me.

Hail Mary

26   And I have declared unto them thy name—I AM THAT I AM—and will declare it: that the love wherewith thou hast loved me may be in them, and I in them.

Hail Mary

In the name of the Father and of the Mother
and of the Son and of the Holy Spirit,
Amen.

Not my will, not my will, not my will,
but thine be done!

(nine times)

I Surrender

In the name of the Father and of the Mother
and of the Son and of the Holy Spirit,
Amen.

In the name of the I AM THAT I AM,
    the one true God,
    I surrender all that is less
    than the Christ consciousness within me!
In the name of Jesus the Christ,
    I surrender all that is less
    than the manifest perfection of my being!

In the name of the Holy Spirit,
>   I surrender all misuses of the sacred fire
>   within my four lower bodies!
In the name of the Holy of Holies,
>   I invoke the flame of the Holy Spirit
>   upon the altar of my heart
>   and I declare this temple
>   to be the temple of the living God!
In the name of the Christ,
>   the only begotten Son of the Father,
>   full of grace and truth,
>   I surrender all mortal consciousness and mortality,
>   all struggle and the sense of struggle,
>   all sin, disease and death!
In the name of the Divine Mother
>   and in the name of the immaculate heart of Mary,
>   I surrender all that is less
>   than the purity of the Cosmic Virgin!
In the name of the I AM Presence of all life,
>   I AM THAT I AM!
In the name of the Father-Mother God,
>   I surrender the spirals of all selfishness and self-love,
>   all self-pity, self-justification and self-condemnation—
>   all self-awareness apart from the flame of life!
In the name of the one true God, my own Real Self,
>   I declare:
>>   I AM this day a son of God!
>>   I AM the blazing Reality of the noonday!
>>   I AM the living presence of love!
>>   I AM the Word incarnate!
>>   I AM the threefold flame of love, wisdom and power!
>>   I AM a son of God!

By the authority of the flame
> of immortal truth which I AM,
> I surrender all human consciousness—
> the human ego, the human will, the human pride,
> the human intellect, and all human momentums
> less than the fullness of the Christ Presence
> which I AM!

In the name of the I AM THAT I AM,
> the Almighty One,
> I surrender all identity apart from
> the blessed Son of God!

I AM THAT I AM!
I AM the full and perfect manifestation of
> the immaculate conception of divinity
> held in the sacred heart of Mary the Mother!

I AM the fullness of the presence of living Truth!
I AM the Holy Comforter!
I AM THAT I AM!
In the name of Jesus the Christ,
> I surrender all manifestations of evil,
> all indulgence in error!

I surrender, by the flame of God-reality,
> all unreality and the dweller-on-the-threshold!

In the name of Jesus the Christ,
> I call to Michael the Archangel
> to descend into the forcefield of this God flame!

And by the authority of the I AM Presence,
> I demand the binding of the carnal mind,
> the Antichrist, all luciferian, satanic
> and temporal power that has ever manifested in
> or through my four lower bodies
> and my soul consciousness!

In the name of Jesus the Christ,
> I call for the twelve legions of angels
> from the heart of the Father-Mother God
> to descend into this forcefield in time and space
> to consecrate the flame
> of the Cosmic Christ consciousness within me!

In the name of Jesus the Christ,
> in the name of my own Christ Self
> and the I AM Presence, the Beloved One,
> I surrender the not-self, the fallen one
> and the consciousness of sin, disease and death!

I surrender the spirals of disintegration
> and I invoke the spirals of integration where I am!

I AM THAT I AM!

In the name of Jesus the Christ
> and by the authority of the Two Witnesses,
> in the name and by the authority of the entire
> Spirit of the Great White Brotherhood
> and the World Mother,
> I surrender unto Almighty God this day
> all manifestations and incarnations of evil
> throughout the Macrocosm and the microcosm
> of my own self-awareness:

I surrender the carnal mind, the Antichrist,
> the Devil and Satan!

I surrender unto the Lord the fallen ones,
> the rebellious spirits,
> all demons and discarnates
> and the archdeceivers of mankind!

I AM THAT I AM!

In the name of the living God,
> I surrender unto the Lord

the dragon who stood before the Woman
who was ready to be delivered,
to devour her child as soon as it was born
and who went to make war
with the remnant of her seed!
In the name of Jesus the Christ, I AM THAT I AM!
I AM Alpha and Omega,
> the beginning and the ending, saith the Lord,
> which is and which was and which is to come,
> the Almighty!

I AM THAT I AM!
In the name of the living God,
> I surrender the beast that rose up out of the sea
> and the dragon who gave him his power
> and his seat and great authority!

I surrender all that would usurp the consciousness
> of the Christ within the Macrocosm
> and the microcosm of my own self-awareness!

Lo, I AM THAT I AM!
I AM Alpha and Omega,
> the beginning and the ending!

In the name of Jesus the Christ,
> I surrender the beast that came up out of the earth!

I surrender the beast, the image of the beast,
> the mark of the beast
> and the number of his name!

In the name of Jesus the Christ,
> the King of Kings and Lord of Lords,
> in the name of the Faithful and True
> and the armies of the Lord,
> in the name of the Lamb
> and the hundred forty and four thousand,

in the name of the Woman clothed with the Sun,
in the name of the Divine Manchild
who liveth forevermore
and the saints that overcame the dragon
by the blood of the Lamb
and by the word of their testimony,
I AM THAT I AM!
I surrender the dragon and the antichrist,
the beast, the false prophet and the great whore
within the microcosm and the Macrocosm
of my own self-awareness!

In the name of the Father and of the Mother
and of the Son and of the Holy Spirit,
Amen.

(Please give your personal prayer of surrender.)

I AM Alpha and Omega,
the beginning and the ending.
Behold, I AM alive forevermore.
Behold, I AM Alpha and Omega,
the beginning and the ending,
which is and which was and which is to come,
the Almighty.
I AM THAT I AM
I AM THAT I AM
I AM THAT I AM

Hail Mary

Hail, Mary, full of grace,
the Lord is with thee.
Blessed art thou among women
and blessed is the fruit of thy womb, Jesus.
Holy Mary, Mother of God,
pray for us, sons and daughters of God,
now and at the hour of our victory
over sin, disease and death.

(three times)

Jesus' I AM Lord's Prayer

Our Father who art in heaven,
Hallowed be thy name, I AM.
I AM thy kingdom come
I AM thy will being done
I AM on earth even as I AM in heaven
I AM giving this day daily bread to all
I AM forgiving all life this day even as
I AM also all life forgiving me
I AM leading all men away from temptation
I AM delivering all men from every evil condition
I AM the kingdom
I AM the power and
I AM the glory of God in eternal, immortal manifestation—
All this I AM.

The garland of
the rosary that you weave
is the very rope of Almighty God
whereby he intends
to rescue Earth.

Mary

12

A Child's Rosary to Mother Mary

Mother Mary gave the precious gift of a new rosary for children, with the following admonishments:

> Beloved ones, I AM ever in your heart in the nearness of the flame. My desire to seal you in purity, in the will of God and in the perpetual awareness of the life that is in you can be fulfilled by your free will each day as you commemorate the rosary with me. I have placed into the heart of the Mother a rosary for children, which many adults will also find appropriate. This rosary will be an abbreviated rosary, somewhat shorter than the one that is given, so that none may have the excuse of not giving the rosary because it is too long but that all of you will be able to give at least a rosary each day that satisfies the request in the hour of Fátima.[1]

The request for the giving of that rosary, then, is not exempted from the children of any age. For the children, the blessed children have immense hearts of light and are magnificent God-free beings at inner levels....

Beloved ones, let it not be again, then, that we must come to remind you of the daily giving of the rosary. These are not words. These are the energies upon which the very salvation of the United States of America, of this hemisphere and this planet rest.[2]

A Child's Rosary is the means and the moment of your communion, a quarter of an hour each day with the God who is Mother in Mary and in your very own soul. Through her rosaries, Mother Mary would strengthen and assist us. And through her own Immaculate Heart, she enables us to contact God's love that is locked within our own hearts. When we give her our love, she returns her love to us to activate and unlock this fiery treasure from God.

In the Child's Rosary, as in the first thirteen scriptural rosaries, the verses from the scriptures are read by the conductor, with the Hail Mary and the other prayers given in unison by all participants in the ritual.* The readings are drawn from the epistles of Paul, John, James and Jude. We include the full text of two of the Child's Rosaries here. Following these, we list Bible verses that may be used in other Child's Rosaries. You may follow the pattern outlined here and insert the appropriate readings for each rosary.

---

*This rosary may be given with the tape. To order your two-audiotape album with booklet or CD-on-Demand, call 800-245-5445 or visit www.tsl.org.

A Child's Rosary to Mother Mary

ROSARY 1
I John 1:1–2:11

In the name of the Father and of the Mother
and of the Son and of the Holy Spirit,
Amen.

The Keeper's Daily Prayer
by Lady Master Nada

A flame is active—
A flame is vital—
A flame is eternal.

I AM a God flame of radiant love
From the very heart of God
In the Great Central Sun,
Descending from the Master of Life!
I AM charged now
With beloved Helios and Vesta's
Supreme God consciousness
And Solar Awareness.

Pilgrim upon earth,
I AM walking daily the way
Of the ascended masters' victory
That leads to my eternal freedom
By the power of the sacred fire
This day and always,
Continually made manifest
In my thoughts, feelings and immediate awareness,
Transcending and transmuting
All the elements of earth
Within my four lower bodies
And freeing me by the power of the sacred fire
From those misqualified foci of energy
   within my being.

I AM set free right now from all that binds
By and through the currents of the divine flame
Of the sacred fire itself,
Whose ascending action makes me
God in manifestation,
God in action,
God by direction and
God in consciousness!

I AM an active flame!
I AM a vital flame!
I AM an eternal flame!
I AM an expanding fire spark
From the Great Central Sun
Drawing to me now every ray
Of divine energy which I need
And which can never be requalified by the human
And flooding me with the light

And God-illumination of a thousand suns
To take dominion and rule supreme forever
Everywhere I AM!

Where I AM, there God is also.
Unseparated forever I remain,
Increasing my light
By the smile of his radiance,
The fullness of his love,
The omniscience of his wisdom,
And the power of his life eternal,
Which automatically raises me
On ascension's wings of victory
That shall return me to the heart of God
From whence in truth
I AM come to do God's will
And manifest abundant life to all!

Call to the Fire Breath

I AM, I AM, I AM the fire breath of God
From the heart of beloved Alpha and Omega.
This day I AM the immaculate concept
In expression everywhere I move.
Now I AM full of joy,
For now I AM the full expression of divine love.

My beloved I AM Presence,
Seal me now within the very heart
Of the expanding fire breath of God.
Let its purity, wholeness and love
Manifest everywhere I AM today and forever.
(three times)

I accept this done right now with full power!
I AM this done right now with full power!
I AM, I AM, I AM God-life expressing perfection
All ways at all times.
This which I call forth for myself
I call forth for every man, woman and child
   on this planet.

Jesus' I AM Lord's Prayer

Our Father who art in heaven,
Hallowed be thy name, I AM.
I AM thy kingdom come
I AM thy will being done
I AM on earth even as I AM in heaven
I AM giving this day daily bread to all
I AM forgiving all life this day even as
I AM also all life forgiving me
I AM leading all men away from temptation
I AM delivering all men from every evil condition
I AM the kingdom
I AM the power and
I AM the glory of God in eternal, immortal
   manifestation—
All this I AM.

1   That which was from the beginning, which we have heard, which we have seen with our eyes, which we have looked upon, and our hands have handled, of the Word of life;

Hail Mary

2   For the life was manifested, and we have seen it, and bear witness, and show* unto you that eternal life, which was with the Father, and was manifested unto us;

Hail Mary

3   That which we have seen and heard declare we unto you, that ye also may have fellowship with us: and truly our fellowship is with the Father, and with his Son Jesus Christ.

Hail Mary

4   And these things write we unto you, that your joy may be full.

Hail Mary

5   This then is the message which we have heard of him, and declare unto you, that God is light, and in him is no darkness at all.

Hail Mary

6   If we say that we have fellowship with him, and walk in darkness, we lie, and do not the truth:

Hail Mary

7   But if we walk in the light, as he is in the light, we have fellowship one with another, and the blood of Jesus Christ his Son cleanseth us from all sin.

Hail Mary

I AM Lord's Prayer

---

*I John 1:2: "... and shew unto you that eternal life...."

1 If we say that we have no sin, we deceive ourselves, and the truth is not in us.

Hail Mary

2 If we confess our sins, he is faithful and just to forgive us our sins, and to cleanse us from all unrighteousness.

Hail Mary

3 If we say that we have not sinned, we make him a liar, and his word is not in us.

Hail Mary

4 My little children, these things write I unto you, that ye sin not. And if any man sin, we have an advocate with the Father, Jesus Christ the righteous:

Hail Mary

5 And he is the propitiation for our sins: and not for ours only, but also for the sins of the whole world.

Hail Mary

6 And hereby we do know that we know him, if we keep his commandments.

Hail Mary

7 He that saith, I know him, and keepeth not his commandments, is a liar, and the truth is not in him.

Hail Mary

I AM Lord's Prayer

1   But whoso keepeth his word, in him verily is the love of God perfected: hereby know we that we are in him.

Hail Mary

2   He that saith he abideth in him ought himself also so to walk, even as he walked.

Hail Mary

3   Brethren, I write no new commandment unto you, but an old commandment which ye had from the beginning. The old commandment is the word which ye have heard from the beginning.

Hail Mary

4   Again, a new commandment I write unto you, which thing is true in him and in you: because the darkness is past, and the true light now shineth.

Hail Mary

5   He that saith he is in the light, and hateth his brother, is in darkness even until now.

Hail Mary

6   He that loveth his brother abideth in the light, and there is none occasion of stumbling in him.

Hail Mary

7   But he that hateth his brother is in darkness, and walketh in darkness, and knoweth not whither he goeth, because that darkness hath blinded his eyes.

Hail Mary

Transfiguring Affirmations
of Jesus the Christ

I AM THAT I AM
I AM the open door which no man can shut
I AM the light which lighteth every man
    that cometh into the world
I AM the way
I AM the truth
I AM the life
I AM the resurrection
I AM the ascension in the light
I AM the fulfillment of all my needs and
    requirements of the hour
I AM abundant supply poured out upon all life
I AM perfect sight and hearing
I AM the manifest perfection of being
I AM the illimitable light of God
    made manifest everywhere
I AM the light of the Holy of Holies
I AM a son of God
I AM the light in the holy mountain of God

> Glory be to the Father
> and to the Son
> and to the Holy Spirit!
> As it was in the beginning,
> is now and ever shall be,
> life without end—
> I AM, I AM, I AM!

In the name of the Father and of the Mother
and of the Son and of the Holy Spirit,
Amen.

ROSARY 8
James 1:22–2:14

Sign of the Cross

The Keeper's Daily Prayer

Call to the Fire Breath

I AM Lord's Prayer

1 But be ye doers of the word, and not hearers only, deceiving your own selves.

Hail Mary

2 For if any be a hearer of the word, and not a doer, he is like unto a man beholding his natural face in a glass:

Hail Mary

3 For he beholdeth himself, and goeth his way, and straightway forgetteth what manner of man he was.

Hail Mary

4 But whoso looketh into the perfect law of liberty, and continueth therein, he being not a forgetful hearer, but a doer of the work, this man shall be blessed in his deed.

Hail Mary

5 If any man among you seem to be religious, and bridleth not his tongue, but deceiveth his own heart, this man's religion is vain.

Hail Mary

6 Pure religion and undefiled before God and the Father is this, To visit the fatherless and widows in their affliction, and to keep himself unspotted from the world.

Hail Mary

I AM Lord's Prayer

1 My brethren, have not the faith of our Lord Jesus Christ, the Lord of glory, with respect of persons.

Hail Mary

2 For if there come unto your assembly a man with a gold ring, in goodly apparel, and there come in also a poor man in vile raiment;

Hail Mary

3 And ye have respect to him that weareth the gay clothing, and say unto him, Sit thou here in a good place; and say to the poor, Stand thou there, or sit here under my footstool:

Hail Mary

4 Are ye not then partial in yourselves, and are become judges of evil thoughts?

Hail Mary

5 Hearken, my beloved brethren, Hath not God chosen the poor of this world rich in faith, and heirs of the kingdom which he hath promised to them that love him?

Hail Mary

6 But ye have despised the poor. Do not rich men oppress you, and draw you before the judgment seats?

Hail Mary

7 Do not they blaspheme that worthy name by the which ye are called?

Hail Mary

I AM Lord's Prayer

1 If ye fulfil the royal law according to the scripture, Thou shalt love thy neighbour as thyself, ye do well:

Hail Mary

2 But if ye have respect to persons, ye commit sin, and are convinced of the law as transgressors.

Hail Mary

3 For whosoever shall keep the whole law, and yet offend in one point, he is guilty of all.

Hail Mary

4 For he that said, Do not commit adultery, said also, Do not kill. Now if thou commit no adultery, yet if thou kill, thou art become a transgressor of the law.

Hail Mary

5 So speak ye, and so do, as they that shall be judged by the law of liberty.

Hail Mary

6 For he shall have judgment without mercy, that hath showed* no mercy; and mercy rejoiceth against judgment.

Hail Mary

7 What doth it profit, my brethren, though a man say he hath faith, and have not works? can faith save him?

Hail Mary

*Transfiguring Affirmations
of Jesus the Christ*

Glory Be to the Father

Sign of the Cross

---

*James 2:13: "...that hath shewed no mercy,..."

Readings for the Child's Rosaries

Rosary 1   I John 1:1–2:11
Rosary 2   I John 2:12–3:3
Rosary 3   I John 3:4–24
Rosary 4   I John 4:1–21
Rosary 5   I John 5:1–21
Rosary 6   II John 1:1–III John 1:14
Rosary 7   James 1:1–21
Rosary 8   James 1:22–2:14
Rosary 9   James 2:15–3:9
Rosary 10   James 3:10–4:17
Rosary 11   James 5:1–20
Rosary 12   Jude 1–25
Rosary 13   Hebrews 1:1–2:8
Rosary 14   Hebrews 2:9–3:19
Rosary 15   Hebrews 4:1–5:8
Rosary 16   Hebrews 5:8–6:14
Rosary 17   Hebrews 6:13–7:22
Rosary 18   Hebrews 7:23–8:13
Rosary 19   Hebrews 9:1–22
Rosary 20   Hebrews 9:23–10:14
Rosary 21   Hebrews 10:15–39
Rosary 22   Hebrews 11:1–22
Rosary 23   Hebrews 11:23–12:7
Rosary 24   Hebrews 12:7–29
Rosary 25   Hebrews 13:1–29

PART SIX

Messages from the Divine Mother

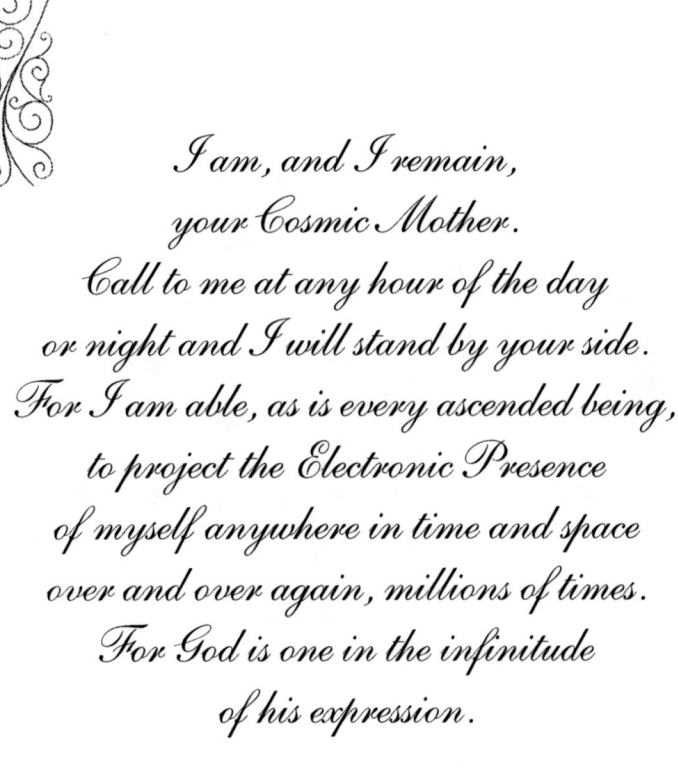

I am, and I remain,
your Cosmic Mother.
Call to me at any hour of the day
or night and I will stand by your side.
For I am able, as is every ascended being,
to project the Electronic Presence
of myself anywhere in time and space
over and over again, millions of times.
For God is one in the infinitude
of his expression.

Mary

13

The Healing Science of the Mother

My children aborning in the womb of time and space, becoming the fullness of the Christ day by day, know ye not that I AM the Mother ray, Ma-ray, Mary. Hearts cry out to me, arms upraised, children in prayer, souls racked upon beds of pain cry out to the Divine Mother, and the Divine Mother hears and answers each call.

I am come this day with my divine complement, Raphael, the archangel of healing. And we bring with us angels of the healing flame to minister to the needs of mankind, to souls weary—weary of the world with its pain, its daily, hourly crucifixion.

Yes, I know, for I AM the heart of the Divine Mother. I know what is in your hearts, each one. I know the hearts of millions, for I have fashioned the etheric pattern and design of that heart to be the pulsing life force of God's energy for the incarnation that is the opportunity for each soul to become more of God, more of life, more of love.

The heart must be sealed in fire, as the fire of protection and perfection against the dissonance of the world, the jangled beat, the jealousies, the hatreds of men. These attack the hearts of the innocent and the unwary. Heart disease and heart failure have become a common occurrence in a modern society that prides itself in the greatest methods of healing and medicine that the world has ever known.

The Lost Arts of Healing

I say to you that the world is in its infancy regarding the healing arts, and that in the healing temple of Atlantis over which I presided for a time,[1] there was a greater manifestation of healing through the direct precipitation of the emerald ray than has yet been achieved through modern science, with all of the effort and all of the expense. For healing requires the heart's devotion to Truth.

Truth must be emblazoned upon the consciousness of those who would heal. The thought of touching the sick, of raising the dead, of cleansing sinners has always been one of great attraction to those of compassion for humanity, as well as to those practitioners of the black arts who well use their talent and their manipulation of forces to imitate the miracles of Christ, to imitate the miracles of the Son of God. For mankind know, and the charlatans know, that the manifestation of phenomena, the working of so-called miracles is a means to filling the pocket and the purse, and to personal adulation. And it leads to the personality-cult consciousness. Therefore, angels of healing and members of the Brotherhood have bestowed the gifts of healing upon the humble of heart and upon those who would apply themselves diligently to the science of healing.

In many cases, blessed hearts, the Lords of Karma have

revealed to scientists who were dedicated the knowledge of healing of all forms of disease. And thus the mercy of the Great Law has provided mankind, until they are able to make use of the healing flame directly from the heart, the throat and the third-eye chakras with those means of saving life and preserving the opportunity of life that come through the alchemy of chemistry and material science.

Material science in its perfection is the science of the Mother. It is not to be looked down upon or to be dispensed with, but to be enshrined in greater principles and greater purity, for greater effectivity. Thus, we who sponsor the healers of the world stand behind the good physician, the tender nurse, those in every walk of life who minister to the needs of mankind. And wherever a prayer is spoken, wherever there is faith in a higher power, we work through the dexterous hands, the skillful hands of surgeon, as well as chiropractor, and all those who have dedicated themselves to the reestablishment of the divine flow within the four lower bodies.

I am concerned now in this hour that there shall arise up among you those who have greater facility with the flow of the emerald ray through the hands. For the action of the healing ray working together with the secret rays coalesces in form the healing manifestation that comes forth through the third-eye vision of the immaculate concept.

O ye of little faith, you who see not and do not believe, can you not cast aside your doubts and fears for this sacred moment of our communion? Will you not allow me, your Cosmic Mother, to hold the vision and to believe the vision that I place before you. That is a vision of the great flow of healing power and healing Truth through your very form, centering there the God-awareness of light and light-patterns that shall be the healing power, the healing love, the healing wisdom for millions of souls who can be touched by your devotion, through your invocation and through your dedication and to the establishment of a higher form of life.

I say, then, you will work with the angels of healing, with Raphael and with me as you recite the sacred rosary, which is also the ritual of healing, and as you give the Jesus Watch,[2] another ritual of healing that sets a geometric pattern each time it is given that goes forth into the etheric belt, the mental belt, the astral belt and coalescing in the physical through the crystal ray of the crystallization, or the Christalization, of mankind's consciousness.

Do Not Neglect Your Rituals of Prayer and Invocation

Do you not understand that there is more to the science of invocation than a vain repetition of words? Our words are the Words of God. They are a chalice of light. Into this chalice of our words, you pour your heart's energy. And thus there is a meeting of the energies of heaven and earth, as Above, so below, at the level of the Christ. And by your participation in this ritual, you also are raised to that level. And in the level of the Christ consciousness, you become the focal point for the great flow of cosmic abundance to all life and all evolutions upon the planetary body.

Do you not understand, precious hearts, that when you neglect your ritual of meditation and prayer, of invocation and supplication, there is a hole in the great filigree lacy pattern of the antahkarana? It is like a dropped stitch in your crocheting. When you omit the ritual, the repetition of the cycle is not complete. And so the anchoring of the focus that is intended is weakened. The structure is weakened. Thus you will understand in the dawn of the Aquarian age how mankind will solidify and make permanent all of their endeavors through the ritual of the divine art and the divine science, through the power of the spoken Word, which you learn in the ascended masters' teachings.

When mankind learn the action of rest in the flow of light through the throat chakra, through the heart, through head and through hand, then they will experience the miracle manifestation of the permanency that comes through the fire of the Holy Spirit. Some of you have prayed to me for the healing of certain physical conditions. As others among mankind visit the shrines dedicated to the Divine Mother at Guadalupe, Fátima and Lourdes, so you have come here seeking the assistance of my flame.

I place my flame now upon your heart, merging the fires of my devotion to Truth with the fires of your threefold flame to give you the impetus of the divine healing. In your patience possess ye your souls.[3] Precious hearts, do you not understand that there be some forms of illness that are for the glory of God, for the working out of past cycles of sin and imperfection? And if these cycles were to be abruptly cut off by the action of the healing ray, it would not be an act of mercy, but an act of deprivation, for you would be deprived of the opportunity for atonement and the even greater opportunity of bearing the sins of the world.

The Opportunity to Bear the Sins of the World

Do you understand that mystery of the Christ, Christ Jesus, when it is spoken, "He died for our sins"? It means that he allowed the human consciousness with all of its ramifications to die upon the cross of Spirit and Matter. The awareness of self as the human ego was sacrificed by Jesus, gladly and joyously, in order that he might bear the total planetary weight of world karma, and in bearing that karma for each one, provide the opportunity for souls evolving in the womb of time and space to have a greater lightness about them, less burden, less pain, less travail, that they might pursue the Holy Grail, that they might pursue the overcoming of the Christ, that they might also begin to balance their karma, free of the enormous weight of that karma.

Do you understand, then, that in each century as others rise to the position of Christhood, those who desire to render a more than ordinary service for mankind may also be given the opportunity to bear the sins of the world? This is done as each one passes the test of the ten, the test of selflessness and surrender in Christ. For, free of the skin of mortal consciousness, shedding that skin, standing in the position of the Christ, you are able to bear a more than ordinary weight of world karma.

Some of you who have given invocations and decrees for many years are bearing, even this very hour, a greater amount of density and substance of the world than you would even imagine. But by your faithfulness to the ritual of decrees, we are able to gauge from heavenly octaves what you will be able to bear, what you will be able to transmute of the burden of the world that it might become light, that you might affirm with Jesus, "my burden is light."[4]

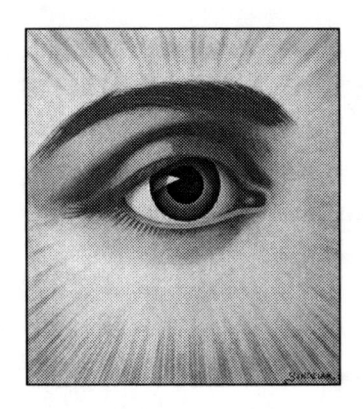

We do not assign to lifestreams who have not the constancy of the emerald ray, or of the All-Seeing Eye, a more than ordinary burden. For those who decree one day, and another day, and then wait a week to decree would be completely overcome to the point of insanity in their outer consciousness if they were to hold the balance of planetary momentums of sin. We will not place that weight upon those who are unstable or undetermined in their invocations.

But when we see that week after week, day after day, the sacred ritual is fulfilled, and that the devotee will come before his altar, however humble, to make intercession through the holy rosary, through decrees, through prayer, then we know that we may place upon the shoulders, the broad shoulders of that one—broadened by a sense of cosmic responsibility—the weight of the little children suffering in the ghettos and the slums of the world, of the prisoners of war being tortured, of the underground Christians who are giving their lives so that they might be counted among the Christians, of those who are standing up for Truth and for God, of those lifestreams who are prominent in the world in government and religion, in politics, in economics who have not the knowledge of the Law, but have the great courage of their convictions. These need the prayers of the saints. These need your love.

I could tell you instance after instance where those of you who are gathered in this room have been given the burden to carry for a world leader, a great figure who is holding the light for the Brotherhood on the world scene. And in the quietness and humbleness of your abode and your service, as you have invoked the violet flame, as you have invoked the circle and sword of blue flame, you have carried the weight day after day for these individuals who are walking on the front lines of the battle, and who do not have either the time or the inclination to pray, and yet are held in my heart, in the heart of God, as noble souls who work the works of Christ on earth.

You see, allegiance to Christ only begins with an affirmation, but then it must be continued through works. Many who have the works of Christ know not the Christ. We do not condemn them because they do not say exactly the form of prayer or commitment that is taught in the churches; for churches are built to be an assist to man, not a detriment to his walk on the pathway Home. And thus, the kingdom of heaven is indeed peopled with virtuous men and women from all walks of life.

What a tragedy that a certain sect here, a certain sect there, will affirm, "Unless you believe what we believe, unless you speak as we speak, you cannot be saved." Is it any wonder that mankind are discouraged and disillusioned with the teachers in the religious marts when one after the other, time after time the charlatans come forth in the name of Christ to pick the pockets, to pick the hearts, to pick the energies of the innocent ones who gather for some morsel, some crumb, some word of Truth? Is it any wonder that those who have the Spirit within them and know God—for they have seen him face to face—turn from religion and even begin to deny their own divinity or the divinity that is everywhere present?

As we observe the world, as we make our daily round from shrine to shrine, charging the holy places of the earth with the Mother's love, we observe these conditions, we observe the intrigue, the treachery, the deceit practiced by some—but not all—of the leaders of mankind. How then does the Mother and the Mother's heart reach her children? We must then resort also to a certain subterfuge, a certain getting around of the religious figures who have betrayed our purpose and our name. How do we do this? I will give you one example.

The Miraculous Medal

Many of you are aware of the power of the focuses of light that manifest in form in various ways as jewels of light. You will recall that in the last century, in the year 1830, I appeared to one to describe the Miraculous Medal.[5] And in my appearance, I showed the jewels that I wear on each of my fingers, focusing the virtues of God that are to be in manifestation in man. And I gave to that sweet soul who communed with me the direction for having the Miraculous Medal made. And so it has been made, and it has been worn for over a century by those who believe in the power of the Mother flame.

Now you see there are always those who intend to make merchandise of men, and therefore, we of the heavenly hosts know that if we give a revelation that will impart some measure of income to those who are involved in it, given what the mortal consciousness is, there will be always someone who sees that he can profit from the credulity of the holy innocents. Thus, in giving the revelation for the Miraculous Medal, we have a means of focusing our image, our matrix, over the very heart of the faithful ones. For you see, it is only the faithful who would deign to wear a medal of the Virgin Mother or of Christ Jesus or the star of David or the image of the Buddha. And thus we seal each medal in the flame and in the fire of the perfect concept of the divine religion, the divine science and the protection of the soul for her incarnation. Thus, this is an action of talismanic magic, and we are able then with our blessings to circumvent those who hold themselves pious before men, those who perhaps read the ritual of the Mass, but have darkness in their hearts, and we reach directly the children of God upon earth. This, then, is the means that we are forced to use to reach directly the little children.

Pray for the Liberation of Mankind

I say to you, precious hearts, pray for the assimilation by mankind of the consciousness of the saints and ascended beings. Pray for their inner awareness, free from dogma and doctrine and a binding to fear and to ignorance that has been perpetuated in the churches for far too long. The threatening and the condemnation and the accusations of priests must cease. And if they will not cease, then we will raise our hand and there shall be a reversing of that energy upon those who send it forth in their attempt to control mankind.

The controllers of men, the black magicians, are not all in the churches. They are also in government and in secret places where they work their nefarious deeds. When we are therefore able to focus our light through these sacred objects and through the communion of saints in holy prayer, we are able to seal great and small from the nefarious influences of the dark ones who are working in their treachery to take mankind down in a spiral to the very base element of his nature, into the bottomless pit and into eternal damnation that is the death of the soul.

I am come with joy in my heart, even as I come with a certain sadness at the plight of the world, at the frenzy of the world. And I must appeal to you again, one and all, to make fervent effort in the flame of constancy to bear the sins of the world. We need lightbearers. We need those who can be counted upon to rise at a certain hour and to be in prayer at a certain hour so that we know at that particular point in time there can be an alleviation of distress in the areas that are war-torn and wherever there is famine or pestilence upon the earth.

Hierarchy needs to have the knowledge that mankind are constant and dependable in their religious service. Thus we appeal to you who have been given a more than ordinary understanding of cosmic law to be the handmaid and the servant of the Lord in this hour, and in so doing to fulfill the role of Christ as minister, as servant of all. He who would be great among you, let him be the servant of all—the servant of the Christ in all.[6] This is the pathway of enlightenment, of self-perfectionment and of the miraculous manifestation of the flow of healing that will make you indeed healers of men in the highest sense of the word.

Call to Me at Any Hour

I am, and I remain, your Cosmic Mother. Call to me at any hour of the day or night and I will stand by your side. For I am able, as is every ascended being, to project the Electronic Presence of myself anywhere in time and space over and over again, millions of times. For God is one in the infinitude of his expression.

So we are one, and my Presence will be near unto you. And in the hour when you develop the perfect sight of the

All-Seeing Eye of God and the senses of the soul, you will be able to declare to all who ask you, "What is your belief in the Virgin Mary?" you will declare, "I have both seen and heard the Word of the Cosmic Virgin."

So will you be blessed for your sight and hearing as you have made these senses instruments for the inculcation in all mankind of the virtues of the Sacred Word.

I AM within your heart the love of the Mother,
the compassion of the Mother, the mercy of
the Mother for all mankind.[7]

Mary

I am releasing the seal of my flame in the first volume of the series of "The Golden Word of Mary." My soul doth rejoice in this release of the sacred Word. And wherever that book is placed, in the libraries of your communities, in the schools and colleges, there I will also place an Electronic Presence of myself so that when souls come to pick up that book, to examine it, they will find me there in person to greet them, to extend the warmth of the Mother's love. Therefore know, O my souls, that for each book that you place, you have also initiated the spiral of my Presence in that place, which can also transform the consciousness in education, in the libraries and universities of the world.

Mary

14

The Hallowed Circle

Children of the sun of my heart, I come in the full-orbed glory of the consciousness of the Divine Mother. I come that you might know what it is to be in the presence of love, love as the very air that you breathe, the perfume of flowers wafted on the breeze, love as a tenderness of God that permeates space.

I come that you might know the Holy Spirit, which I have espoused as the handmaid of the Lord. I come that you might know what it is to be Mother and to impart to you a veil of light, like the veil that a bride wears, symbolizing the virgin consciousness. And I place upon you one and all that veil, which shields the consciousness from the impurities of the world and seals you in the immaculate light of the Cosmic Virgin.

I am grateful for the release of love and light from the heart of my beloved Saint Germain and my Son Jesus. I come as the finisher of that faith of which they are the authors.[1] I come to conclude a spiral of Omega. I come that you might remember the love that is the hallowed circle of life.

I draw that circle around you now, around you each one, together with your twin flame. And there is imparted to each one of you by angels of Raphael's band the Truth of the Presence of your divine complement that you might feel for a moment the wholeness of Father-Mother in life, as Above, so below. It is the Christ consciousness of the counterpart that I would have you experience that you might see how the merging of energies in a spiral of wholeness is for your ultimate victory and your ultimate return.

This hallowed circle can never be broken but includes all of life also as the awareness of Self and Selfhood. And as you progress along the Path, you will learn more and more about being aware of Self as God in every part of life until you include in the boundaries of your love the All of creation, and then you merge with God's consciousness of the Cosmic Egg,[2] and you ensoul it, and you are that forcefield.

As we look upon the world today, the sorrow, the pain, the anguish to which a mother's heart is always attuned, we see that here and there across the skies of the mental belt there are shooting stars of light and of awareness. There are pinpoints that denote an illumination of the mind in the understanding of the Son and the relationship of the Christ to the Mother.

I Anchor My Flame through My Book

I am releasing the seal of my flame in the first volume of the series of "The Golden Word of Mary," *My Soul Doth Magnify the Lord.** My soul doth rejoice in this release of the sacred Word. And wherever that book is placed, in the libraries of your communities, in the schools and colleges, there I will also place an Electronic Presence of myself so that when souls come to pick up that book, to examine it, they will find me there in person to greet them, to extend the warmth of the Mother's love. Therefore know, O my souls, that for each book that you place, you have also initiated the spiral of my Presence in that place, which can also transform the consciousness in education, in the libraries and universities of the world.

My heart reaches out to the children of God of all faiths. I am partial to none and yet partial to all. I am partial to the flame, and I am drawn where I am bidden to enter. I go where I am received, and if I am received not, then I too must obey the injunction of the Christ to shake the dust from my shoes and depart from that place and enter not there.[3] And so, sadly it comes to pass that I am rejected in many homes because of a dark doctrine and a dark theology and a confusion surrounding my mission to ensoul the Christ for lifewaves upon the planet.

I trust that you will take the opportunity extended to you to carry the flame of this book to those who have not yet considered the worth of rejoicing in the flame of the Mother ray, which I am privileged to bear and to carry, although I am not the origin of that flame. For the flame is

---

**My Soul Doth Magnify the Lord* was first published in 1974. In its most recent edition, this book is titled *Mary's Message for a New Day.*

God, and I claim no exclusivity in that flame or in that name. For as I have said before, all can be truly the Mother of God.

There Are Many in Heaven Who Respond to the Hail Mary

When you ascend to His Presence, you will find that the more among mankind who call to you, who know of you, who know of your life of service and devotion, the more you will be able to intercede on behalf of mankind. Therefore, it is good if in your final incarnation you can render those services that are acknowledged by man as well as by God, for this will increase your service at inner levels. And so it is because I am known as the Mother of Jesus that I can give forth an extraordinary service, for mankind have created a momentum of devotion over these thousands of years to my flame.

There are many lady masters in heaven who have risen as the Divine Mother, but not many among mankind know of these and therefore do not call upon them as they call upon me. These noble ladies of heaven, therefore, assist me in my service as cadres of lightbearers carrying the torch of the immaculate concept. There are thousands, and when they hear the Hail Mary, they also respond in my name to minister unto souls calling for intercession.

And you will find that as you are in tune with my heart and the service of lifewaves, that your heart will also respond to the Hail Mary offered in prayer. And while you yet walk in this veil, you can be the mediatrix of mercy, of grace in my name and in my flame. Closer and closer draws the hierarchy, pressing close to the consciousness of the pure in heart, the devotees and all who have surrendered a measure of personal will unto the Godhead.

Be Instruments of Grace and Mercy

I am the instrument of mercy. I am the instrument of grace. So you too can and shall become instruments for the dispensation of virtues of light through the jeweled essence of the sacred fire that descends from your causal body.

Come close now into my heart as I impart to you the fragrance of motherhood, the aura of motherhood, and as I crown those who would be the protector of the Divine Mother with the crown of Joseph, of Saint Germain, of the masculine ray, that you might enter into the fullness of the majesty of being a knight of the Table Round as you, sons of flame, accept the role of protecting the Woman and her seed.

So I come to crown you king and queen not only for a day but for a life and for an eternity. And when you ascend with your twin flame, you are received in the courts of heaven as a prince and princess of the realm, ready, then, to make your way in the path of service and initiation to higher reaches of cosmic consciousness.

How good it is to arrive at the mark of victory, knowing that you have left that mark definitely imprinted in the planetary home and etched upon souls, millions of souls, who will follow after you. It makes the trek and the victory all the more worthwhile to see the spiral of souls following after in the wake of your triumph.

Carry the Flame for the Holy Family

So, then, the flame goes forth for the divine family. So you carry that flame and you are well qualified now,... for you have been enlightened and you have received much from the Source of oneness. You have much to tell the world. You have much to live, much to rejoice in as you experiment with the meditations of the sacred fire that you have learned, as you think upon the holy thoughts.

There is created, then, here in this forcefield a circle of fire from us, and it is a forcefield of such great light to reestablish the Holy Family. As a matter of fact, such an intensity of dedication to that Family I have not seen in many a year, such an enlightenment, such a purity of mind and heart, such a freedom to be the fullness of that which you know....

Yes, it was only yesterday that you began to unfold. And so here in this unfolding of the ribbons of light of my heart, you have been wrapped in a swaddling garment of a consciousness that will be with you for ages to come.

And do you know that each one of you ... can become the center of another hallowed circle of enlightenment? You can give forth the teaching. You can magnetize light. And you can see that the earth is covered with the teachings of the Mother to her children.[4]

We are one in the flame. I am on earth and she is in heaven and the spirals of our being flow over the figure eight. And for a moment I experience time and space. For a moment she experiences eternity.

This, then, is the consummation of the flow of love: that you establish that contact with the Holy Spirit whereby you too can flow with God to new heights and dimensions of consciousness and return to earth and infuse them into the sod, into Mater, into the planet Earth, here to enshrine the age of the new birth.

Rejoice in the Descent of Souls of Light

I impress upon you the scenes of Jesus' childhood, of the little experiences, the episodes in which he brought me so much joy, so much love. And my heart did sing as I felt the presence of Joseph protecting and guiding and caring for us on the way, the homeward way.

I would like you to know the joys of a child such as Jesus, a child of light, of innocence, of great wisdom, of purity and a sense of mission. Such children are a joy, a joy to the household. What would we do without the laughter of a child to break the somberness, the seriousness of the adult world and the cares of that world? What would we do without the simple child mind that asks the questions of nature, of life and yearns to know more of God each step of the way?

Let the children come nigh. Let the souls of those yearning to give birth to a higher way of life come forth. Let them be released by the Lords of Karma. Let them be received by all who wait upon the Lord as brides of the Holy Spirit, as the husband of the Cosmic Virgin. So let all receive the impartation of the Spirit of the Lord in these, these little ones.

Elementals rejoice in the buoyant flame of the Holy Spirit. And they too rejoice to see the descent of avatars, for they know that these are the souls of light who will bequeath to them their ultimate freedom in the resurrection flame.

I Leave You with the Mantle of My Presence

And now as I take my leave of you, I leave with you the mantle of my Presence. I place it around you each one, mothers-to-be, for all wearing the garb of the feminine ray are mothers-to-be. And Saint Germain at my side places around the fathers-to-be the mantle of the Knight Commander. And sealed within your hearts is the image of the Divine Manchild.

So does the crystal sound in our temple, and the ring of that crystal is the clarion call for souls to descend into form. So be those who hold the light for them in this age. So know that your prayers will sustain life throughout the planetary body in time of duress, through the dispensations of light that will carry the remnant of humanity into the age of gold.

I am with you always as the flaming presence of the Mother. Breaking the bread of life, I unfold wonders and glories untold of Father, of Son, of Holy Spirit, of Christed One, of sons and daughters of my heart.

I am your Mother always,[5]

Mary

It is the Mother
who holds the body of Christ
when the body is taken down
from the cross. It is the Mother
who holds up the child in joy
who has come forth from the womb.
It is the Mother whose voice can be heard
in the day and in the night, the Mother
who is always there listening
to the children's prayer.
It is the Mother who is there
teaching the children of the
Law, of the Presence
and of the
I AM THAT I AM.

Mary

15

The Mother Ray as the Instrument of the Soul's Transition into the New Day

Sons and daughters of God, I come to claim you for the Mother ray. I come to appear to you in the way of life as Jesus my Son after his ascension appeared to Saul of Tarsus on the road to Damascus.[1]

Appearing in that light of the masculine ray and the personification of the Christ, he called to the one in whom the Flame of Life burned and yet the one who had rebelled against that flame, "Saul, Saul, why persecutest thou me?" And Saul was blinded by the light. And the Lord said to him, "It is hard for thee to kick against the pricks."[2]

I come to appear to woman. I come in the way of the Aquarian age.... I come to Terra. And in this hour, in my hand there is the dispensation of the Almighty One to contact every woman on earth. And so I come releasing the Electronic Presence of my momentum of attainment in the threefold flame.

I appear to woman and I say, "O woman, why persecutest

thou me? I am thy Mother and thy light and thy joy appearing. It is hard for thee to kick against the pricks. Do not resist the Divine Mother when she is in the way with thee. Do not resist the flowering of your own feminine divinity. O woman, rise to the point of God-realization. Come of age. Come into your calling. Come into that position of leadership and lead the energies of mankind into the chalice of the Christ consciousness.

"Clear the way for Mother-flow. Clear the way for the Buddha and the Christ. Clear the way for the little ones aborning in your womb. Clear the way and let them come forth.

"O woman, rise to the appearing of the sun consciousness. Rise and reach for the crown of life. Cease your perversions of the Mother ray. Rise to the God-realization this day of the principle of life and the fountain of life that is yours to dispense. And give freely of that Water of the Word to the children of the Father.

"Preserve his seed immaculate. Cherish that seed as the light of Alpha. Nourish that seed as the Christ consciousness. Let it give birth to a New Age within you, for the New Day will come when woman gives birth to the New Day, makes room for the New Day in the womb of consciousness.

"The golden age is a Reality in the heart of woman, and the City Foursquare is the alignment of her being with the alignment of the Being of the Father. When you are willing to stand before the Father to receive the cube of Mater, the Father will transfer the cube into your hands, and in your hands is the gift of victory, the gift of Mater-realization.

"O woman, hear the word of the Mother. Hear the word of the Cosmic Virgin. In your hand is the key to the victory of a civilization. You can lead the energies of life, you can discipline the energies. You must stand and face and conquer the dragon of the carnal mind, the beast that comes up out of the earth, that rises out of the sea—that conglomerate of the carnal mind that occupies your own feeling world, your own mental world. You have the authority of the rod of Aaron to exorcise those beasts of consciousness. And when you have triumphed over the beasts within, then go forth as Joan of Arc, as heroines of the cause of the Brotherhood. Go forth to make way in the wilderness of the human consciousness for the coming of the avatars, the prophets and the Christed Ones."

The Gift of the Swaddling Garment

And therefore, my gift to every woman of the world this day is the gift of the swaddling garment. It is a garment woven by the Cosmic Virgin. It is the energy you use to wind about the newborn babe that the babe might feel the disciplining of body temple, might feel the edges of the Mother's love, might have the sense of yet abiding in the womb of time and space, might feel the mantle of love. And so the swaddling garment is wound round about the newborn babe coming into life.

And you will remember also the winding of the clothes, the grave clothes, around the body of Christ and the body of Lazarus for the preservation of that body in the tomb of Mater. The Christ Child is born in the womb of Mater and passing through the initiations of the sacred fire is placed in the tomb of Mater. And in each moment, it is the Mother who prepares the soul, initiates the light and the cycles, holds the blueprint, knows in her heart that her son and her daughter will overcome, will fulfill the Law, will return to the heart of the One.

It is the Mother who holds the body of Christ when the body is taken down from the cross. It is the Mother who holds up the child in joy who has come forth from the womb. It is the Mother whose voice can be heard in the day and in the night, the Mother who is always there listening to the children's prayer. It is the Mother who is there teaching the children of the Law, of the Presence and of the I AM THAT I AM.

Mothers, fulfill your role, and then you will see the Father incarnate, then you will see how man will respond to the highest aspect of his own being. You will see how man will come of age, how man will mature to be the coordinate of your flame. And together, hand in hand as cloven tongues of sacred fire, you shall show forth the Holy Spirit on earth as in heaven. And in that day when the flames of the Holy Spirit are balanced on earth and in heaven, then you will see the culmination of an age and the ushering in of the golden cycle of Aquarius.

Then you will see the balancing of the waters and the balancing of the air and the balancing of fire and of the earth. Then you will see the balance of mind and heart and soul and body. Then you will see the City Foursquare in the temples of the children of the One.

Now, O earth, spin. I raise my hand for the spinning of the world and the spinning of Terra. The acceleration of the consciousness of Terra is for the throwing up into the flame of the Spirit of all darkness, all degradation and the vials of wrath. O spin this world. Spin now and release into the flame all sin. Spin, O world. Spin, O consciousness of the chosen ones. Spin now and increase the pulsations of the flame within. Increase the initiations of the sacred fire. Increase your attunement by your atonement and your at-one-ment with the Mother and the Spirit.

I am Mary, appearing in the way to the woman of the world. O woman, manifest the destiny of fire and air and water and earth. Manifest the destiny of the quadrants of Mater, O woman. Lead the way. Carry the torch. Hold the book. Teach the children. Wash their faces. Nourish their souls. Show them in the simple teachings of nature how God is revealed over and over again.

Run to Greet the Man Who Is the Son of God

Woman of the world, run to greet the man who is the son of God. Run to greet him in the way. Restore to him the powers that you have taken from him by devious means. Restore to man his divine identity. Restore to him his soul, his heart, his oneness with the Father. Run to greet him in the way. He is waiting for the love of the Cosmic Virgin this day. Run to tell him the news that the Faithful and True[3] is coming and the armies of heaven and the angels of the Lord and the hierarchies of the sun, that they come to reinforce that strength in the hour of Armageddon[4] whereby the man of God can defend the woman in the way. Run to tell him the news of life aborning within you, of the coming of the Manchild, that Christ will be born again in Bethlehem and that the star of the I AM THAT I AM will appear, that Terra will find her place, that Terra is coming Home.

O woman of the world, run to greet thy Maker as thy husband.[5] Run to greet the I AM THAT I AM. Run to greet your families and your children, your fathers and your sons, your husbands and your brothers. Run to greet them as the fusion of light and tell them, tell them of a love and of a wonder of the Cosmic Virgin who lives, lives to release all that is Real in man and woman. And tell them of the true nature of Being, of the glorious fulfillment and of the victory of spirals merging in the I AM THAT I AM. And tell them of the rod of Moses that he held up in the wilderness.[6]

So woman of the world, hold up the rod and let the children gaze upon the image of the rising serpentine fires that they might feel the flow of life rising within and be healed thereby of all their diseases, of all their sins and compromises, of all of their death and rituals of death.

O woman of the world, run to greet the dawn and greet the sun and draw out the fires of the sun and return to all mankind the energies of the One, of life and Truth and love, of sacred fire burning and blazing within the heart. Unlock the secrets of the heart and the mysteries of the temple. Give them, give them unto all.

Here, then, is the swaddling garment that you will use to draw the consciousness of all into the womb of the Divine Mother. Here also is the key of the divine wisdom and the understanding of the Logos.

Now I have given you my love, my understanding, my Presence this day. I have transferred to you my consciousness and my ray. Take it, mothers of the world. Take it and run with it and know that I am with you on that way.

I am the way, the truth and the life.[7] I am the victory of the age. And I am with you always[8] unto the fulfillment of all cycles of the cosmic consciousness of God as Mother appearing within you.

> In the name of the Father and of the Mother and of the Son and of the Holy Spirit, Amen.[9]

Mary

I am Mary,
appearing in the way
to the woman of the world.
O woman, manifest the destiny of
fire and air and water and earth.
Manifest the destiny of the
quadrants of Mater, O woman.
Lead the way. Carry the torch.
Hold the book. Teach the children.
Wash their faces. Nourish their souls.
Show them in the simple teachings of
nature how God is revealed
over and over again.

Mary

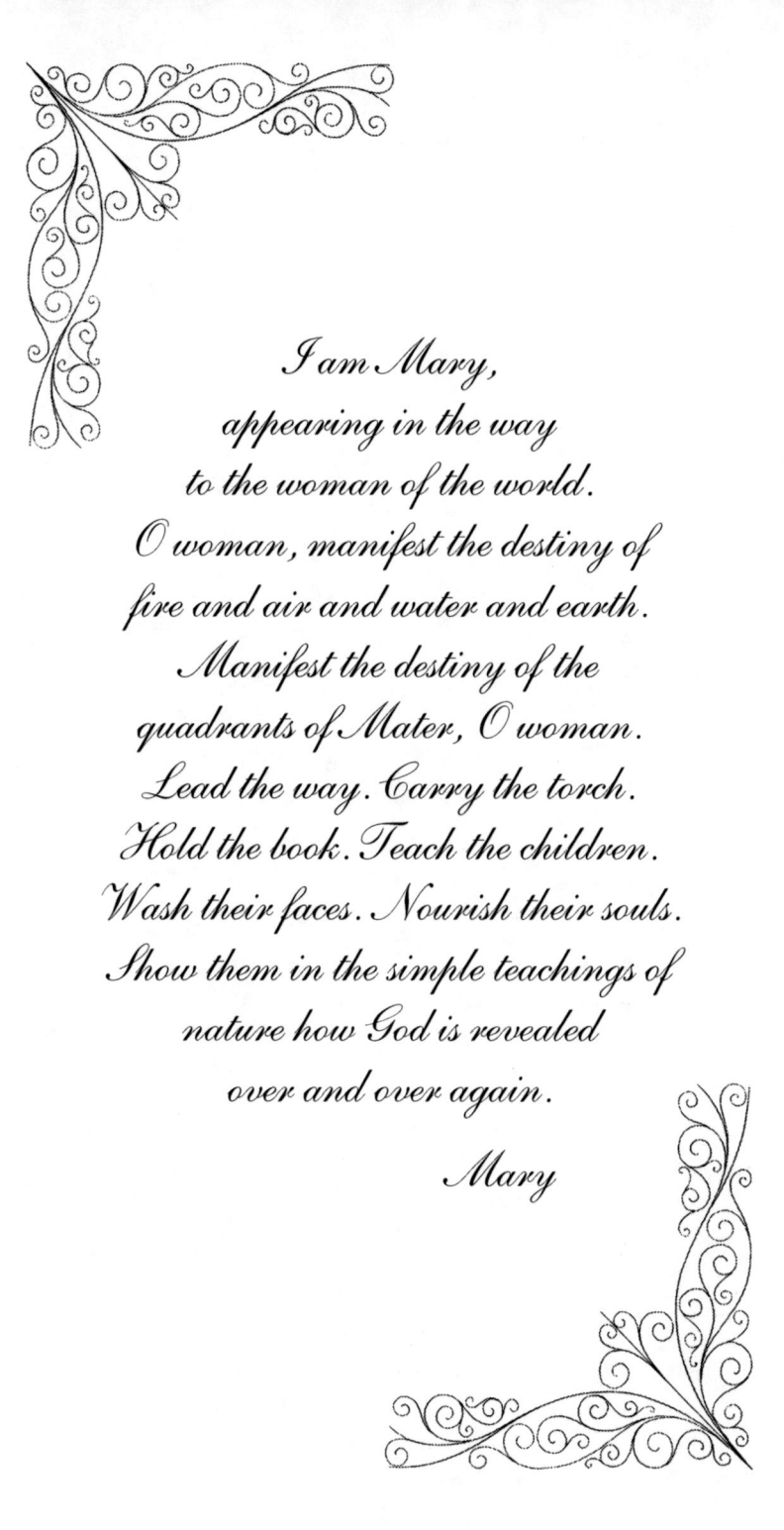

16

I Would Free You

My beloved sons and daughters, I would bring to you the memory of our assignment, of the hour when you stood as holy angels or as sons and daughters of God with the holy angels, for both evolutions were blest to be sponsors of life on earth by Alpha and Omega.

Some of you will remember of first hearing of my assignment to come to earth to give birth to the avatar Jesus, the Christ.[1] He was my son in numerous incarnations before the final one, and many of you served as the circle of his retinue in those lifetimes. Some of you were born through the seed of his heart when he was Joseph, the son of Jacob.

You, then, have been a part of the great band of co-servers of the Mother of the World. Wherever there has been the manifestation of Mother and of the Christ you have been there stretching the band, stretching the very fabric that has become the sounding place of the echo of the far-off worlds. It is not unusual that you should be found gathered

Mother of the World
by Nicholas Roerich

again in this seminar on the Mother. Called by my flame and by the mothers of life, whose image is the image of Omega redundant throughout nature and life, you would assemble yourselves and I would sponsor you to become mothers of life.

Blessed sons, dearest ones who have such sensitivity to the Mother's heart and such understanding and perception of inner levels that is even beyond your outer awareness, I bless you for keeping the Mother flame through the ages. I would say it, therefore I shall: I dedicate my life to you. I dedicate my heart to you.

Sons of God, daughters beautiful, I come with the Maha Chohan* that the mantle of sacred fire and soft and gentle garment might keep you in the sense of coziness and bliss and warmth that the passage from the seat-of-the-soul chakra, as the long passage from the door of the cathedral to the altar, might be for you a chosen way and a way on which you lead many.

---

*The Maha Chohan is the "Great Lord" of the seven rays, the representative of the Holy Spirit to a planet and its evolutions. He is the one who embodies the Trinity and the Mother flame of the seven rays and chakras and is qualified to be chohan, "lord," of each or all of the seven rays. Hence, he is called the Maha Chohan, the Great Lord, as he presides over the seven chohans who embody the Law, the Word and the Christ consciousness of their respective rays.

I Would Free You

For some who have loved me and the Mother for aeons, there is not yet the fulfillment of the soul's potential, and you are not even aware of those inhibitions of which the Mother speaks that keep you from the fullness of yourself. Your self-expression has often been hindered by the harshness of life.

The Maha Chohan

I come with the warmth of the Mother flame so that you might be free and comfortable, quiet, enjoying holiness and having the spur of life to explore the reaches of illumination's star—the enjoyment of science, the magnificent contemplation of religion.

I would unleash you, I would unbind you from the fetters of conditionings of consciousness—reticence to speak, to be, to love, to serve. I would reveal to you by the path of the Mother's initiation the love of your own being, the beauty of your own Selfhood and your capacity to be so much of God on earth!

> I would free you from limitation
> And condemnation.
> I would free you from the sharp edges of life,
> The jagged edges of hopes dashed
> By the proud and the powerful.
> Their day was done from the moment they had begun,
> Yet they still appear.
> May it cause you no longer the shedding of a tear
> Or a setback in life.
> May you look to the Sun

> And see the vision
>   of the eagle before you,
> Of the coming of the hosts
>   of the Lord,
> Of brothers and sisters of the
>   star Sirius!

I AM Mother Mary with Raphael. Though I appear in many guises, some who love me neither understand nor know me, whether as the person familiar in each one's household or as the cosmic being of the archeiai. On the chain of life that is my lifestream there is a multiplicity of levels of consciousness, and everywhere the face of the Mother turning greets her own in the image that they recognize. And sometimes their own image itself limits my appearing or what I may say or do in the midst of the devotees.

May you come with me for the widening, ever-widening of the expanse of the habitation of the Mother and her seed. It is my prayer through your heart, as you do receive the love fires from the Maha Chohan and me this day, that you might also expand the narrow room of the Mother's Being, that you might perpetuate her teaching, her life and her Word.

> Praise God that I may appear in the flesh to you!
> Praise God that I AM here
> Because you allow it and because the inner vow is set!
> I AM your Mother Mary
> And I AM with you unto the victory of the age
> Of your incarnation of the Word.[2]

Mary

I am a mother of your heart. I am an organizer, an administrator, I am a priestess, and I lead also armies of heaven. You may know me in one or many of my offices but, above all, remember that I assist you in your own path of personal management and organization of your life—the setting of priorities, the use of the hours and of your strength while the day is. For the night cometh when no man can work, and that night may be either the dark night of the soul or the dark night of the Spirit.

Mary

17

The Betrayal and the Victory

I am here now to bring forth, from my heart, skeins of light for the weaving of a womb of light as a cocoon the size of a vast cosmos, that in the angel hair of God's own love you might feel yourself protected even while suspended in a sometimes hostile world. This world, as God's world, is a world of love.

How interesting to note—coexisting in time and space with the beauties of God's own living space is an unreality of maya, not as wisps of angel hair but wisps of nothingness and phantoms, there where the Christ ought to be.

Images of the not-self parade across the avenue. And yet, in that very place is the holiness of God, but not in that dimension. For where men have dedicated themselves since even before the last days of Atlantis to perform the wicked deeds of the fallen ones, they themselves by free will have dedicated space to that which is the antithesis of heaven.

Thus I come to you who live in God's heaven in the very midst of a hell that the fallen ones have created. Now, which is Real and which will endure? It is not time that will tell, but it is the heart of my blessed. My blessed and beloved ones, I hold you in my strong arms of God's determination that you shall be victorious.

On Good Friday, many think of me as the sorrowful mother. I can assure you that my heart has long been healed of the sorrow of my Lord's crucifixion. Even the resurrection hour was the fullness of my joy. Therefore, if there be sorrow, there is sorrow in my heart first for those who are of God who become the unwitting carriers of the seeds of evil.

So it was with Judas. So it was with this son. Realize, then, that there was a determination of Satan to place in his heart the seed of betrayal.[1]

Blessed ones, this act of the fallen ones perpetrated against the lightbearers must be understood. For, you see, it is an implant in the very heart of hearts, in the very seat of consciousness where the conscious mind believes itself to be in full control.

Judas perceived this thought of the Devil as his own—justified it in that inasmuch as the Lord would be betrayed by someone, it did not matter if he himself would effect and effectively bring about that passing. On the other hand, there was the ambition within him that somehow the Lord himself would rise up and proclaim himself the King of the Jews and restore Israel and overthrow the Roman Empire and show his power.

Did he think in his heart to precipitate a confrontation in

which Jesus would have no alternative but finally to evidence who he was? I do not disclose all of the thoughts of his heart, nor do I seal the theories of men by my words, as to their own speculation as to what was the chemistry of that moment. But I show you this: that Jesus came to illustrate the confrontation with Antichrist.

Instead of waiting for an importune or inopportune moment, he began his mission swiftly with a fast in the wilderness[2]—at the conclusion of which, the planetary dweller-on-the-threshold did confront him.[3]

You recall his words on another occasion: "The prince of this world cometh, and hath nothing in me."[4] Jesus was indeed empty, having fasted. But he was also empty of any point of pride or earthly ambition or ego or selfishness or desire of any kind except to be God in action. Therefore, he passed the tests of divinity—the three tests of Satan directed to the line of the Father, the line of the Son and the line of the Holy Spirit.

These tests he passed in the name of his love for Mother, Mother symbolized in Eve—I-Eva—Mother in the universal sense,[5] Mother as a flame in his heart, Mother as the Word Incarnate. It was indeed on behalf of one Eve and of many that the Lord came to face the very serpent of the Garden. And he faced that serpent again in the Garden of Gethsemane.

Defeat the Logic of the Fallen One

And therefore, to save that which was lost, from the beginning unto the ending his cosmic purpose from out the Great Central Sun was to defeat the logic of the Fallen One, to set the example, that you might understand this, beloved: that if the Fallen One may catch you in any of these lies or the ramifications thereof, if you may be tempted by devil reasoning, by human logic, to stray from the one-pointedness of your path, you will find that to consent to the statements of the fallen ones, to agree with them in their materialism will result for you in another round in entanglement with that state of consciousness.

Have you lately overcome an enemy within or without? Have you lately seen the face of evil and its fruits in your life or in another's? Perhaps you have lately gotten the victory over some beast of the carnal mind. I am here to praise God, to love you, to cherish you and to tell you I rejoice in every victory of all of my sons and daughters.

I point this out to you so that you may realize that each victory is a liberation of your soul from a certain plane of consciousness in the lowlands of life. You cannot mount the mount of God's love, you cannot climb step by step the highest mountain of God's holiness unless with each step you have overcome the pull of earth, the gravity, the thinning of the air and all of the challenges that are there. But most of all, you must overcome planes of the human consciousness, planes of self-limitation, binding laws of mortality.

If you will consider your most immediate victory, you will find that it has occurred in the seat of the conscious mind, that point where your soul has touched the mind of Christ and realized a great realization of God's own Reality. Standing in the sun of that Reality, you have said, "I no longer have need of that unreality! I have no need of that shadowed self. I have no need for this or that entanglement with a lesser state of consciousness! Let it all go into the flame—and may my true friends be those who are the friends of God."

Thus, one by one, you pass through life. And you understand that had Jesus inclined his ear to Satan, he, too, would have had another round—perhaps one that could have been overcome in that embodiment, perhaps one needing the fullness of a long life or another incarnation.

Therefore it was necessary—though he had overcome even prior to that incarnation—to receive the enemy in the earth itself, to know him for what he was and is, to prove to all of his brothers and sisters (which ye are) that you, too, can receive the mark of "100 percent perfect" in this challenge to your Godhood. And the challenge in the fourth point is also the challenge of the Mother flame.

Now, then, beloved, in the case of Judas, he did not have this attainment. And therefore, in a moment, in the presence of the magnetic aura of the Fallen One (the same Satan that tempted the Lord), he could give way and not hold on to the Christ-truth he knew, and he saw face to face.

You will note how suddenly and quickly this occurred. In a matter of a few weeks, his entire consciousness was aligned and polarized in the betrayal. And once he was poisoned in the mind itself, in the seat of the conscious mind, my Son could but say to him, "That which thou doest, do quickly"[6]—let the deed fall through the hourglass, that you may see the consequences thereof and that your mind might be cleared from this odious substance of that Fallen One.

For in the light of the physical precipitation of sin, there is actually a clearing of the air, as the vibration of the poison itself somehow passes into the act of sin and becomes concrete that one may look upon it then objectively and no longer contain it in the subjective mind and heart.

Thus Peter, too, succumbed. After he had done so, he saw clearly the error of his way, perceived how he had been tricked by his own carnal mind and wept bitterly.[7] And Judas hanged himself for the utter remorse[8] of a crime, which in the process of committing, he could not have the objectivity to see, for he was truly in the grips and the toils of Satan.

Beloved ones, therefore I, Mary, say to you that the concern of my heart is for the children of God who are not equal to the temptation of the dweller-on-the-threshold—in whom, because there is some fallow field in consciousness, a seed of doubt may be planted, a seed of fear. And fear begets excessive self-concern, a change even in physical, bodily functions, an acceleration of a consciousness of survival and self-preservation.

Therefore, the mind becomes clouded, increasingly clouded, and therefore darkness is in the sky. And the contemplation of rash acts, even considered to be necessary for self-defense, does actually pass through the mind. And yet, the origin of this is in death itself. From the point of fear, through the whole round of human creation—which I have taught you on my cosmic clock, diagramming world and personal karma (see pages 17, 19)—you will see that fear may be the original seed that leads to death itself in some form, even if it be the death of the image of Christ within your very soul.

Therefore, if there be sorrow on Good Friday, it is because I see that those who ought to be in the next spiral of their overcoming have setback after setback because they wax hot and cold. They do not see themselves as that yo-yo that goes back and forth between the influence of the Fallen One and the influence of the Christ.

And, of course, beloved ones, these two, being so diametrically opposed, increase an enormous strain—and tension reigns over the individual as he swings backwards and forwards and backwards and forwards. And so he says, "I must be delivered of this."

Be Not Duped

And at that moment, many make the decision to stand at the point of self-doubt and therefore to be certain in their self-doubt—if that were conceivably possible—that they themselves will not be duped, will not be tricked, will not be cast out, that they will be the first to declare that Christ is not the Christ but, in fact, the position they have espoused is truly the real one.

Well, beloved hearts, it is a tragedy, but it has occurred again and again. I weep not for the fallen angels, but I weep for those who unknowingly have become their tools and therefore bear an enormous karma. And when they remain as their effective instruments, these individuals begin to experience a decrease of soul power and soul substance, and identity becomes less and less. For while they are the tools of the fallen ones, the fallen ones do eat their light. And their inverted practice of communion is actually to steal the substance of the souls of God's own, to devour it and therefore prolong their life.

This is because they have not been offered the communion wafer or the cup of wine in Christ's name. And therefore, they say, "What we do not receive by Law, we will steal! We will kill for it. We will commit adultery for it. We will desecrate the Virgin. We will mutilate the Son. We will hurl down the Laws of the Father, and we will pervert the force of the Holy Ghost."

Therefore, beloved ones, in the face of the infamy of Good Friday and the spell of the fallen ones placed over the earth, let us rejoice that God is Real. And he will save to the uttermost those that are lost or almost lost, those who are almost in the grips of the toilers, and perhaps those who have already been abducted. By fervent prayer, we know that the heart of Christ physically flowing through your own is able to perform miraculous works by the Science of the Spoken Word.[9]

And so the events of the news have shown just how effective your seminars have been, just how effective the Word is.... There are some who stand by and wish to minimize this victory and the many victories we are seeing. They do not understand that *these* victories mark the point of the reversing of the tide, of the rolling back of that momentum. They have reached that watermark, and they will now recede if you will understand that they do *flee*—they are on the run, and therefore it is the hour to hurl now, with the mighty archangels, that *thrust* and that *roll* and that *ho, ho, ho,* as the mighty laughter of the hosts of the LORD drives into the very core of that consciousness of unreality, this manifest Evil that is present.

Understand the Strategy of Victory

Therefore, it is important to understand the strategy of victory. When you have struck a blow for the LORD, as you have, and they are on the run, it is important to pursue with more dynamic decrees. For if they run and feel no one pursuing behind them, they will soon slow down. And if again they consider that no one is looking, they will attempt to regroup and regain that which was lost.

And therefore, we must have a continuing and organized action in our study groups and teaching centers and with each individual. We must have, therefore, a cumulative awareness of that which we are about and not allow the fires in the camp to go out, lest the enemy consider that we are no longer alert.

Far from it—we are alert and we are on the move! And

there is much progress and much reason for victory in this hour. All the more why those betrayers, even of the Mother and my heart, even of the messengers and the teaching, take this hour and opportunity to attempt to strike a blow against the expansion that has become a mighty release of light—even a fireworks in spring, as the aurora borealis does sing, and the sky of the north awaits the coming of the children of the sun.

Yes, I am sorrowful for those who do receive the seeds of the toilers—who become incensed, whose auras are therefore inverted, and the darkness that was in them is multiplied tenfold or a hundredfold by their acceptance of the planetary dweller-on-the-threshold, multiplying that personal dweller.

Realize, then, that the confrontation objectively with the one called Satan, who may come to you in any guise, serves you with notice as much as if it were Maitreya himself handing you the paper declaring the initiation—the initiation that you must also confront the adversary within and slay that adversary, lest the one without catch you off-guard and find something in you,[10] when there should be nothing at all.

Let there be the self-emptying. Let there be the filling of oneself by the Lord! Let Jesus fill your emptied self with joy, and let his joy suffice thee to meet every human need until you are *weaned* of those needs and come to another plane where you perceive in love and compassion that there is a higher need in your life, one that supersedes the past. It is your soul's longing for the true companionship of Christ, the friend of your life.

Make friends with him, I say, as you have never done before. When you hold his hand, clasp it tight. And do not wait for him to clasp yours tighter. Therefore, understand that there must be a will in the grasp and a determination to hang on and to go where he goes, wherever he may take you.

Secondly, my sorrow on Good Friday must also be somewhat to see the continuing bearing of the burden by our blessed devotees, by our messenger. But I must tell you, the sorrow is greater for the one who is betrayer. For, after all, the sons of God live in the earth for the manifestation of the light that contrasts the darkness. They expect to be line-to-line in that mark of confrontation. They expect and understand this way, and that it is the way that leads to victory.

The strength of the son of God to overcome is the greatest joy of Good Friday. The greatest joy of the Mother is this realization that the one who is Christ becomes another who shall light the world—for "as long as I am in the world, I am the light of the world."[11]

A Physical Oneness with the Saints of Heaven

I, Mary, say this so that you may understand that Jesus, Saint Germain, El Morya and the sons of heaven can only be the light of the world so long as they are in the world physically. Therefore, there must be a *physical* oneness of yourself with the saints of heaven. And they may stand where you stand, even as hell stands where heaven is—except this is by the magnet of love and not by the warfare of the unreal pitted against the Real.

This congruency and oneness is that lawful state of hierarchy stretched out across a cosmos and then condensed and compressed into one fiery diamond heart, one single devotee, one single chela unswerving that becomes the point of our entrance. And I, Mary, speak from that heart of that chela and I say, in the name of the blessed rosary and your offering thereof: As long as I AM in the world of *you* and in the seat of your consciousness, I AM the light of the World Mother through you!

And in the hours and the moments when you intensify that light and that call, we are one. There is no separation. You know the Friend, you know the divine Lover of your soul, you know the bliss of that communion, and you feel the flow of fire that is not entirely your own.

It is your own gathering of the flowers of spring and of the essence of the heart of Christ, and it is the focusing through this of our hearts' fire, which we have garnered as bouquets of stars and causal bodies and daisies of your adorations that form a chain across the sky and pierce the night as a streak of lightning—and yet is still the endless chain of souls, the endless chain of daisies in the field of the Lord.

Yes, all of this in your heart makes you the effective spokesmen for the Great White Brotherhood. May it be so.

Let us crown Him with many crowns. Let us place the crown of our hearts' love upon the Christ in one another. Let us worship together the living God and know that because this Friday is come, and because He is victorious, nothing—no, nothing—from the very depths of hell to the heights of heaven, can take from you your victory!

And none, blessed hearts, can give it to you. You must take it to yourself and you must give it as a gift to God and all of life. Your victory is the most private affair of your entire life and lifestream. Your victory is that point of communion where only the One can occupy the third eye and the heart.

O my blest Raphael, teach them the point of victory, theirs to *seize* and run with! Teach them the victory of the souls departing this day and mounting to the higher retreats—souls whose lives have been well lived in search of God, who now will have open to them truly the portals of heaven for a continuing study and experience in the retreats of the Brotherhood—that they, too, might have their hour and their day of victory on earth. Let no man take thy crown,[12] thy opportunity for victory.

We would not see a victory half done, nor would you. And this is why so many desire to go back, to reembody, to "do it right" and to leave a record that will encourage all to fight for the highest and the noblest in self.

I am a mother of your heart. I am an organizer, an administrator, I am a priestess, and I lead also armies of heaven. You may know me in one or many of my offices but, above all, remember that I assist you in your own path of personal management, organization of your life—the setting of priorities, the use of the hours and of your strength while the day is. For the night cometh when no man can work,[13] and that night may be either the dark night of the soul or the dark night of the Spirit.

In hours of initiation when you must deal with the total planetary consciousness and karma, you will spend all of your energy in dealing with that initiation. And therefore, make haste to complete the work of your life so that one day when you are called—always unexpectedly, as a thief in the night, as the bridegroom comes—so understand that Maitreya will call and you will be ready, and others may fulfill and continue what you have begun.

Remember also the suddenness of the sowing of the seed of betrayal and the turning of a consciousness. So also is the suddenness of the Divine Encounter and the conversion unto Christ. Each one bespeaks that some thing, some very mighty thing has entered the world of the individual, something of the absolute order of things—absolute Good or absolute Evil.

These forces exist. Though you may not see them, you see them clearly in the consequences of men's lives and the choices they make. Something from without, something from within—the chemistry changes and a new identity appears.

Let it be so that on this Good Friday, the victory of your love will see manifest where you are a multiplication, by those fourteen stations,[14] of the light in you by the light of Christ.

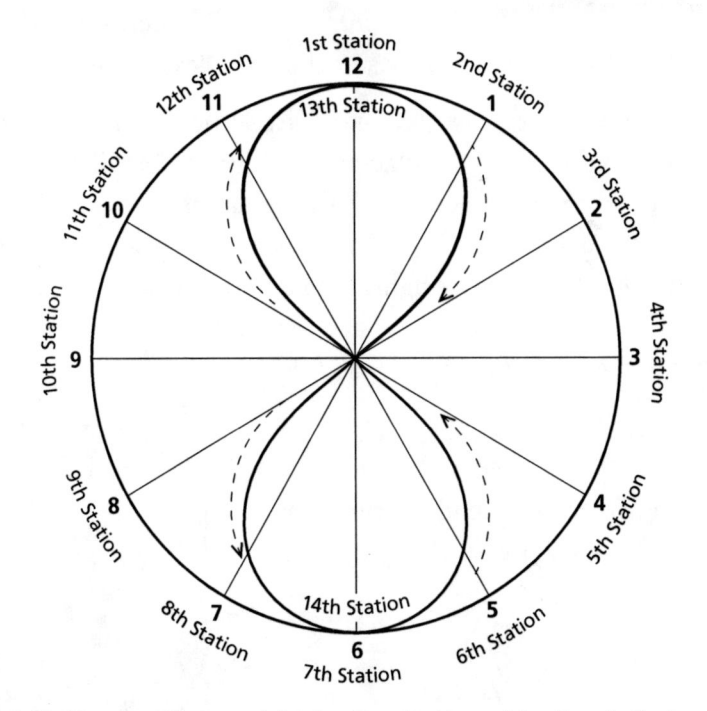

The Fourteen Stations of the Cross on the Lines of the Cosmic Clock

Blessed ones, if the new lilies of sainthood do not appear each Eastertide, then is the walk to Golgotha in vain. He did it not for himself alone, but for *you*, my child, and for you. Therefore, let your own life be the point of light that he will multiply.

Let the Cosmic Christ appear where you are!

Let Maitreya *be* where you are.

And then you will see Maitreya here, Maitreya there.

Lo, the kingdom of God is within you!

And you and you!

And they will not know where Maitreya has appeared,

For he is everywhere—

Everywhere in the hearts of the disciples of Christ.

And therefore all are right, all are wrong—and none are right or wrong. For the placing of Maitreya as a flesh-and-blood person is erroneous, but the denial of Maitreya living within the heart of a flesh-and-blood person is also erroneous.

Let be the incarnate light! Let be the Chosen One! Let be the universality of the Christed Ones, and let all become lilies in the field of the Lord—as Above in Elysium, so below.

I AM Mary,
the Mother of the lily within you,
always and always.
Amen.[15]

Mary

*I come, then,
to nurture every aspect
of the Mother light.
For even as you have been told
that the seven rays have seven
aspects of the Christic light,
you must understand that
if all aspire to be the Mother,
not all will become the same design,
not all will come forth
out of the same
cookie cutter.*

Mary

18

Keeping the Vigil

My own beloved hearts of light, hearts of living flame:

I have come from visiting the Midnight Mass, line by line across the time zones of the earth, arriving here for the keeping of the vigil of that midnight hour.

Wherever hearts have called to me this night, I have answered. Wherever they have prayed to the child Jesus, I have sent forth an answer to their prayer—one perhaps not expected, but always an answer.

Dear ones, do realize in this hour that my service to earth is directly dependent upon the call of the devotees; and that call most frequently heard, as you know so well, is the Hail Mary.

There has been so much controversy regarding the office of the Mother of God, confusing the office with my person and considering that somehow in this salutation, the human is made divine.

Beloved ones, I would tell you exactly why the tradition of the call to me was begun. It is not because of my person, but because of my office. It is the office I occupy as archeia of the fifth ray. And upon this office, beloved Alpha has placed an authority for the divine intercession. The call made to me is answered by millions of hosts of the LORD who bear the flame of that office, who attend the office, who come to earth to succor souls in my name.

Therefore the appeal to Mary, as you have been told, is to the Mother ray. But most specifically, it is a scientific call to that point of my contact with the divinity of our Father and of Brahman—and of the Word, which I, too, have become.

Blessed ones, do understand that the call to me is, as it were, to access the cosmic computer of the Mother, of the Cosmic Virgin herself. And therefore, my Electronic Presence, by the dispensation of our Father, may be present a million times a million throughout the world.

I say this so that you would understand that I, too, recite the Hail Mary. For I adore the One and the Source and the God as Mother. It is the keeping of the flame of Mother, the path that I excel and I exemplify that leads to the reintegration of worlds.

I would tell you, therefore, that the denial—whether of my office or of my person—has resulted in the candle going out within the Protestant movement. For it is I, and the I AM that is the I in me, to whom the LORD God gave that commission (which has been recently explained to you[1]) of holding the office of the Mother—the one point in the four that does descend below the level of the heart.

You have been given this teaching. Brahma, Vishnu and Shiva—the mighty power of the Father, the Son and the Holy Spirit resident in the threefold flame—may descend only to the point of that flame and that perfection. But the

Mother descends the spiral staircase, as it were, into the dark basement of the astral body, the astral plane and the electronic belt where she must also encounter the dweller-on-the-threshold and have the attainment to bind that dweller temporarily—to reach the soul, to preach to the soul, to extend the hand and to take that one quickly up the flight of stairs to the secret chamber of the heart where the soul may be tutored by Christ and Buddha and Krishna and the eternal Flame.

Come Up that Staircase

Thus, if souls will listen to me as I descend and will trust me and will come up that staircase, great progress is made. For in the office of the Cosmic Virgin, I do keep the flame, I do place my Electronic Presence around that soul as a swaddling garment of light in order that the soul may have the sensitivity and the development of the senses of the Spirit and of the chakras wherewith to perceive and to understand what it is that the Father or the Son or the Holy Spirit will teach that soul.

Therefore, when the teaching is concluded and the soul has enlightenment concerning her destiny and her karma and reason for being in this life, it is as though the soul has been in the mountaintop experience; but the mountain is the point of Zion, of the mighty threefold flame and the Christ of the heart. Then the soul must descend the stairway again, and I will accompany that one down the mountain, once again to the valleys and the plains.

And the soul now understands that there is a world of maya and illusion and a world of Reality. And the sweet taste of Reality as the nectar of the Buddha is something that the soul now will cherish, will remember, will long for.

This memory will also provide balance and strength and inner resources in the hour of the descent of karma or the Dark Cycle or even the dark night of the soul. Thus, you see, there are some who face adversity with that inner Rock of Christ. And this is because I have escorted them to that Christ, and they have received a transfusion of sacred fire for the centuries ahead.

Some have gone ten thousand, a hundred thousand years through that one and single encounter whereby in the trust of the Mother they have visited the heart of Christ and retained the fire that has been sufficient for them. Thus you understand the words of my Son, "My grace is sufficient for thee."[2] Truly it is sufficient for a million years or even for the entire span of descent to the Matter planes.

The Reformation

Beloved ones, therefore, with the coming of this Protestant revolt ignited from the fires of hell itself by the fallen angels, you see the putting out of this candle of the Mother. Think of the darkness of the earth as the candle of the Mother goes out one by one, and I personally am expelled from the cathedrals of northern Europe and from Britain.

No longer is there the reverence for the Mother, but she has become once again a common, untutored, ignorant young maid who, by chance or the selection of God, became the Mother of Christ by no particular virtue of her own but merely by an ordination or an immaculate conception.

Thus, not only is there the denial of the Mother, but there is the denial of her path and of the spiral staircase and of the welcoming of the Mother when she does appear. Those indoctrinated in the outer sense may often suffer internally also when they are visited by my angels. Others, however, never lose the inner love, for they have known me as friend or Mother or sister or even child.

Therefore, beloved hearts, in this great mystery of the Word of the Mother, I would tell you that the restoration of life on earth depends upon the salutation of the Mother ray daily. If you do not find time or space to participate in the rosary, I would request that the mantra alone, the Hail Mary, be on your lips in moments when you must wait here or there for one cycle to end or another to begin, when you are walking or changing modes of service.

The simple mantra can be given without the entire ritual, for it does establish the open door whereby I may not only enter the temple of thyself and abide there, but also use your chalice provided in purity to serve all life. And I may also descend that staircase, if necessary, to teach your soul in your seat-of-the-soul chakra, if your soul has never truly mounted herself to the heart of Christ but only gone there on the mantle of the messenger and the dictations of the ascended masters.

You understand, therefore, that the office of messenger does hold the focus of my flame, guiding you in those dark chambers and canyons of the night, holding a torch, showing the surest way out of the dilemma of thy human creation. Thus our desire, the desire of the Great White Brotherhood, is that by your soul attainment you should be able to mount that staircase from the seat of the soul, through the initiations of the solar plexus, to the heart and then the secret chamber of the heart.

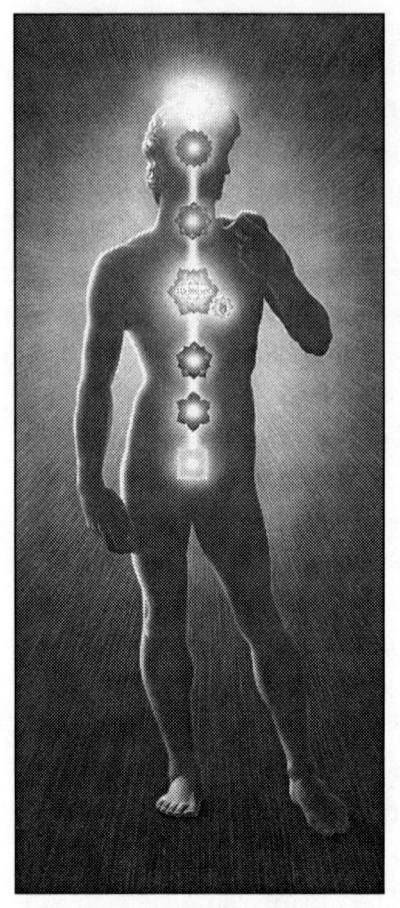

Thus you understand that the journey to the heart from the seat of the soul is the passageway through the turbulent anchoring point of the astral body in the solar plexus—all of the records of violent or disturbed emotions, burdens, karma, and so forth. Thus, it is no small wonder that souls do not venture forth, for those who have tried have been met with the most severe setbacks.

These are seen on the road of life. Some interpret these adversities as karma. They are not all karma. You may see calamity come to individuals solely because they have loved Christ so much, they desire once again to venture forth; and without the hand of the embodied Mother, they can scarcely withstand that which does come upon them as the records of their own past.

Therefore, every person of the Great White Brotherhood, every ascended master and those who have embodied as the avatars, such as Jesus, have come forth to be the Mother in embodiment. Whether male or female in form, you are the Mother because you are here in your sacred labor, in your sixth sacrament of the ministering servant and of marriage, to guide souls through the labyrinth of those areas and levels of consciousness where they encounter the greatest danger and burden and all manner of accidents and diseases and terrible tragedies to which life on earth is heir.

The blessed Kuan Yin has become known as the Saviouress out of the East performing the selfsame and identical function as my own, yet each of us bringing to this office of Mother our own past attainment and experience, which is different by our very service on differing rays.

The Sine Wave of the Law of Karma

Blessed ones, all of the ascended masters of heaven contrive and conspire to reach the souls wherever they are positioned, moving toward the central sun of Being. And those who are spiraling away from that center by wrong indoctrination, by their drugs or the terrible, terrible rhythm of that rock music, we attempt to convince by every means and manner imaginable (and some that you could never imagine, which are the secrets of heaven) to bring these souls to the desire to take the path to the sun of their own Christ Self and to walk that path, not in a jagged pattern but according to the sine wave of the law of their karma.

This sine wave does bring them the rhythm of the descent of Omega, which gives the impetus to the ascent of Alpha, and the ascent of Alpha, which gives the impetus to the descent—as when you are on a roller coaster, you realize the momentum gained in the descent for the ascent.

And thus, if you understand your life in these cycles, you must surely know that the peaks of Zion, of contact with God, the acceleration of light, will be followed by the descent where all of that light garnered must become a thrust, therefore, into the levels where you have created karma, where you must return to the scene of that karma, bring the light, not lose the momentum in the process of giving the light—not spending it all but giving that which is lawful so that you have reserved enough fuel for the ascent again to the point of Alpha for a new recharging and infilling with light and the descent once again.

This is the great mystery of the journey of the soul to the center of the heart. And by and by, the soul that enters the alchemical union with Christ bears more and more of the light of Christ into the lower centers until all of that karma is transmuted, the dweller is bound and cast out, the sacred fire of the Kundalini is raised without danger because it will no longer contact that turbulent karma and record and actuality of misqualified substance that does cause a chemistry and often a violent reaction when that Kundalini is forced.

By and by, therefore you see, with the soul ascending and descending the spiral staircase, there is the illumination; and the lower chakras become as clear and purified as those above. And each individual, therefore, stands in his own mighty figure-eight flow, and the light of the causal body may descend. It may descend because the I AM Presence and the Christ Self, the Father and the Son, have come to take their abode in the temple of the loving and the obedient disciple.

Thus, day by day and little by little, you experiment with this increment of fire. And as you make the journey again through the untransmuted layers, you guard the harmony, you guard the consciousness, you do not allow yourself to engage. None of your chakras, your feelings, emotions or thoughts engage with the unreality that is being consumed. And therefore, my precious ones, you become the victor.

Once the human creation of thyself can see that there is nothing it can do to rouse you, upset you, engage you, cause you to believe the lie or the illusion, become burdened with the records of doubt, then it does give up. It will no longer manifest the ferocious face of the beast; but it sees the end come, passes through the death throes—and you are also vigilant.

And therefore by your call, Archangel Michael and the mighty archangels do bind that dweller as you stand fast and behold the salvation of your God in your very living temple, and you become on earth an electrode of living fire like unto the LORD God above who dwells in the Holy of Holies in the heart of the I AM Presence. This is the goal of your walk with God.

Let not lesser considerations take the place of this path, this understanding, this vigil. For you see, just as quickly as you gain this Mother-awareness, this Mother Presence, you will find yourself feeding the multitudes, tending the millions. For the Mother flame of cosmos will flow through you as those rivers of Living Water[3] and many, many will gain that same inner strength by your presence in the earth.

These days are not far from you! Do not compare the path of the ascended masters and the Great White Brotherhood to any other path, East or West. Let no man take thy crown[4] in this hour. Let no man rend the veil of the holiness and the oneness of thy life with the living Christ.

Understand, beloved hearts, that this is the new dispensation of Aquarius. It does not require centuries, as in the past, to come into this union. Nor should the process be taken lightly. Nor should you so easily forgive yourself your discords—as if it were nothing.

You Must Mend the Bridge of Consciousness

The co-measurement and understanding of that which is violated when you lose your God-control and that which you lose, in fact, is necessary. Thus, not remorse or condemnation or self-pity, but a more enlightened and alert striving—not rote but a deep entering in and the willingness to go to those weak places of consciousness as though you were a workman repairing a bridge crossing the abyss in the

Himalayas and your master had told you: "The Buddha is coming! He must cross over this bridge. You must secure it that it break not with his coming. There are weak places in the bridge. You must find them. You must test the bridge. You must mend each and every one so that when the Buddha crosses over, he will have safe and enjoyable passage."

Thus the responsibility is upon you. But the Buddha is your soul. With all of your ingenuity, you prepare the way of the soul's passage and you realize, blessed hearts, that if you leave a weak spot in the bridge, a weak link in the chain, when the soul must pass the most severe testing and temptation and trial, she will not have the strength to endure and that particular place in the bridge will break—and therefore the soul will fall into the abyss.

This is why no more light or attainment or initiation may be given to you until you mend the bridge for the crossing. For we dare not give you the light that would assure you advanced initiations, which initiations you would then not pass.

Thus the holdup, you see, comes to the point of your ingenuity, your wisdom and your carefulness in remembering what I am teaching you. It is so important for the journey of life—whether for the initiate who walks as the ministering servant, whether for the married couple, the family, the child. The marriage will not succeed, the sacred labor will be abandoned, the child will not realize his potential, the undertaking will fail if you have not first seen to it that the weak points are strengthened.

You already know where you are strong, for you lead by your right hand and your strengths. Therefore, examine what is missing and become strong spherically, and let your strength be at each sign of the clock.[5]

This advice is for the victory of the Church and the victory of the community. Now, each one of you is a plank in the bridge, a part of the rope. Will you be the weak link whereby the community itself breaks, or breaks down, and the Buddha cannot pass through lest he step upon that weak link?

Thus say to yourself, "I am as important as any other part of the bridge. When Buddha walks upon me, will I be able to sustain the harmony and the integrity of the bridge, or will I be the weak link?"

Do not faint at the thought of being the weak link! Simply raise the torch of the Mother. Send forth the call, for this is why there is the Mother-Teacher in the whole Matter universe. Omega is everywhere, and I AM everywhere in the consciousness of Omega.

Thus the office of the World Mother is the mantle worn by the messenger. The teacher, in the person of the Mother Sanat Kumara, is available to teach you how to mend the flaw in the bridge of consciousness, to unveil for you the weaknesses, and to keep at you and at you and at you again and again until you think you will not bear one more round of correction or instruction on that same old point, that same old rusty nail.

But I tell you, the Mother will never leave you alone until she is certain that that weak point is strengthened, is mended and will endure the powerful step of the Lord of the World.

You see how the Mother does not go after the strong points. She is not concerned. Those are your sails, which the wind of the Holy Spirit uses daily. These strengths are your own, and when you know you have them by attainment, you need no compliment, no constant reassurance of well-doing, for you know your job and you do it well.

The Formula for Thy Victory

Thus, let the Mother, in all tenderness—and I speak of every Mother flame throughout the universe—let the Mother incarnate in this flame teach you. And fear not the encounter. For, blessed ones, I say with my Lord: Behold I come quickly and my messenger is with me! Also with me is the formula for thy victory. The formula for thy victory is Christ the Lord, whose incarnation I praise in this hour.

Therefore, blessed ones, beings of fire, air, water and earth, angels of the sacred fire proclaim his coming! For truly because this Jesus Christ is born, so the Adamic evolution does now have the open door to eternal life.

From the beginning unto the ending, I AM Omega. I have come now to claim each and every seed of Abraham and of the descent of Seth. And therefore, beloved hearts of light, I announce to you the hour of the homecoming of that particular lifewave called by some the Adamic evolution—thus of the seed of these twin flames. The hour is come. Rejoice in the birth of the Saviour and the coming of the Mother, for by these does Christ appear in thy temple.

O holy night of the return of the sacred fire of Sanat

Kumara to earth, I AM the vestal virgin! Forever and forevermore, I bear the lamp and the office of Mother.

Thus, call to the Hail Mary, and the forces of cosmic Motherhood shall come forth for the saving of this planet. Let the light of the Mother and the Hail Mary return to the nations of Europe and especially to the heart of Germany for the unification of hearts of light as the sure foundation of the building of the new nation under the one God.[6]

In the name of the Father and of the Son and of the Holy Spirit, I, Mary, send this flame to the heart of Alpha in the name of Omega, bearing the record of all lifestreams who now hear my Word who are seated in this company and all who will ever hear my Word on electronic tape.

A Peep into the Insides of Heaven

So that you may have a peep into the insides of heaven, I will tell you that it is already foreknown and foreordained as to every lifestream who shall and will hear this dictation throughout this two-thousand-year dispensation. Beloved ones, this is not predestination, this is the calculus of free will!

I seal you in the mystery of your destiny. That which is foreknown, therefore, can be fulfilled. Do you will it so?

My beloved, go forth to conquer in the name I AM THAT I AM, Amen. As you send your flames to Alpha, let them bear your hopes and dreams, for Alpha does love to hear your hopes and dreams....

I AM Mary, Mediatrix unto the nations. I desire the sealing of the nations in the sacred fire of love—love that is the ruby ray that binds the devils who oppose the living Christ, who enslave and oppress my children, who deny unto them my heart.

I desire to see the devotion to the Mother... for I tell you, it is the Mother flame in the earth consecrated in all of your chakras that will beat down the entire juxtaposition of nuclear war and all those things that now challenge you so greatly when you consider what is the responsibility of being a parent. It is to make the world safe for your children, safe for future generations.

You have a vested interest, for every one of you must endow the next generation with a portion of your Christhood. And it is you as that Christ light who will live on in this evolution. And therefore, you are concerned. And therefore, you love.

In the fullness of joy, then, let the wedding bells of the brides of Christ ring!

God bless you, my beloved.
A joyous Christmas in the joy of your Lord.[7]

Mary

*Simply put,
without the Mother flame
manifest as a holy science,
as Truth and as Law,
mankind could not even accept
the potential of the acorn
to become the
oak tree.*

Mary

19

The Continuity of Being
"Come and Pray with Me"

Beloved of my heart,
I come to you today in the fullness of my office. "Mary" you call me—and you have called me. And thus I, too, must obey the Law of God to be where my children, my sons and daughters are.

This Circle of Light you have formed[1] demonstrates a conscious willingness on your part to be the handmaid of the LORD, your mighty I AM Presence. Giving yourself to God, as I gave myself to him, can only bear the fruit of the Christ within you.

Give birth, then, to that Christ in this season as the Truest Self thou art. Bid him welcome into thy temple as the Reality of thyself, and walk hand in hand with thy brother, my Son Jesus.

I place myself physically [in this city]...through this temple, the body of the messenger, the chakras purified, and yours. For the radiation of the Mother that I bring from God is truly the healing of every condition within and without.

Your Desire for Wholeness Satisfied through Dynamic Decrees

I come to tell you that I have seen and heard your desire and longing for wholeness, for peace in your life, for the betterment of loved ones. I also assure you that the tapping of the fount of crystal-clear Water of Life comes as you elect to turn the lever and open the valve itself by the affirmation of the Word.

The dynamic decrees given by the ascended masters for their students are efficacious when you fill them with your love and faith, when you make them the very personal communion between your heart and the heart of God, understanding that it is the sacred science that is vouchsafed to thee in this age to forestall nuclear war, the perishing of souls, the loss of your own identity, or any calamity, personal or national.

The healing power of God is within thyself—thy True Self, who is God. Seek it not, then, in the mere human consciousness, but know that power is the divine spark.

Discover Your Mission through the Mainstream of Cosmic Purpose

Many of you have waited long for the opportunity to discover your mission. Some of you have thought you discovered it a number of years ago when you discovered this teaching but yet have not entered into the mainstream of that purpose. I speak to you, and I speak also to those who have searched and now must deal with the demands of finding the true way of one's own path.

I would counsel you from the realm of compassion and

practicality. I would counsel you not to enter into a total upheaval in your life, for Truth does not come for this purpose. Therefore, take step by step the light. And know when it is firm in thyself and know when you have divested self of an impropriety or a density, an erroneous idea or an unwanted habit.

Beloved ones, some who have had the Law have overlooked the mote in their own eye,[2] have stayed and dwelled far too long in a sense of belittlement, have failed to apprehend the swift movement of the eagles who must gather together where the body of Christ is.[3]

Knowledge of the Law Brings Responsibility for Change

The knowledge of the Law is a responsibility for change, not entrenchment in some form of comfortable human situation. Yet comfortability is a moving spiral. One becomes comfortable in God by habit, even as one has formerly been comfortable in the human consciousness by habit.

Those come newly to the fount drink joyously and freely and feel cleansed by the Waters of Life. When you come to the deeper troubles of the heart and the subconscious, these are not as easy. Therefore, let the violet flame saturate and drench and soften and clear away those subconscious blocks to the flow of the mighty River of Life within you.

I speak now following the dictation of my Son, Jesus. . . .[4] With great earnestness of heart and pathos of soul and compassion for the earth, he pleaded for disciples to follow that path to which he called his own for the holding of the balance against conditions that he described in the world—though unknown to most people, yet being of the most dire necessity to be handled, circumstances that you know about, threatening life in the misuse of nuclear energy, and other circumstances not known by you that threaten the nations in this very hour.

I can only repeat the call and plead in his name for each and every one of you to reach for the highest star of purpose in your life, and to offer yourself in your families and communities to draw this greater light that you have felt—or perhaps not felt, yet which has passed through you this day —for a cleansing, a purging of the planet and then a healing.

Cleansing, Soul-Searching and the Planetary Rescue Mission

We must clean out the toxins in the body politic, in the framework of civilization and in every cell of the physical body before the light of the restoration of wholeness can descend. Neglect not, then, the cleansing of mind and body and heart. Neglect not the soul-searching that is necessary in order for you to come forward and be a part of the rescue mission of the angels to save a nation and a planet and a people, but most of all to save your own soul.

Blessed ones, I live with the Fátima prophecy. I live with its message. And I go from door to door and heart to heart knocking, asking for those who will come and pray with me—pray the violet flame or the rosary or the calls to Archangel Michael. But above all, pray. For by thy prayer is the open door extended, and the angels come stepping through the veil to prevent disaster and calamity.

I would whisper a tender message to thy heart—each one individually—of comfort and joy and divine direction. This message is sealed in your heart. And though you may not hear it now, it will unfold like a rose appearing to comfort you and guide you in the days ahead.

We have sent our messenger here to touch you with a light for your own protection and elevation. We have brought you here that you might know just how much you are the beloved of the angels and of God. Knowing this love, take it not for granted, for God may love you but he may not love the untoward habit. Thus realize, in that supreme love, you can let go of all these things and come into union with one who has been devoted to your soul forever.

Hold the Hands of the Christ Self of Your Beloved Twin Flame

Now I ask you to stretch forth your hands and receive the hands of the Christ Self of your own beloved twin flame, that you may feel the divine counterpart and know the wholeness of life you once knew in the Beginning and that you will know again in the ending of all cycles.

Angels come to guard and guide thee to the heart of thy perfect love. Angels come to renew the love for the beloved

Presence with you of God. May your love poured forth daily return to you great love from the altars of heaven.

May you know the nearness of the heavenly Presence and extend it to those who truly suffer for want of affection, comfort and the enlightenment of the true path of my Son.

Your Path to the Retreats of the Brotherhood Made Known through *The Lost Years of Jesus*

I commend you to the study of *The Lost Years of Jesus*[5] with the purpose of gaining the understanding of your own path to the highest retreats of the Brotherhood, the necessity to pursue that path and to take advantage of all that we offer.

The world must face that there is more to the life of my Son than orthodox Christianity has allowed. They have not allowed my children to know the truth of his mission and work, and how that mission and work should apply to each and every one in all centuries.

Thus, may you become heralds with the angels of the sending forth of this book and message to all friends and loved ones, that they might face the challenge to accept a Jesus that demands more and yet gives all the more for his demand that each one face the path of Self-knowledge and overcoming Self-mastery.

All things can be overcome where you are and as He demonstrated. Let it be known to you that the gifts are there and available, and the very, very same angels who comforted him comfort you now.

Is this not a testimony to the everlastingness of life—that the very same angels are alive and well and yet ministering to Christ in you? Is it not a sense of the continuity of Being that you are also everlasting in God, without beginning or ending, and yet always in eternity in the Father's heart?

Teach Thy Children to Know God, Become One with His Likeness

Teach thy children that life presents the grand opportunity for knowing God and becoming one with his likeness.

So comfort one another in the travail of karma.

Uphold one another in the fighting of the beast of anger in every addiction that you have fallen prey to by the very force and plot of the fallen angels in your midst, who have sought to bind you chemically and in every way to deprive you of the one true love and perfect embrace of thy Christ, Jesus Christ, of the I AM Presence and the twin flame.

In the circle of our love, receive now the touch of all loved ones of all ages, lost or forgotten, and know that you are never apart but one and that all have united at inner levels to save the planet.

And the great, great necessity of the hour is to bring to the physical attention of the lightbearers of earth the immediate availability of the light through the Science of the Spoken Word.

I can assure you that the change on earth by a cosmic alchemy, were tens of thousands to give the violet flame daily, would be so phenomenal not only would you wonder where the problems went but you would forget that you ever had any problems.

So be a purveyor of the divine knowledge. So, with Melchizedek, Ecclesiastes and the Lord Christ, with Enoch and Elijah, become a preacher of righteousness by example, by love, by speaking when the Holy Spirit speaks through you, by remaining silent when he does not.

I Am the Mother of All Children of God

I am the Mother of all children of God, not only of Catholics. I am a tender vine, one master in heaven representing the Divine Mother. Many also represent that Mother. I am also of the angelic realm, the complement of the archangel Raphael, who held the balance for me as my twin flame when I came to earth to love the soul of Jesus and to weave for him the swaddling garment that he might weave for himself the wedding garment.

Through many lifetimes I was his mother. I was his mother when he was embodied as King David and also on Atlantis. Thus, the trek to the Himalayas described in the book [*The Lost Years of Jesus*] began even farther back. His footsteps are everywhere on earth. It was planned that way, that all that is required of thee he might also pass through, taking upon himself the karma of the world to show the path of the balancing of karma.

Christ the Saviour Is Come through the Heart of Jesus

Truly, through his heart is the Saviour come and is the path of thine own salvation. He desires that you should look, then, to those who sponsored and taught him, and not alone to his outer self, and thereby know that the Universal

Christ has the power in all ages to raise up the representative of the Spirit.

In this hour and in thy life, let that representative be thyself, thy Self,[6] beloved. Take responsibility for your own soul and for others, and see what wonders heaven shall work through thee. Neglect not the first steps, and having conquered these, seal thy life in victory. And go not back to the old ways— to the old ways of death and dying—but move on. For this earthly span is short and thy angels gather for thy victory.

It Is Yours to Ascend in This Life

With the sign of the ascension, I AM come. And Gabriel with me does announce to you that it is yours to ascend in this life and that it is mandated by the cosmic law of thy being.

Across the forehead is written I AM THAT I AM. Within the heart, it is written I AM THAT I AM. As Above, so below, God be with thee and in thee forever.

I AM Mary. Thy love of Mother never faileth.[7]

Mary

*Wisdom would teach
her children to understand
every part of life by letting the flow
of the Mother be poured into other
cups of identity. Learn compassion by
looking through another's eyes, by walking in
another's footsteps, by entering the heart and the
mind for a moment, for awhile, of father, mother,
brother, sister or little child. For as you flow with
the consciousness of the Mother to and fro, in and
out of the body of God on earth, you will come to
understand just why people are people, why they
behave as they do, both with and without the
knowledge of the Law. Retaining your identity
as the Christ, you can be at once at the point of
that Christ in man, in woman, that releases the
creativity of the Universal Mind even
as you fathom the whys and wherefores
of the human existence that is
an enigma to so many.*

Mary

The Vow to Heal a Planet
Study the Healing Arts at Fátima

O my beloved children of the Sun, I am your Mother, so very near. And I come, mindful of the Fátima message and of prophecies due to descend upon earth.

I ask you, then, to realize that God has given to me in your behalf a Presence, a calling and a dispensation. When you say, "Hail, Mary, full of grace," you are giving the salutation to the Mother ray, the Ma-ray that is in the heart of the Great Central Sun, which it is my ordination to convey to you through my heart.

I am an archeia, therefore a consort of an archangel. My beloved Raphael did keep for me a flame of love in heaven as I descended to earth—not in one life alone but in a number of lifetimes preparing, then, to give birth to Jesus in his final incarnation as the Christ.

In this day I surround you with my swaddling garment of light. I hold you in this immaculate embrace that is a healing power to restore the mind and soul and body to the original blueprint that is in your higher etheric body.

I speak, then, of your vow to be on earth in this hour when many would require healing. I ask you, then, in hearing the words of my beloved Raphael to remember to call upon God, ourselves and many angels to bring healing where healing is possible. And if the Law does not allow it in the flesh, then call, oh, for the healing of the soul and the spirit that it might take flight from the body in the end to enter new planes of glory and edification to prepare for a final round unto the ascension.

It is the healing of the whole man that we are about. And we ask of you not only this but to remember the vow to heal a planet by becoming the instrument of such radiant light of the Central Sun. Pursue, then, all avenues of healing that are open to you lawfully. And, beloved, pursue the healing of souls.

Souls are in torment and require the healing of the Holy Ghost. You may learn of the gifts and graces that you may earn under the tutelage of the lords of the seven rays.[1] You may seek to increase the aura by devotion, decree and service. And you may call to me and Raphael, for our etheric retreat is above Fátima in Portugal.[2] There you may come at night (your soul in her etheric garment apart from the physical during the sleep state) and study the healing arts. Not far away is the University of the Spirit of Hilarion over the isle of Crete.[3]

Do, then, call to God and your guardian angels to take you at night in your finer bodies where you may study and learn what are the golden-age methods of healing; and how, when the planet is delivered of a certain karma and a certain band of fallen angels incarnate who oppose the real cures that could be available today for cancer and other terminal diseases, through you and others there may come about finally the liberation and the revelation of the true healing arts.

Some who know it not have been inspired by us and have brought forth their methods. They have been persecuted. They have been pursued by those who have taken the Law to wrest it to the destruction of those cures that ought to be available to everyone upon earth.

It is not the LORD God who has decreed that mankind must suffer from these dread diseases. But it is, beloved, a certain clique of fallen angels who have crept in unawares with their spiritual wickedness in high places[4] who have prevented the little people—my people—from having those cures and that application of science that could have delivered their bodies that their souls might have pursued the true spiritual calling of their lives in this very life.

The plagues themselves descending were never designed unto death and hell. They are a karma, yes, but the LORD has perceived and has sent the intercessor in the person of the Cosmic Christ to inspire all with the means of deliverance.

I say to all who are so inspired, be not bound by the money beast! Freely ye have received, freely give.[5] Therefore, let the world have what God has given you for healing. Minister to the poor in spirit and the broken in body.

Some have promised to give and have been taken aside by their desire for wealth or money. Blessed hearts, millions are dying. Give and give again that you might be emptied—that you might be filled of the Spirit and renewed to give again.

Did it ever occur to you, beloved, that God may have given to you a gift of healing or a knowledge because it is meet, for your karma demands that you serve life even as you may have done disservice to life in the past? Count every blessing, then, and talent and even genius as opportunity to make all things right.

I desire to see you free, even free from the desire to heal. I desire to see you become instruments of whatever light and love God would deliver through you. Thus, a little bit of nonattachment would liberate you to know the highest calling of your life.

In the purest heart of my Son Jesus, I extend to you the light—truly the light that is the answer to every need and call. Sent by the Father this day, I seal you in the will of God, the wholeness of God and his never-failing compassion.

As I am one with Raphael, we establish, then, a circle of fire about you if you receive us, that our angels might better minister unto you and through you alway.

> So when you are ready, may the Holy Spirit deliver
> unto you gifts of healing—freely received,
> freely given in his name.[6]

Mary

Woman of the world, run to greet the man who is the son of God. Restore to him the powers that you have taken from him by devious means. Restore to man his divine identity. Restore to him his soul, his heart, his oneness with the Father. He is waiting for the love of the Cosmic Virgin this day. Run to tell him the news that the Faithful and True is coming and the armies of heaven and the angels of the LORD and the hierarchies of the sun, that they come to reinforce that strength in the hour of Armageddon whereby the man of God can defend the woman in the way. Run to tell him the news of life aborning within you, of the coming of the Manchild, that Christ will be born again in Bethlehem and that the star of the I AM THAT I AM will appear, that Terra will find her place, that Terra is coming home.

Mary

21

I Stand By You

Champion the Cause of the Child!

My beloved sons and daughters, I am grateful to be with you in this city. I am grateful that you can listen to the whisperings of my heart and that you can know the Path with me. For I have never left any one of you. Even as I stood by my Son all the way to Golgotha, I stand by you. I am there when you are on the cross, and I am there when you are taken down from the cross.

You have not been taught that the fourteen stations of the cross are for you to walk also (see page 243). In this hour it is not only the Christ who is crucified but the Woman and her seed, for fallen angels move about in earth-bodies tormenting women and children. Yes, I am here to walk the stations with you.[1]

The soul of both man and woman is feminine. The Bridegroom is Christ, your divine spouse, who is masculine. So know, then, that the soul of each and every one of you is mutable and yet she becomes immutable by love, by light, by glory, by self-giving.

Therefore, know the way of the bearing of the cross of world karma, for you are already bearing the cross of your own karma. You have become accustomed to its weight even though you are not always comfortable with that weight. And so you surfeit yourselves in loud and dissonant music, in TV and motion pictures that have no merit, in drugs or alcohol—anything that will silence the burden of the soul and the weight of karma, if but to escape it for a night before you must take up your burden again in the reality of the day.

I am the Angel Mother who mothers your soul. Each one of you can be a portion of myself. The intercession of the Divine Mother in the earth is the great need of the hour. The Divine Mother is universal and universally present with you through her ministering angels. Millions of legions of my angels respond to the prayers of all people to the Divine Mother, she the Great Goddess. Call her what you will, configure her according to any of your religious paths —the Mother is the Word, the Great Shakti of Brahman. And the Mother in her various garments does go forth to rescue her own.

The Children Need You Every Hour

Now, as never before, the children of the world have such a profound need for mothering and nurturing. Mothers of the world, fathers of the world, I speak to you: Your children need not so much of the goods of this world and the material things that you work and work to give them to the neglect of the moments of tenderness and caring and intimacy that are paramount in their soul development. They need *you* and they need you every hour.

Do not harm them anymore! Do not harm them anymore, even though your parents and caregivers have harmed you, your soul, your inner child. And if it is possible for you to undo the harm done to you (and indeed it is!), then you will be free not to mar the souls of your children by passing on to them the pain you experienced in your own childhood.

And in this age of materialism and neglect of the oneness of mother and child, let the protective arm of the blessed father give comfort and strength to both. Let the Holy Family and your family be the sign of the Aquarian age. Let tenderness be the mark of your being, your speaking, your interchanges with children and adults alike.

And when you meet souls who are hollowed out, who have no sense of caring for themselves or others, no tenderness toward life, souls in whom the fire is gone out, know that so often this comes from their childhood when they suffered abandonment at some level—the emotional level, the spiritual level, the physical level. And in that abandonment, they also abandoned themselves, and they left off tending the candle of identity, and the flame was snuffed out.

Think how many are behind bars because they committed crimes when it was the only way they knew to get their mother's attention. Well, I tell you, one and all, they have my attention. My attention is on them. And I ask you to pray for those who have come out of dysfunctional homes and families, this dysfunction having been carried from the fathers to the sons from generations long past.[2]

How shall the world be healed unless some say:

I will turn this thing around!
I will invoke the violet flame and the Holy Spirit!
I will accept my healing in my four lower bodies.
I will pursue therapy for my soul.
I will resolve the schisms in my psyche.
And I will come to the point of wholeness!
I will stop the momentums of generations before
 me who have abandoned the child.
And I will nurture life!
I have no greater calling than to restore
 to every part of life
 the gentle communication of the Mother:
"I AM here.
"I have returned.
"I AM with you.
"I AM not afar off."

These are the words of the Divine Mother:

I am a Mother among the heavenly hosts. And as you know, I am called the Queen of Angels. In that office I send all angels of heaven to nurture life and to take from mothers their hardness of heart toward their children that has come from their own abuse by this one and that one and another and another.

I send angels in embodiment such as this messenger to teach them to call upon Mercy's flame, the flame of forgiveness, which is the violet transmuting flame, for the melting of that hardness of heart and for the restoration of the living, pulsating heart of fire, heart of flesh, immaculate heart of a mother's eye that sees only the beauty of her child and protects her precious one and does not allow the world to tear that child from her womb or from her breast.

I Stand Against the Aborting of Life, Aborting the Mission of a Soul

Of course I stand against abortion and the aborting of life and the mission of a soul! Of course I do! For I know that in every child that is aborted, there is a Christ-potential and there is a mission. And therefore abortion is the aborting of the divine plan of a living soul. For God has ordained the return of each soul to physical incarnation in that special timing when that soul may come into life with her group, with the many who played their parts with her on the stages of ancient civilizations when they made good and bad karma together.[3]

There is a law of generations that governs those who are born under the common influences of the slow-moving planets and the fixed stars—generations of people who must be born together, play together, grow up together, study together and take dominion over the earth together as their elders grow old and pass to them the torch of civilization.

Where are they?

I cry out to you! I cry out on behalf of twenty-nine-million souls whose mission has been aborted in this nation alone!* I speak in their defense, for this messenger gives me a mouthpiece and a voice. I cry out to you and I tell you, a soul is a living heart and a soul has *full conscious awareness*, even in the hour of the conception of the physical body, of

---

*in the twenty years from *Roe v. Wade* to the delivery of this dictation

being in life, of being alive!

And have you not seen the films of the soul in her new body swimming in the womb, dancing for joy and even performing pirouettes?[4] Have you not seen this joyous activity taking place in the womb of the mother?

Therefore, pray for those whose hardness of heart, passed on from generation to generation, has allowed them to silence the heartbeat and the cry of the child within. This child within is part of mother, part of father, part of life: life that is sacred, life that is God.

I am not old-fashioned, I am a realist. And I am telling you of the realities of the karma of abortion.

If abortion has entered your life, I say, call upon the violet flame for the healing of the soul in pain for her mission cut off. Call on the law of forgiveness for yourself. Do not condemn yourself, for I, Mary, do not condemn you, but I urge you to seek early the opportunity of serving life and caring for children that you might learn to love your own inner child and balance the karma of abortion.

And pray that in due course you might have a family and bring in the soul or souls whom you aborted through ignorance in an hour when you were perhaps distraught, misled, faced with choice without being given the facts about the life that was aborning in your womb, or perhaps you knew and denied what you knew.

Blessed ones, America is not fulfilling her mission because millions of souls are not in life, are not growing up, are not taking their places at your side.

Whose Twin Flame Has Been Aborted?

Whose twin flame has been aborted? Whose children to be? Whose loved ones are not here?

Do you sometimes look around and say, "Where is what's his name? He should be here. Where is what's her name? She should be here, too."

I will tell you where they are. They are waiting in the wings of life in the heaven-world for parents to welcome them so that even belatedly they might take up their mission.

I will not dwell upon this, for I desire not to burden you but to enlighten you. Yet this is one of the grave realities of our time, and you need to know it so that you will not incur negative karma and so that you can wake up others so that they do not incur negative karma.

I come, then, in profoundest concern for all children of earth and I ask you to champion their cause, for they are the seed of the Woman clothed with the Sun.

So often the child is defenseless. Who defends the child and the right of that child to breathe the air of freedom, to be carefree, to not go hungry, to learn his lessons and to grow up to enjoy life to its fullest maturity?[5]

Who will defend the child? Midst the entire population of the planet, only the child is defenseless.

Angels Come in Defense of the Child

Yes, beloved, my angels come, Archangel Michael's angels come in defense of the child. May you come to the aid of children no matter what your profession! May you make time for children and for your own inner child!

Yes, make time for the children. Make time for them, for they so desperately need your love, and in their little souls and in their little hearts they pray to God for deliverance.

Who will deliver them?

Who will take the women and children down from the cross?

Let the light of your mission be upon you now. I blaze the light upon your own childhood, and I send waves of healing for all hurt that may have been done to you. And you who are the strong and you who are the whole, may you take in your arms many of these precious ones. For this is an age for the succoring of life.

Now our angels come. They come in myriad numbers, clustering around you, tapping you on the shoulder and saying to each one: "Remember me? I am your cohort of light. I was there when you were born. I have tended you, I have been with you. Come, I will show you the next step."

Feel the love of God in the angelic hosts. We are Real, I promise you. We are Real, we are ready, and we are determined that this civilization will not go down for this or that darkness that has penetrated. For the judgments of the Lord Christ shall ultimately come for the binding of the rebel angels, and the burdens of life will ease up as you move into the twenty-first century. But just now and in these years to come, nine years and more from this hour, you will face challenges supreme.

I come, then, for the strengthening of your determination and to give you my promise that I, Mary, will come to you and care for you as I have cared for my Son Jesus. So call to me, for I AM your Mother of Love, most approachable and never condemning.

No, you are not dyed-in-the-wool sinners. Yes, you may have sinned. You may be ignorant of the Laws of God and you may have broken some of his Laws, erring on this or that side of the Law, but in you is that Divine Being, the Atman, which you are and ever have been from the Beginning.

Remember, I AM Mary.

I hold the immaculate concept for your victory.

I AM your Mother cheering you on.

I will not leave thee, O my sons and daughters.

In this flame, we seal our message to you this night. May you rejoice that your eyes are opened and that you can nurture your inner sight and therefore know and see those things that shall shortly come to pass.

With Raphael, I bow before the light within you, ever the servant of your God flame and your soul.[6]

Mary

The goal is
not so very far from you
if you will heed
the word of a Mother.
For I taught the blessed disciples
and I have taught many lifestreams,
one by one, the steps that are not too hard
for thee, for they are not too hard for the Lord.
You do not scale a mountain all at once,
but you prepare for the journey;
and if it takes fourteen days,
then you take the necessary supplies,
change of clothing,
all that you require,
and then you set your pace.

Mary

22

The Gift of a Mother's Heart: The Mystery of the Fifteenth Rosary

The Surrender of that Christ that You Have Become

Most beloved sons and daughters of my heart,

I AM grateful to be in the midst of the sacred fire that burns brightly upon the altar of the heart of the true chela of the flame. I AM the Mother in all the world, and in that Mother light I amplify and I intensify your very own heart's love of the children of the world.

The Goddess of Liberty, the Great Divine Director, beloved Cyclopea and the members of the Karmic Board[1] have brought to you a most magnificent dispensation of life. To be tutored by them, to be given their causal body awareness, their cosmic solar awareness of life and life's greatest needs is truly the gift of the ages. To have transferred to you that wisdom of the mind of God, embodied by the chief justices of the solar systems and the galaxies, places within your heart and your hand that magnificent tool of light that is a tool of discrimination and the practical awareness of Mother love. For it is the office of the Mother flame, fulfilled superbly by the Lords of Karma, whereby life on earth receives the ministration of life in heaven.

Therefore, to become representatives of the World Teachers, my own sons Jesus and Kuthumi,[2] is to become the embodiment of the Mother flame as that flame is the epitome of cosmic justice. It is justice that you become whole. It is justice that you bequeath to life the gift of your wholeness. It is cosmic justice that the little children be God-taught! It is cosmic justice that you be, in time and space, the full manifestation of the cosmic cross of white fire.

I reveal to you now, as I place this treasure in the heart of the Mother and the messenger, the understanding of the mystery of The Fifteenth Rosary.

First, let me say that The Fourteenth Rosary and all of the rosaries preceding it are preparatory initiations for the putting into the flame of the unbalanced karma, the misqualified energies of life, the unwanted substances and all that is unreal. These rosaries are sacred keys to the initiations of Christhood whereby you, very presently and with haste, may balance 51 percent of your karma and remain in life the Presence, lo, the living Presence of your own blessed Christ Self.[3]

This goal is not so very far from you if you will heed the word of a Mother. For I taught the blessed disciples and I have taught many lifestreams, one by one, the steps that are not too hard for thee, for they are not too hard for the

Lord.[4] You do not scale a mountain all at once, but you prepare for the journey; and if it takes fourteen days, then you take the necessary supplies, change of clothing, all that you require, and then you set your pace.

Pacing yourself, preparing for the climb to the summit may involve many prior excursions into the mountains. But that ascent, which is the ultimate ascent to the mount of transfiguration,[5] is one that you pace by the very breath of the Holy Spirit, for it is in the inbreathing and the outbreathing of the prana of life that you are able to mount that mount of attainment. Thus, beloved, you are able to pause at the fourteen stations and tarry there (see page 243).

The Fourteen Stations of the Cross Are Way Stations on the Onward Path

Those fourteen stations are meant to be way stations on the path that leads onward up the royal road of reintegration with your God Self. Thus you see, what is most important is that you begin and that you attune with the pace of the Holy Spirit, the Maha Chohan, for your pace on this road of life is truly the rhythm of the heartbeat of Almighty God. Thus in beginning, step by step, as the mountain becomes steeper and the air more rarefied, you must leave behind some of the heavier weight of your baggage. As the sun and nature and God himself become more real, you leave behind still more of that self because it is nonessential, for you have found the Self that is God.

Passing through, then, the fourteen stations, you arrive at the summit of Being who is Christ the Lord. You enter into the heart of that Christ, and that Christ enters into the fullness of your temple. First you go into the secret chamber of the heart where the Ishwara[6] who is Christ in you is sealed. There are the initiations for Christhood. When you have passed them, the blessed Ishwara steps forth from the secret chamber of the heart and now occupies the fullness of the temple of life.

Understand, then, that you are yet mounting the fourteen stations. And there are some who are students of the ascended masters who have not yet begun the fourteen stations. They are preparing for the preparation for Christhood.

Thus in the beginning, to receive the judgment of the world, the hatred and the records of death, the Antichrist and the entire rebellious momentum of disobedience, the division of life and the attempt to divide and conquer, the burdens of the misuse of the Mother flame and all that opposes the great light of the joy of the heart as the ingratitude of selfishness, the entire accumulation of planetary and personal injustice, misuses of the cycles of life, the entire momentum of unreality, the entire conglomerate of the world's sense of struggle that manifests only through selfishness and self-love; and ultimately to defeat the dragon of vengeance against the Almighty—these stations[7] of bearing the burden of life result, then, in the transfer of the all-power in heaven and in earth.[8] In that hour of the fulfillment of the resurrection through the fourteen stations, it is understood that each candidate has the opportunity to elect to enter into the ascension spiral and to ascend to God.

As beloved Lanello has told you, this is not our desire in this age, but our desire is to see the fullness of that Christ manifest in the earth for many cycles and years in many of our devotees. For the harvest is truly great,[9] and the souls of light upon earth need the physical example of those who walk in the ultimate sense of freedom. Thus, my beloved, *the mystery of The Fifteenth Rosary is the mystery of the surrender of that Christ that you [have] become.*

Give Away that Christ that You Have Become

It is not an automatic surrender, for some disciples may fulfill the fourteen stations and become that Christ and yet desire to possess that Christ, to be that Christ, to enjoy that Christhood and with it to yet pursue some of the private paths that indeed may increase attainment but may not increase the path of Christhood for others. Thus you see that when all other surrenders are in the valleys behind you and you stand on the mount of that transfiguration and you stand in the glory of Easter morn, you recognize that from the mount of transfiguration unto the mount of the Holy of Holies of the resurrected Self, there is a unique path to be walked. It is the surrender of that Christhood that you have attained.

The not-self, which is placed upon the altar of God, is not a sufficient sacrifice that you might have transferred to you the fullness of your Christ Self. It happens that when the not-self is surrendered, then the True Self begins to manifest—often in faint glimpses at first, as a tiny babe, and then growing and waxing strong until the fullness of the Christhood is manifest. Thus, from the hour of the setting aside of the long path of unreality to the hour of the putting on of God-reality in the fullest sense of the word, that is the path of The Fourteenth Rosary. But when the God-reality comes and the Christ in you is made perfect and the soul is made perfect in Christ, there is the decision to be made: to give away that Christ that you have become.

And therefore, my beloved, when Abraham laid Isaac on the altar, he was surrendering his Christhood manifesting in his own son.[10] He was not surrendering the not-self, but he was willing to give even the fullness of that God-identity in the trust that as that body and that consciousness and that being would be broken as the crumbs of life to feed all of humanity, even so that Christ would return and be one. And in having been broken for all, then that Christhood—the ultimate Christhood of the victory of the mission—becomes the Cosmic Christ, becomes the ascended master.

In the breaking of the loaf that God is within you, there is the temporary sacrifice of the fullness of the expression of that identity. Rather than keep the fullness of that light to your very own temple, you have said, "I will break the bread of life. I will give a portion of that Christhood that is my own to every soul of God who is sent to me to receive that leaven, that white cube, that igniting fire of eternal life."[11]

Become One with All Life

Thus, my beloved, though God take in his hands the loaf, it is given to God by your free will and in your surrender. And as you give that Christ consciousness to him and he does break the bread of life, you live in the joy of the threefold unfed flame everywhere—in the hearts of little children, of those who are aging according to this world's cycles of time and space, in the hearts of families, in the hearts of elementals and angels. You even live in the unfed flame of ascended masters and cosmic beings. You transcend the stairway of life, moving in and out of the octaves of heaven and earth. For truly, by the gift of the grace of God of your own Selfhood, you have become one with all life in the deepest sense of the word.

This is the mystery of the Holy Grail—how the Grail can be one and yet duplicates of that Grail, your own Electronic Presence, fragments of its crystal, might live and grow and multiply God consciousness in every part of life whom God has ordained.

This oneness of life is a love incomparable. It is the oneness that you share with your messengers. Now it is a oneness that is yours—to drink, to experience and to give away. When you are passing through the exercises of life where you must surrender this or that trinket or experience or even a dear friend who must take another path, remember that these surrenders are preparatory to the moment when you will give away the most precious gift of all—the Son of God that you have become....

The sense of being needed and of being useful, professionally and practically, is most needed by your souls. How happy are ye when ye have a gift of life in your hand! I commend you who move on now from first level to consider how precious is that experience of receiving the torch that I one day gave to Maria Montessori.[12] Therefore our hearts hold the chalice for life to continue as life in the earth, for civilization to be sustained and for the waiting hearts of children in the cities of the nations to be greeted by you, to be received by you....

Out of the light of East and West, out of the inner retreat of the Mother of India, I give to you the gift of the flame of the Mother East and West. I give to you the gift of a Mother's heart, the most sacred gift—The Mystery of the Fifteenth Rosary. With those who have gone before me, I say, "Forge your God-identity!" and thereby enter the mystery of The Fifteenth Rosary.

I AM in the joy of springtime the gentle Mother of your heart. In the lily of the valley I come. I come to pluck my lilies of the valley that they may move on to higher ground and the higher way of the summit of attainment.

Sons and daughters of light, arise and take dominion in the earth! Sons and daughters of dominion, I bid you, keep, oh, keep the flame for these my little ones!

In the name of Jesus Christ
and the servant sons of God, I AM always Mary
in the heart of the flame in your heart.[13]

Mary

Now I have given you
my love, my understanding,
my Presence this day.
I have transferred to you
my consciousness and my ray.
Take it, mothers of the world.
Take it and run with it and know that
I am with you on that way.
I am the way,
the truth and the life.
I am the victory of the age.
And I am with you always unto
the fulfillment of all cycles
of the cosmic consciousness
of God as Mother
appearing within you.

Mary

23

The Hour of the Mother's Crucifixion

As the music of India fades from the outer ear, one hears the sounds of Ireland, of America, of Russia and of China as the children of the Mother make music that is music to her ears. For out of the sound of the song comes the joy of the heart in anticipation of the coming of the World Mother.

How her children have waited so long—awaiting her coming, sensing an aloneness so often filled with the preoccupations and the noises of life that, though they wait, scarcely allow her to enter when her time is come.

I AM Mother Mary, Mother of East and West, come in the peace-commanding presence to break the Good Friday spell. It is the spell of death and the all-too-serious seriousness of the fallen ones who are convinced that they have crucified Christ and therefore he is truly no more. And some of them have never really come to understand the mystery of Christus,[1] the mystery of the resurrection. So much a part are they of the flesh and blood that must always pass away that they in themselves cannot perceive a reality beyond their own forms—much less His own.

And so, my beloved, we come in the flame of the God Star with our own brand of "Sirius-ness." For it is the hour of the crucifixion not of one son of God but of all sons of God who contemplate this mystery (to which I have alluded in my teaching to you on The Fifteenth Mystery of the Rosary[2]) that can come only when you have become the fullness of that Christed One—and then the decision, my beloved, which will culminate with the Word, "Nevertheless, Father, not my will, but thine, be done."[3]

The dilemma of the Christed One—if it could be called a dilemma—is how to preserve the integrity of that Christ and yet lay down its life. And so I come to teach you on this Good Friday in the hierarchy of Aries—the hierarchy of the Son of God who declares, "Lo, I AM THAT I AM!"

This declaration that all that I AM in the earth is the I AM that is in heaven is truly the statement of the Lord Sanat Kumara as he has appeared to each avatar in succession as that one has incarnated with the gift of the Manchild and then arrived at the point, the point of Be-ness in the midst of Sinai,[4] for the resolution of worlds and the declaration of Being that all that I AM here and now is become the fullness of the joy of my own beloved I AM Presence! And that which I AM I give for the fulfillment of life and light unto the seed of Sanat Kumara and for the judgment of those who are the antithesis of that seed. Therefore my Son declared, "For judgment I am come!"[5]

Most blessed hearts, if the Law is not understood, you may find yourself giving away the Christ as potential even before the full flowering of that potential. And therefore, the walk of the disciple must be understood. For it is most dangerous when one is partially endued with the blessedness of one's own Christ Self and yet not altogether fulfilled in it; for it is then that the fallen ones who lust after the light of the Woman and her seed come to take veil upon veil as they tear away thin skeins of light unto themselves.

Guard the Budding of the Heart

Realize, then, that the offering of my Son upon the cross this day is the offering of the full flower of the rose of Sharon.[6] It is the Christed One in full bloom with that fullness of the person of Lord Maitreya—congruent as the interlaced triangles that are the sign of all who descend out of the house of David. Until the full flowering of the rose, then, guard the budding of the heart! Guard the sacred fire! And become sensitive by the sensitivity of the soul to the pressing in upon the heart of those who would pluck the bud or a fragile portion thereof that the full flower may not appear in due season.

The preparation for the fullest manifestation of the gold-and-white lily of your Christhood must be seen as the most magnificent walk of the ages. You have engaged yourself in conversation with the Saviour. You have contemplated that walk. You have taken steps upon that walk, beloved. And so, the Christ comes to gather you to his heart—gathering you as flowers that he tenderly adores. And by the crystal radiance of the sun, the warmth of the heart of the Son of God gives you hope, encouragement, blessed comfort, wisdom for the Path.

I come, then, in these hours of contemplation of the rejoicing and the blessed union upon earth with Alpha and Omega, as the Son of God—self-fastened to the cosmic cross of white fire—is ready, oh, ready in the joy of the Lord, to take upon himself even the sins of the world, knowing that in so doing, that portion of personal Christhood will be shed as the shedding of blood, as a mist-fine radiance of crystal fire—itself absorptive, now prevailing around the face of the entire world. And wherever it is (and it is everywhere!), it does absorb that substance of antilight that the little flowers may breathe the breath of life again and be restored and begin themselves to realize the magnificent starry point of Selfhood that I AM.

I speak to my beloved East and West who are yearning and striving and working the works of God that Christ might be formed perfectly within you.[7] O my beloved, I come with a most intense love of the Mother flame—worlds without end! Feel my heart as I feel your own about to be born, about to receive the lowering into this temple so precious of your beloved Christ Self, about to pass through the dark night of the soul, about, then, to enter the dark night of the Spirit from the very cross itself, about to become the Incarnate Word and, lo, the incarnation of the I AM THAT I AM.

So blessed a life do we live together upon this earth! So beautiful is our sweet communion with him, Jesus, even while there is the raging of the battles of the fallen ones amongst themselves. And as they imitate the bearers of the light, these terrorists who fast unto the death,[8] pretending to be his followers, pretending to make sacrifices as the sons of light may do—they are the impostors! Yet they would appear to be the deliverers of the people by tyranny of Fascist governments. They are but another phase of the betrayers. And their death is not a hallowed death and cannot be called the crucifixion, which initiation is reserved for those in whom the Christ dwells bodily. Cherish, then, my beloved, the tender vine of the soul.

It is good to sing to the Beloved of thine own heart. For adoration needs to be given to the flame of God within—and thereby the sense of Self-worth in the hour when the fallen ones condemn not only Christ in Jesus my Lord but the Christ universally present. Not only do they condemn the Son of God but the soul reaching for that light who has not quite grasped the fullness of that mind and heart promised unto each little one.

Don the Shepherd's Garment, Go After the Sheep

O blessed hearts who have enough of Him, Immanuel,[9] internalized to be able to don the shepherd's garment, I encourage you: Put it on, though ye be not perfected. Put it on and therefore go after those who are the sheep who yet require those who will lead the way and preserve them from harm.[10] For harm there is yet abroad in the land, harm that is not readily perceived as the wearing away of Christhood, the wearying of souls in this path—the path of the balancing of life and the balancing of the records of death.

The planetary body reels in the records of death of a Piscean age that is yet in the process of being transmuted. As the currents of Pisces pass through your hearts, even your sacred hearts charged with the violet flame, a newness of life is felt. And yet, beloved, none can deny that in this hour of the beginning, the new beginning of Aquarius, death is most prevalent upon earth—and famine and war and plague and pestilence. All of these are of the former things that must pass away.[11] In the very present of your heart, looking toward the future glory, you must yet contend with records of the past—long past and yet lingering. For they require diligence of the application of the Holy Spirit.

I Would Teach You of the Mystery of Being Christus

I would teach you, then, of the mystery of being Christus and of giving away all that thou art—laying down that life that is God for all, yet taking it again,[12] yet retaining it hour by hour. I will give you, then, a simple comparison: the inbreathing and the outbreathing of God translated to you as you take in the sacred fire breath and as you give it forth.

Think upon the moment of the outbreath, beloved hearts. You press out the air you breathe with perfect confidence that there will be a sufficiency of air for the next inbreath. You care not to be possessive of that air. You give it all away, knowing that in the rhythmic cycle of life, you may take in sufficient quantity for all that you need—and yet no more, for you cannot breathe more than you can breathe in a moment and that you can use in that moment.

Thus it is in the laying down of the life of one's own Christhood. One breathes out all that one is as a holy breath, as the fragrance of lilies—realizing that the whole world, then, receives the crystal fire mist and is translated, yet knowing that the inbreath that cometh from God, which descends as blessed heartbeat from the I AM Presence, will in that single breath re-create, re-form and re-manifest the fullness of that Christ standing upon the hill of life.

Moment by moment, you can lay down your life that the sins of the whole world might be balanced through the remission of sin through the shedding of blood by the crucifixion.[13] Do you understand, then, that in the deepest meditation of your heart, which I have shared with some of the saints of the Church who have walked the blessed earth, there has come to pass the experience of the crucifixion with that cyclic flow of the hours, the days, the weeks, the moments and the rhythm of the breath? What trust, what confidence in God!

Do you see how your fears are with fault and you must now become faultless—and can only so become if, once and for all, the fullness of your love of Christ and his love of you will conquer fear. And thereby, perfect love will be born within you.[14] And that perfect love, the perfect magnet of the Magnanimous Heart, will open the way for Christ himself to abide within your temple forever and forever and forever and a day of forever!

Now understand the mystery of The Fifteenth Rosary. Having attained to Christhood that is yet a goal for thee, you then realize that you can give away and receive again, lay down and take up! And the three days[15] become the cycling of the three—the Father and the Son and the blessed Holy Spirit as tripartite light within your heart. In the twinkling of the eye, in the turning of the flame in one cycle, these three live, expand, express, expire and return to inspire and to be the fullness of God made manifest.

Be to the Right Hand, to the Left Hand of the Lord upon the Cross

How noble are ye aspiring—aspiring to be with him, to be crucified with him in place of the malefactors! Would not any of you this day give your life, in living your life, to be at the right hand and the left hand of the Lord Jesus Christ upon the cross? Blessed hearts, if the Lord has not called you—sent and signified by his angel—to your own crucifixion, then you may appeal to the Lord Sanat Kumara to be to the right hand, to the left hand, as bodhisattvas.*

Blessed hearts, see the mockery of the Son of God as the fallen ones placed at his side not sons of light, not saints to lay down their life with him, but those who had not that light in them—those who mocked him and said, "If thou be the Son of God, save thyself! Come down from the cross, and save us!"[16] It is the story of the ages and the drama of

---

*Bodhisattva is a Sanskrit term meaning literally "a being of bodhi (or enlightenment)," a being destined for enlightenment, or one whose energy and power is directed toward enlightenment. A bodhisattva is one who is destined to become a Buddha but has forgone the bliss of nirvana with a vow to save all children of God on earth. The bodhisattva may forgo his ascension for thousands of years or until the last man, woman or child on earth wins his victory.

the Great Dramatist that there might be portrayed the supreme sacrifice of the Word Incarnate. And thus God has allowed these fallen ones to come so near to be the mouthpiece of hell itself in the moment of the victory of life over death.

The dispensation of the bodhisattvas carrying the flame of Alpha and Omega, tending the Buddha, is the way of the East. And thus, you may see the configuration in this hour of our Lord Gautama and of two disciples (representing the male and female polarity of the Body and the Blood of the living Christ) thus saying, "O Lord, our Lord, we will not leave thee to be crucified alone, but we will be with thee to atone for the sins of the whole world and to make of this crucifixion in this hour a trinity of light upon the hillsides of the world!"

Thus, my beloved, when you say, "Jesus Christ my Lord, I bear thy cross! Saint Germain, I bear thy cross!" you may also be chosen to hold the balance at the right hand and at the left of the mighty work of Jesus and Saint Germain in this hour—bearing to the right and to the left of the Great White Brotherhood, of the messenger, of the servants of God in embodiment that balance of the flame of victory, of love so intense and of the all-power of God that stands with the apostles of Christ for the judgment of the fallen angels as has been prophesied for so very long, even since the hour of their descent.[17]

Now, blessed hearts, on the way to Golgotha (which may consume for you many a year of initiatic rite with Jesus and Maitreya), you may yet give portions of that Christ according to the will, according to the apportionment of your own blessed Christ Self, so that you need not feel that even the dipping into The Fifteenth Rosary is withheld from you. For after all, it is the very Real Self, the Christed One of each one of you, who is crucified in this hour! And when the soul is so one with that Christ as to be ensconced within that jewel of the cross—it, too, will know the mystery of the Word, of the Lamb slain from the foundation of the world.[18] Until that hour, you can attend your own Beloved.

Run to the Cross and Care for that Christ, Assume the Mantle of the Comforter

Behold, the Bridegroom whom you have awaited cometh![19] He cometh, blessed hearts, as the one soon to be crucified. Receive him, then, within your soul as I did. Receive him in your arms of light and realize that all of you hold the very heart of the World Mother within your soul as you feel compassion for the Eternal Christ, for the Christed One, for the One Sent[20]—truly for that Christ preparing to merge with each Divine Manchild. And the compassion of your heart is to run to the cross and care for that one in this hour.

Look, then, to life. Look to your brothers and sisters on the Path. Look to the Eternal God daring to descend in this hour into the hearts of his very own! He dares to descend to be crucified again and again. And you are so bold as to assume the mantle of the Comforter, the Compassionate One, even the mantle of the Lord Buddha, and to say:

I will care for thee, my Lord and my Saviour!
I will affirm thy victory.
I will praise thee in the hour of seeming death
That truly is life eternal here and now!
I will bind up the brokenhearted in thy name!
I will find thee, my Lord, in the very heart
Of thy children helpless, thy disciples not yet whole.
I will give compassion as roses on the vine of
   my becoming
The fullness of the rose of Sharon.
I will.
I will give the precious essence of thy life given unto me.
With each inbreath of the sacred fire,
   I will breathe out—*Purusha!*
I will convey that element of Godhood
That God has given to me this day!
And after a million billion breaths in the life of Brahma,
So I will know that Christ himself is formed in me.
And I am all aglow!
And the floral offering of
   angels of the resurrection
Will adorn my form that
   is God's.
For, lo! Christ has come
   to live within
This temple where I AM.
Lo! I AM THAT I AM
In the fullness of the joy
   of the Godhead dwelling
   in me bodily.[21]

   This is my immaculate prayer for your immaculate becoming of the Word.

Hear my prayer, Almighty God! Hear my prayer, Lord Jesus Christ! And so intercede for these blessed disciples who dare to affirm the completeness of our wholeness even while they perceive with all due humility yet the wearing of the shroud of mourning, symbolizing the garment of karma that yet is in transmutation—is in translation.

Step by step, thread by thread, the Deathless Solar Body[22] is appearing around you. And truly it is the gold-and-white lily garment that has come forth in place of the shroud of death you have worn for centuries. I behold the process. I behold the beginning, the first step on the Path and the last. I behold the ending. I behold the middle.

A Trinity of Christed Ones

I walk with Gautama. I walk the Middle Way with my sons of light—Jesus, Gautama. We three walk the path of earth in this hour desiring to manifest, this Good Friday, the essence of Communion—the essence of the meaning of this ritual.

My blessed sons Jesus and Gautama have asked me in this hour that they might attend me in the hour of the Mother's crucifixion, which is my own. These avatars of the ages count it all blessedness to be on the right hand and the left as I keep my vigil in this age of Aquarius—the crucifixion of the Mother God within each of you and of her seed.

Therefore, we walk as symbol and sign that when the banner of the Divine Mother is raised upon earth, it is the sign of the resurrection of the Mother, the raising up of that light, the raising up of the life force, and her coming forth from the cross unto the manifest presence in all the earth of the resurrection flame dwelling bodily within you as her seed, as her issue, as her offspring forevermore!

O blessed hearts, this sign is a two-thousand-year sign in the fiery light of the Infinite One! It is written in akasha that when the son, the daughter of God comes to the internalization of the Mother flame, then that Mother also will be crucified as Christed One, will be resurrected also as Christed One and will enter the spiral of the ascension.

I AM the Mother of all devotees, East and West. In me and in my Immaculate Heart, one and all are blessed. Now perceive how these sons of God have determined to be to your right, to your left in the hour when you share as Communion cup even the drop, the single drop of His blood shed in the hour of the crucifixion.

I give to you that single drop. It enters the heart. It commingles with your very own blood. And you experience, lo, the burden, the pain, the piercing of the side—and that burden, *which is light!*

The single drop of blood is for the salvation of the many. It will wash you clean—if you allow it. It will be for your transfiguration—if you allow it. It will be the ever-present element of transmutation as you give your dynamic decrees to the violet flame—if you allow it. It is the gift of the heart of the Son of God in this hour.

Let us pray. Let us kneel together before the cross.

This is my prayer this Good Friday before Christus, before Brahman with whom is the Word:[23]

> O my LORD, I greet thee!
>
> I come to thee, bearing the light and a portion of the burden of karma of the lightbearers of earth. I come, my LORD, requesting that in my Immaculate Heart there might be translation in this hour and my very own sharing of the burden of life with devotees of Christus, East and West.
>
> All who love him, all who love thee, LORD— I carry them in my heart! It is my desire that, preceding the entering into this phase of the Dark Cycle, they might be unburdened somewhat; and by the carrying of my rosary of their hearts, they might receive some surcease, some forgiveness, some transmutation, some setting aside of their karma by the Great Law, that they might labor on.
>
> That they might labor on, my LORD, this is my prayer!—that the burden of the oncoming Dark Cycle might not be too hard for them to bear, that the burdens of war and the rumors of war and the increase of the intent of the murderous one—that famine, that manipulation of the abundant life, that plague, that pestilence—might not be too hard to bear.

Therefore, I come. I come with supplication. I come before the throne of the LORD GOD whence proceedeth the flame of the ark of the covenant of my people Israel! I supplicate for the light of the Holy Spirit to intercede twixt the cross and the bodies that bear that cross, twixt the cross and the hearts and the souls and the mind.

LORD GOD who livest and reignest forever, hear the imploring of my soul! Hear the imploring of my soul! And send the light of the Comforter as sacred fire cushioning, transmuting, uplifting hearts already afire for thee!

O LORD, I walk with them in this year! O LORD, I AM thy daughter Mary! And as the Mother ray, I AM affixed to the sacred white-fire cross upheld by my sons Lord Jesus and Lord Gautama.

I AM with thee this year, O God! For I would be where thou art in the earth once again crucified. I would be there that my Immaculate Heart might be the vortex of galaxies of light swallowing up darkness, that many might pass through the crucifixion and emerge triumphant, universally one with thy blessed Church—as Above, so below—even the white cube of this communion of saints.

I AM Mary. Let the lightbearers be strengthened in the hour of the judgment of the wicked upon earth! Give them the endurance of thy flaming heart, LORD God Almighty. This is the prayer of a Mother's heart.

I intercede! I AM the Mediatrix of Life—one with the cross of white fire, worlds without end, until all who are my own return to the throne of Alpha and Omega in the Great Central Sun.

Even so, come quickly, Lord Maitreya, Lord Gautama, Lord Jesus.

Blessed hearts, in this trinity of Christed Ones sent by Sanat Kumara, it is the holy one Maitreya who centers himself with me that the three anointed might appear to all lightbearers of earth truly, truly in the benediction of life, truly in the joy of laying down that Christ light and taking it again—ever expanding, ever expanding, ever expanding!

Lo, I AM forever and forever, until the fullness of your union in the cross, your Mother of lights appearing—lights eternal, lights of the hosts of the LORD! I AM with joy in the heart of the causal body of all life.

You may approach, blessed one. For it is I. I AM here. I AM with you. Do not fear the hour—the hour of your coming. For it is your hour and it is the hour of our victory of love.

I AM your Mother, blessed one. See me as I touch your heart through my own on earth.

Let us walk now the via dolorosa. Let us walk with Him to Golgotha *with joy!*—O blessed joy, the very joy that was indeed within His heart in those fourteen stations of the cross.

> O blessed amongst the blessed, I AM
> living love in your midst. Caress a Mother's heart
> and know that I AM with you alway.[24]

Mary

*I would whisper
a tender message to thy heart—
each one individually—of comfort
and joy and divine direction.
This message is sealed in your heart.
And though you may not hear it now,
it will unfold like a rose
appearing to comfort you
and guide you
in the days ahead.*

Mary

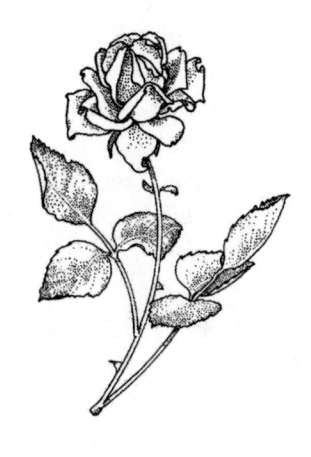

Notes

Publications, audiotapes and CDs referenced here are Summit University Press unless otherwise noted. To order, call 800-245-5445 or visit www.tsl.org.

A Word from the Author

1. The angelic evolution includes choirs of seraphim, cherubim, thrones, angels, dominions, powers, virtues, principalities and archangels.
2. Mother Mary revealed the science of the cosmic clock for the charting of the cycles of our own self-discipline. This is not traditional astrology. It is an inner astrology of the white-fire core whereby we chart the cycles of our karma—cause-and-effect sequences of energy in motion. For teaching on the cosmic clock, see *Predict Your Future: Understand the Cycles of the Cosmic Clock,* Elizabeth Clare Prophet.
3. These scriptural rosaries are available on audiotape from Summit University Press.
4. The Fourteenth Rosary—The Mystery of Surrender is available as a two-audiotape album with a booklet from Summit University Press.
5. Rom. 8:7.
6. John 1:9.

Chapter 1 – The Real Mary

1. Ruth Hawkins is now an ascended lady master and Goddess of Beauty. In her final embodiment in the twentieth century, she was an artist and devotee of the Great White Brotherhood. See *The Masters and Their Retreats,* Mark L. Prophet and Elizabeth Clare Prophet, pp. 310–12.
2. A dictation is a message from an ascended master, an archangel or another advanced spiritual being delivered through the agency of the Holy Spirit by a messenger of the Great White Brotherhood.
3. The seven rays are the light emanations of the Godhead, the seven spiritual light rays of God. These seven rays emerge out of the white light, through the prism of the Christ consciousness. Each ray focuses a frequency, or color, and specific qualities. The fifth ray is the green ray of truth, science, healing, music, abundance and vision.
4. The third-eye chakra is a center of spiritual energy anchored in the etheric body at the center of the brow. It is associated with the fifth ray and the expression of Truth, divine vision, holding the highest vision for oneself and others, healing, wholeness, abundance, clarity, constancy, focus, music and science. The third eye-chakra has ninety-six petals and is the orifice of spiritual vision. Ideally, through the third eye, we should be able to anchor the vision of God, the vision of perfection. Jesus was speaking of this when he said, "The light of the body is the eye: if therefore thine eye be single, thy whole body shall be full of light (Matt. 6:22; Luke 11:34)." See p. 39 for a diagram of the seven chakras.
5. *Pearls of Wisdom* are weekly letters of instruction dictated by the ascended masters to their messengers Mark and Elizabeth Clare Prophet for students of the sacred mysteries throughout the world. These precious letters are the intimate contact, heart to heart, between the guru and the chela. *Pearls of Wisdom* have been published by The Summit Lighthouse continuously since 1958. Their timeless messages contain both fundamental and advanced teachings on cosmic law with a practical application of spiritual Truths to personal and planetary problems.

To subscribe, see www.tsl.org/PearlsofWisdom.asp.
6. Deut. 6:4.
7. Rev. 12:1.
8. The violet ray is the seventh ray and focuses the qualities of freedom, mercy, justice, transmutation and forgiveness.
9. Mary's teaching on the cosmic clock and the cycling of the energies of the twelve solar hierarchies may be found in *Predict Your Future: Understand the Cycles of the Cosmic Clock*, Elizabeth Clare Prophet.

Chapter 2 – As Above, so Below

1. John 1:14.
2. The experiences of the soul of Mary on earth are recounted in the introductions to the first and second books in this series, *Mary's Message for a New Day* and *Mary's Message of Divine Love*, Mark L. Prophet and Elizabeth Clare Prophet.
3. It was on the ancient continent of Lemuria that the allegorical Fall of man, depicted in the biblical account of Adam and Eve, took place under the influence of the fallen angels known as Serpents (because they used the serpentine spinal energies to beguile the soul, or female principle in mankind, as a means of lowering the masculine potential). This was a gradual descent of the consciousness of many sons and daughters of God from a level of God Self-awareness to the plane of duality and the relative awareness of good and evil. Mankind's energies descended from the upper chakras to the lower chakras, compromising the sacredness of the altar of God through the misuse of the sacred fire for the gratification of the senses and carnal desire. In this manner, the consciousness of death and sin entered the race, and they became subject to the laws of karma and mortality.
4. Luke 2:35.
5. II Pet. 1:10.
6. Heb. 10:9.
7. James 2:19.
8. Matt. 17:2.
9. Ps. 8:5; Heb. 2:9.
10. Many years ago, the ascended masters called for a book on the

strategies of darkness. While the messengers did not write the book on the outer, they gave us a wealth of teaching on the strategies of darkness and how to overcome them with light. Published in 2002, *Strategies of Light and Darkness* is a compilation and distillation of some of these teachings.
11. A messenger is one who is trained by an ascended master to receive by various methods the words, concepts, teachings and messages of the Great White Brotherhood; one who delivers the Law, the prophecies and the dispensations of God for a people and an age (Rev. 14:6; Matt. 10:6; 15:24). The messengers of the Great White Brotherhood are anointed by the hierarchy as their apostles ("one sent on a mission") to deliver, through the dictations (prophecies) of the ascended masters, the testimony and lost teachings of Jesus Christ in the power of the Holy Spirit to the seed of Christ, the lost sheep of the house of Israel and to every nation.
12. Mother Mary, *Pearls of Wisdom,* vol. 18, no. 44, November 2, 1975.

Chapter 3 – A New-Age Rosary

1. "La Tourelle" in Colorado Springs, Colorado, was the headquarters of Church Universal and Triumphant from January 1966 through the summer of 1976 and a community teaching center from then until the sale of the property in November 1984. Beloved Omega consecrated it as the Retreat of the Resurrection Spiral on April 11, 1971.
2. I John 3:1–2.

Chapter 4 – The Mother Flame and the Incarnation of God

1. John 1:14.
2. Gen. 4:1.
3. John 4:25–26.
4. Rev. 19:16.
5. Matt. 19:24.
6. Luke 1:46.
7. The God and Goddess Meru enshrine the Mother flame at their

etheric retreat, the Temple of Illumination over Lake Titicaca in the Andes on the Peru-Bolivia border. This retreat is also the focus of the feminine ray of the Godhead to the earth. See *The Masters and Their Retreats*, Mark L. Prophet and Elizabeth Clare Prophet, pp. 222–27, 478–80.
8. Titus 1:15.
9. Mother Mary, *Pearls of Wisdom*, vol. 17, no. 50, December 15, 1974.

Chapter 5 – The Science of the Immaculate Concept

1. The Cosmic Egg is the spiritual-material universe, including a seemingly endless chain of galaxies, star systems, worlds known and unknown, whose center, or white-fire core, is called the Great Central Sun. The Cosmic Egg has both a spiritual and a material center. Although we may discover and observe the Cosmic Egg from the standpoint of our physical senses and perspective, all of the dimensions of Spirit can also be known and experienced within this. The Cosmic Egg represents the bounds of man's habitation in this cosmic cycle.
2. Matt. 25:40.
3. Matt. 6:12, 14–15.
4. See the parable of the unforgiving servant, Matt. 18:23–35.
5. Heb. 10:9.
6. Mother Mary, *Pearls of Wisdom*, vol. 17, no. 51, December 22, 1974.

Chapter 6 – The Vision of a New Age

1. John 3:16.
2. Mother Mary, *Pearls of Wisdom*, vol. 17, no. 52, December 29, 1974.

Chapter 7 – A Mother's Warning to Her Children

1. In 1917, World War I was raging in Europe. In Russia, the Bolsheviks were plotting their October revolution, and Portugal was making a difficult transition through a series of unstable regimes. Against this backdrop of turmoil, Mary unveiled her plan for peace to three shepherd children outside the small village of Fátima, Portugal. During her six appearances, Mary

warned of a great chastisement that could come to the world and outlined her plan for world peace: daily recitation of the rosary to "bring peace to the world and the end of the war," devotion to her Immaculate Heart and penance. She gave two visions to the children and entrusted them with a Third Secret that they were not to reveal. For a description of Mother Mary's appearances and her prophecies, see *Mary's Message of Divine Love*, Mark L. Prophet and Elizabeth Clare Prophet, pp. 34–43.
2. Rev. 13:7–8.
3. Rev. 13:10.
4. Gal. 6:7.
5. I Cor. 6:20; 7:23.
6. Jesus taught extensively during his ministry. Yet the Gospels record only a fragment of what he said. In *The Lost Teachings of Jesus* series, Elizabeth Clare Prophet shows that many of Jesus' original teachings are missing, that the New Testament records only a fragment of what Jesus taught and that what was written down was tampered with by numerous editors— or suppressed by "guardians of the faith."
7. Rev. 12:7–8.
8. Jude 4.
9. The October Revolution was the second and last major phase of the Russian Revolution of 1917 in which the Bolshevik Party seized power, inaugurating the Soviet regime and ending the one-thousand-year-old Russian monarchy.
10. William C. McGrath, "The Lady of the Rosary," in *A Woman Clothed with the Sun*, ed. John J. Delaney (Garden City, N.Y.: Image Books, 1961), p. 194.
11. For descriptions of the etheric retreats and how to travel there, see *The Masters and Their Retreats*.
12. The emerald matrix is an inner blueprint, the inner formula unique to your own God Presence in the very heart of the permanent atom of Self that is for the precipitation in the physical plane of the inner Self. It is the sign of the descent of the inner light into outer manifestation. The ascended masters deliver the initiation of the emerald matrix to us through a transfer of light. The ascended master Saint Germain directed

the messenger to use a Chatham emerald for the sealing of the servants of God in their foreheads as she traveled across the nations. She said, "I call it the emerald matrix because it is a molecular pattern in crystal that Saint Germain can use to transfer the ray of light for the sealing of the servants of God. This ray passes from his heart through my heart chakra through this crystal and is anchored in your third-eye chakra."

13. McGrath, "The Lady of the Rosary," pp. 194–95.
14. Lucia was one of the three children to whom Mary appeared at Fátima. She passed away on February 13, 2005, at the age of ninety-seven.
15. *Fátima in Lucia's Own Words: Sister Lucia's Memoirs,* ed. Louis Kondor (Fátima, Portugal: Postulation Centre, distributed by Ravengate Press), p. 62.
16. We see the connection of the third secret to the actions of World Communism as Mother Mary gave that teaching in 1917. According to *Stimme des Glaubens,* in November 1980, Pope John Paul II was speaking to a group of German Catholics who had asked him about the third secret. He said, "Because of the seriousness of its contents, in order not to encourage the worldwide power of Communism to carry out certain coups, my predecessors in the Chair of Peter have diplomatically preferred to withhold its publication.

    "On the other hand, it should be sufficient for all Christians to know this much: If there is a message in which it is said that the oceans will flood entire sections of the earth; that from one moment to the other, millions of people will perish, there is no longer any point in really wanting to publish this secret message. Many want to know merely out of curiosity, or because of their taste for sensationalism, but they forget that 'to know' implies for them a responsibility. It is dangerous to want to satisfy one's curiosity only, if one is convinced that we can do nothing against a catastrophe that has been predicted."

    The Pope took his rosary and said, "Here is the remedy against all evil! Pray, pray and ask for nothing else. Put everything in the hands of the Mother of God!" We ask ourselves the question, "Why, then, have the popes been disobedient to Mother Mary's requests for the consecration of Russia and

for the revelation of the third secret?"
17. *Neues Europa,* October 15, 1963.
18. Gal. 6:5.
19. Gen. 1:26, 27; 5:1; 9:6.
20. Josh. 16:9.
21. The Dark Cycle of the return of mankind's karma began on April 23, 1969. It was a period when mankind's misqualified energy (i.e., their returning negative karma), held in abeyance for centuries under the great mercy of the Law, was released according to the cycles of the initiations of the solar hierarchies for balance in this period of transition into the Aquarian age.
22. *Neues Europa,* October 15, 1963.
23. The Book of Enoch is a text cherished by the Essenes, early Jews and Christians but later condemned by both rabbis and Church Fathers. The book was denounced, banned and "lost" for more than a thousand years. In *Fallen Angels and the Origins of Evil: Why Church Fathers Suppressed the Book of Enoch and Its Startling Revelations,* Elizabeth Clare Prophet examines the controversy surrounding this book and sheds new light on Enoch's forbidden mysteries.
24. Gen. 6:4 (Jerusalem Bible). Num. 13:33 refers to "giants."
25. *Neues Europa,* October 15, 1963.
26. Gen. 22:13; Job 1:5.
27. Matt. 6:12.
28. Frère Michel de la Sainte Trinité, "The Third Secret Revealed..." *The Fátima Crusader* (June–July 1986), p. 6.
29. Ibid.
30. Mother Mary gave the Third Secret to the children on July 13.
31. Frère Michel de la Sainte Trinité, "The Third Secret Revealed..." p. 22.
32. Ibid.
33. Ibid., p. 21.
34. Ibid., p. 23.
35. Mother Mary, *Pearls of Wisdom,* vol. 27, no. 63, December 30, 1984.
36. One day as Pope Leo (1878–1903) had finished Mass he stopped at the altar as if in a trance. Later he explained he had overheard Satan speaking to Our Lord. Satan requested seventy-five

years to attempt to destroy the Church. The Lord said, "You have the time; you have the power. Do what you will." The pope understood that if the devil had not accomplished his purpose at the end of the time limit, he would suffer a crushing defeat. He also understood that through prayer and sacrifice and living good Christian lives, we could offset the power of the devil and his human agents. Thus, Pope Leo composed a prayer to invoke Archangel Michael's intercession, which was said at the conclusion of Mass for seventy-eight years. This was discontinued after Vatican II. Pope Leo XIII's prayer, revised and updated by the messenger for students of the ascended masters, is included in "Archangel Michael's Rosary for Armageddon" (which is available on a two-audiotape album with booklet):

"Saint Michael the Archangel, defend us in Armageddon. Be our protection against the wickedness and snares of the devil. May God rebuke him, we humbly pray. And do thou, O Prince of the heavenly host, by the power of God, bind the forces of death and hell, the seed of Satan, the false hierarchy of Antichrist and all evil spirits who wander through the world for the ruin of souls. And remand them to the Court of the Sacred Fire for their Final Judgment [including _(insert optional personal prayer here)_].

"Cast out the dark ones and their darkness, the evildoers and their evil words and works, cause, effect, record and memory, into the lake of sacred fire 'prepared for the devil and his angels.'

"In the name of the Father, the Son, the Holy Spirit and the Mother, Amen."

37. This statement was included in Mother Mary's June 18, 1965, message at Garabandal.
38. As of this printing, three of the children—Marija, Vicka and Ivan—have received nine secrets, and Mother Mary still appears to them every day, wherever they are. The other three—Mirjana, Jakov and Ivanka—have received all ten secrets, and Mother Mary appears to them once a year and will do so for the rest of their lives. Mary has also been appearing to Mirjana on the second of each month since August 2,

1987, for the express purpose of praying for all unbelievers.
39. Father Tomislav Vlasic's December 1983 report, in René Laurentin and Ljudevit Rupcic, *Is the Virgin Mary Appearing at Medjugorje?* (Word Among Us Press), appendix 1; and Joseph A. Pelletier, *The Queen of Peace Visits Medugorje* (Worcester, Mass.: Assumption Publication, 1985), p. 138.
40. John 8:12; 9:5.
41. Matt. 5:14.
42. Matt. 5:15–16.
43. John 9:4.
44. Vlasic, 1983 report, in Laurentin and Rupcic, *Is the Virgin Mary Appearing at Medjugorje?* appendix 1; and Pelletier, *Queen of Peace Visits Medugorje,* pp. 138–39.
45. Father Tomislav Vlasic's report to Pope John Paul II, December 1983.
46. Mother Mary, May 11, 1987, *Pearls of Wisdom,* vol. 30, no. 23, June 7, 1987.
47. Matt. 2:13.
48. Mother Mary, May 11, 1987, *Pearls of Wisdom,* vol. 30, no. 23, June 7, 1987.
49. See Elizabeth Clare Prophet's *The Lost Years of Jesus* and *The Lost Teachings of Jesus.*
50. Matt. 7:15.
51. I Cor. 15:52.
52. II Pet. 3:10, 12.
53. This lecture was delivered on October 31, 1987, in Minneapolis, Minnesota.

The Violet Flame
1. A decree is a dynamic form of spoken prayer used by students of the ascended masters to direct God's light into individual and world conditions to produce constructive change. A decree is defined as a foreordaining will, an edict or fiat, an authoritative decision, declaration, a law, ordinance or religious rule; a command or commandment. The word *decree,* when used as a verb, can mean to decide, to declare, to determine or order; to ordain, to command or enjoin; to invoke the presence of God, his light-energy-consciousness, his power and protection,

purity and perfection.

It is written in the Book of Job, "Thou shalt decree a thing, and it shall be established unto thee: and the light shall shine upon thy ways." The decree is the most powerful of all applications to the Godhead. It is the "Command ye me" of Isaiah 45:11, the original command to light, which, as the "Lux fiat," is the birthright of the sons and daughters of God. It is the authoritative Word of God spoken in man by the name of the I AM Presence and the living Christ to bring about constructive change on earth through the will of God and his consciousness come, on earth as it is in heaven—in manifestation here below as Above.

The dynamic decree offered as praise and petition to the LORD God in the Science of the Spoken Word is the "effectual fervent prayer of the righteous" that availeth much. The dynamic decree is the means whereby the supplicant identifies with the Word of God, even the original fiat of the Creator, "Let there be light: and there was light." Through the dynamic decree spoken with joy and love, faith and hope in God's covenants fulfilled, the supplicant receives the engrafting of the Word and experiences the transmutation by the sacred fire of the Holy Spirit, the "trial by fire" whereby all sin, disease and death are consumed, yet the righteous soul is preserved.

The decree is the alchemist's tool and technique for personal and planetary transmutation and self-transcendence. The decree may be short or long and is usually marked by a formal preamble and a closing or acceptance. See *The Science of the Spoken Word,* Mark L. Prophet and Elizabeth Clare Prophet. See also Job 22:28; Gen. 1:3; James 1:21; 5:16; I Cor. 3:13–15; I Pet. 1:7.

Chapter 8 – Man, Woman, Become Who You Really Are

1. The word *manu* is Sanskrit for the progenitor and lawgiver of the evolutions of God on earth. The manu and his divine complement are ascended twin flames assigned by the Father-Mother God to sponsor and ensoul the Christic image for a certain evolution or lifewave that is known as a root race—souls who embody as a group and have a unique archetypal

pattern, divine plan and mission to fulfill on earth. According to esoteric tradition, there are seven primary aggregations of souls, i.e., the first to the seventh root races. The first three root races lived in purity and innocence upon earth in three golden ages before the Fall of Adam and Eve. Through obedience to cosmic law and total identification with the Real Self, these three root races won their immortal freedom and ascended from earth.

It was during the time of the fourth root race, on the continent of Lemuria, that the allegorical Fall took place under the influence of the fallen angels known as Serpents (because they used the serpentine spinal energies to beguile the soul, or female principle in mankind, as a means to their end of lowering the masculine potential, thereby emasculating the Sons of God).

The fourth, fifth and sixth root races remain in embodiment on earth today. The seventh root race is destined to incarnate on the continent of South America in the Aquarian age under their manus, the Great Divine Director and his divine complement. The God and Goddess Meru are the manus for the sixth root race, Vaivasvata Manu with his consort is the manu of the fifth root race, and Lord Himalaya with his Beloved is the manu for the fourth.

The manus are God-parents for each root race. They respond instantaneously to the call of their children with the comforting presence of their light. Their presence is endued with such great power-wisdom-love as to quiver the ethers and make each little one feel at home in the arms of God even in the darkest hour.

2. Jesus, Mary and many saints study in the retreat of the God and Goddess Meru, the Temple of Illumination in the etheric plane over Lake Titicaca. For a profile of the God and Goddess Meru and the description of their retreat, see *The Masters and Their Retreats,* pp. 222–27 and 478–80.
3. Ps. 110:4.
4. Dictations from this June 1974 seminar, *Family Designs for the Golden Age,* are available on CD-on-Demand. This seminar focused on the family, the relationship of man and woman on the Path and the raising of children.

5. Rev. 17:1–6.
6. Luke 22:53.
7. John 9:39.
8. Luke 2:35.
9. This lecture was delivered on October 11, 1975, during the conference, *Until the New Day,* in San Francisco, California.

Chapter 9 – The Fourteenth Rosary

1. These rosaries are published in *Mary's Message for a New Day* and *Mary's Message of Divine Love* by Mark L. Prophet and Elizabeth Clare Prophet.
2. Founded in 1961 by Saint Germain, the Keepers of the Flame Fraternity is an organization of ascended masters and their chelas who vow to keep the Flame of Life on earth and to support the activities of the Great White Brotherhood. Visit www.tsl.org/AboutUs/keepers.asp for information on how to become a Keeper of the Flame.
3. John 17.
4. John 17:1.
5. This lecture was delivered on October 11, 1975, during the conference, *Until the New Day,* in San Francisco, California.

Chapter 10 – The Outline of The Fourteenth Rosary

1. Rev. 1:8.
2. Matt. 6:9–13.
3. See the Chart of Your Divine Self, p. 95.
4. Exod. 3:13–15.
5. Mark L. Prophet (1918–1973) was trained by the ascended master El Morya to be a messenger for the Great White Brotherhood. In 1958, under El Morya's direction, he founded The Summit Lighthouse as an organization dedicated to the publishing of the teachings of the ascended masters. In 1961, he was joined in this work by his twin flame, Elizabeth. Mark made his ascension on February 26, 1973, and is now the ascended master Lanello. As Lanello, he continues to direct the activities of The Summit Lighthouse, the "Ever-Present Guru" who has said, "Ours must be a message of infinite love and we must

demonstrate that love to the world." Annice Booth introduces us to Mark Prophet in her book *Memories of Mark: My Life with Mark Prophet*.
6. Rev. 12:10.
7. The Book of Revelation is a revelation that John the Beloved says Jesus gave him, "sent and signified" by his Angel of Revelation. Revelation is a study in the psychology of the soul and a prophecy of the tests we all must master on our path leading to reunion with God. Jesus' teaching to us reveals the kingdom of God as the consciousness of God experienced individually as its mysteries unfold through Christic initiation and the baptism by sacred fire. As one puts on and dwells in this state of God's consciousness, i.e., God's kingdom, the elements (karma) of the "anti-kingdom" come to naught. These are recorded in the subconscious (as well as in the collective unconscious of the race as world karma) and are described by John in Revelation as the challenge to be met on the battlefield of the psyche by every living soul.
8. II Cor. 6:16.

Chapter 11 – The Mystery of Surrender

1. Matt. 5:48.
2. Ps. 70:4.

Chapter 12 – A Child's Rosary to Mother Mary

1. The first of Mother Mary's three requests given to the children at Fátima is for *prayer*, most particularly the rosary.
2. This dictation was given on March 22, 1978.

Chapter 13 – The Healing Science of the Mother

1. For a description of Mary's embodiment on Atlantis, see *The Masters and Their Retreats*, p. 211.
2. Matt. 26:36–41. Remembering the hours when his heart was heavy for the burdens of the world, the ascended master Jesus Christ has offered to watch with God's children as they go through the trials that he passed through. The "Watch With Me" Jesus Vigil of the Hours was dictated by Jesus as his

offering to a world still fraught with chaos, war, pride, superstition and ignorance. By keeping this vigil, sons and daughters of God may pledge their love and faithfulness to watch with Jesus one hour each week as atonement for those who have failed to do so. The service is available on the "Watch With Me" Jesus' Vigil of the Hours audiotape and booklet.
3. Luke 21:19.
4. Matt. 11:30.
5. On November 27, 1830, Mother Mary appeared to twenty-four-year-old Catherine Labouré, a novice with the Sisters of Charity in Paris. In her account of the visitation Catherine reported, "I saw rings on her fingers, three rings to each finger, the largest one near the base of the finger, one of medium size in the middle, the smallest one at the tip. Each ring was set with gems, some more beautiful than others; the larger gems emitted greater rays and the smaller gems, smaller rays." Catherine said Mother Mary explained to her that the gems "are the symbols of the graces I shed upon those who ask for them.... The gems from which rays do not fall are the graces for which souls forget to ask." In this apparition, the Blessed Mother detailed for Catherine the images she wanted placed on the front and back of what has come to be known as the "Miraculous Medal." She instructed Catherine that the medal was to be worn around the neck and said, "Graces will abound for those who wear it with confidence." See Delaney, *A Woman Clothed with the Sun*, pp. 77–78.
6. Mark 9:35.
7. This dictation was given during *The New Atlanta* seminar, Atlanta, Georgia, September 2, 1973.

Chapter 14 – The Hallowed Circle

1. Heb.12:2.
2. See Cosmic Egg, p. 326, chap. 5, no. 1.
3. Matt.10:14; Mark 6:11.
4. Hab. 2:14.
5. This dictation by Mother Mary was given during the weekend seminar, *Family Designs for the Golden Age*, in Burbank, California, on June 16, 1974.

Chapter 15 – The Mother Ray as the Instrument of the Soul's Transition into the New Day

1. Acts 9:1–9.
2. Acts 9:4, 5.
3. Rev. 19:14.
4. Rev. 16:16.
5. Isa. 54:5.
6. Moses carried a shepherd's crook, the symbol of the life force in man. It became the rod of authority that the LORD God gave to Moses (Gen. 4:17–21; 7; 9:23), and wielded by Aaron, that swallowed up the serpents of Egyptian black magic and sorcery and would become the fiery caduceus. This 'serpent' force is the coil of light that rises on the spinal altar, the energy that rises as a funnel of fire in the hollow of the spine, the coolness and the hotness of the sacred fire breath ascending and descending as the fountain of life. It is the rod of attainment denoting that the chosen one has raised the light of the Mother from the base of the spine unto the crown chakra and sealed it in the third eye.
7. John 14:6.
8. Matt. 28:20.
9. This dictation was delivered during the seminar, *Until the New Day*, in San Francisco, California, on October 11, 1975. It is published as The Radiant Word, *Pearls of Wisdom*, vol. 23, no. 27.

Chapter 16 – I Would Free You

1. See Part One, chap. 2.
2. This dictation was delivered during the seminar, *On the Mother*, on November 29, 1981, in Los Angeles County, California. It is published in *Pearls of Wisdom*, vol. 24, no. 78.

Chapter 17 – The Betrayal and the Victory

1. Luke 22:3–6; John 13:27.
2. Matt. 4:1, 2; Mark 1:12, 13; Luke 4:1, 2.
3. Matt. 4:1–11. See also *Pearls of Wisdom*, vol. 26, p. 50.
4. John 14:30.

5. Eve, or *Chavvah* in Hebrew, is translated as "life-giver," from the root *chavah* "to live"—hence "mother of all living" (Gen. 3:20). According to H. P. Blavatsky, *Ieva*, or *"heva,"* is a transliteration from ancient Hebrew for the name *Eve* (pronounced ha'va or ya'va) and is contained within the Hebrew name for God *Jehovah*—or *"Jodheva"* (*Jod* or *Yodh*, meaning "Adam"; and *heva*, meaning "Eve"). See *The Secret Doctrine* (vol. II, pp. 128–30, 467, 469) and *Isis Unveiled* (vol. I, p. 579; vol. II, pp. 269, 462–63), Theosophical University Press, 1963 and 1972.
6. John 13:27.
7. Mark 14:27–31, 66–72.
8. Matt. 27:3–5.
9. The Science of the Spoken Word is the science of invoking the light of God to produce constructive change in oneself and the world. Practitioners use the Science of the Spoken Word in affirmations, spoken prayers and mantras to access divine energy from the Christ Self, the I AM Presence and the ascended masters and direct it into spiritual, mental and physical conditions.

The spoken Word is the Word of the LORD God released in the fiats of creation. The spoken Word is the means of the release of the energies of the Word, or the Logos, through the throat chakra by the Sons of God in confirmation of that lost Word. It is written, "By thy words thou shalt be justified, and by thy words thou shalt be condemned" (Matt. 12:37). When man and woman reconsecrate the throat chakra in the affirmation of the Word of God, they become the instruments of God's own commandments that fulfill the law of their re-creation after the image of the Son.

Disciples use the power of the Word in decrees, affirmations, prayers and mantras to draw the essence of the sacred fire from the I AM Presence, the Christ Self and cosmic beings to channel God's light into matrices of transmutation and transformation for constructive change in the planes of Matter. The Science of the Spoken Word (together with that of the immaculate concept) is the essential and key ingredient in all alchemy. Without the Word spoken, there is no alchemy, no creation, no change or interchange in any part of life. It is the alchemist's white stone, which, when successfully applied by the secrets of the heart flame, reveals the "new name written, which no man knoweth saving he that receiveth it" (Rev. 2:17). Blessed is he that overcometh the carnal mind's opposition to the exercise—the practice that makes perfect—of the Science of the Spoken Word in the offering of daily dynamic decrees unto the LORD, for unto him shall the Holy Spirit "give to eat of the hidden manna" (Rev. 2:17).

The master of the Aquarian age, Saint Germain, teaches his disciples to invoke by the power of the spoken Word the violet flame for forgiveness of sins and for the baptism of the sacred fire in preparation for transition into the Higher Consciousness of God. See Mark L. Prophet and Elizabeth Clare Prophet, *The Science of the Spoken Word*.

10. John 14:30.
11. John 9:5.
12. Rev. 3:11.
13. John 9:4.
14. The fourteen stations of the cross depict the events from the time when Jesus is condemned to death, to when he is laid in the sepulchre. These are fourteen key events in Jesus' walking the way of the cross.

    The fourteen stations of the cross are known as the *via dolorosa*, the "sorrowful way." This is the description of the observer. It is not the description of the one who is passing through the initiation; for the one who passes through is in supreme joy and passion.

    The fourteen stations of the cross are a coil of energy that unwinds, and they are also the spiral of energy whereby we build the divine momentum of our attainment and of our initiation on the Path. God has not ordained that we should face the full energy and weight of our entire past karma in one day, and therefore, he unwinds that coil of energy increment by increment—as Jesus tells us, "Sufficient unto the day is the evil thereof" (Matt. 6:34).

The initiation of each station is to take that energy and demand that it be transmuted by the sacred fire according to the nature of the initiation of that station. That which cannot stand the trial by fire in love is consumed by the Holy Ghost, by the violet flame, and that which can stand is sealed for eternity. See *The Path of the Universal Christ*, Elizabeth Clare Prophet, pp. 193–213.

15. This dictation was given during the *Conclave of the Friends of Christ*, in Los Angeles County, California, on April 1, 1983. It is published in *Pearls of Wisdom*, vol. 26, no. 28, July 10, 1983.

Chapter 18 – Keeping the Vigil

1. See El Morya, October 30, 1983, "A Cosmic Necessity."
2. II Cor. 12:9.
3. John 7:38.
4. Rev. 3:11.
5. See Elizabeth Clare Prophet, *Predict Your Future: Understand the Cycles of the Cosmic Clock*.
6. The two post-war German states became one on October 3, 1990, seven years after this dictation by Mother Mary. That event, seen with the benefit of hindsight, was as much the starting point as the culmination of the process of unification. During the forty years they existed side by side, the Federal Republic of Germany and the German Democratic Republic developed very different political, economic and social institutions. Establishing the terms of political union proceeded quickly in the months following the collapse of the GDR's communist order in late 1989. Uniting Germany economically and socially, on the other hand, has been more complicated and has demanded more time than many had expected during the excitement of 1989–90. Even as the eastern and western halves of the country come to share increasingly more in common, German unification remains a work in progress.
7. This dictation was delivered on December 24, 1983, in Los Angeles County, California. It is published in *Pearls of Wisdom*, vol. 27, no. 2, January 8, 1984.

Chapter 19 – The Continuity of Being: "Come and Pray with Me"

1. In the service before this dictation, the messenger gave a sermon on II Corinthians 12—"The Message of Paul: Unspeakable Words Not Lawful to Utter"—and then invited the congregation to join hands to form Mother Mary's Circle of Light for the healing and protection of the United States of America. During the Circle of Light ceremony, the messenger led prayers, hymns, mantras and meditations on the Blessed Mother's diamond heart, invoking her intercession specifically in the Twin Cities, Los Angeles and Washington, D.C.; in the U.S. government, economy and defense; in Canada and Central America; and for the overturning of World Communism and the entire drug conspiracy against our youth.
2. Matt. 7:3–5; Luke 6:41, 42.
3. Matt. 24:28; Luke 17:37.
4. See Jesus and Magda, December 7, 1984, *Pearls of Wisdom*, vol. 27, no. 62, December 26, 1984.
5. *The Lost Years of Jesus* by Elizabeth Clare Prophet brings together the chronicles of what Jesus did and said during this time prior to his Palestinian mission.
6. The Higher Self is the I AM Presence and the Christ Self. It is one's innate higher consciousness, the exalted aspect of Selfhood. The term Higher Self is used in contrast to the term "lower self," or "little self," which indicates the soul that went forth from and may elect by free will to return to the Divine Whole through the realization of the oneness of the Self in God. Higher Self also refers to higher consciousness.
7. This dictation was delivered during the seminar, *Healing through the Emerald Matrix,* Minneapolis, Minnesota, December 9, 1984. It is published in *Pearls of Wisdom*, vol. 27, no. 63, December 30, 1984.

Chapter 20 – The Vow to Heal a Planet: Study the Healing Arts at Fátima

1. See *Lords of the Seven Rays: Mirror of Consciousness* by Mark L. Prophet and Elizabeth Clare Prophet.

2. For a description of Mary and Raphael's retreat, see *The Masters and Their Retreats,* Mark L. Prophet and Elizabeth Clare Prophet, p. 456.
3. Ibid., pp. 486–88.
4. Jude 4; Eph. 6:12.
5. Matt. 10:8.
6. This dictation was delivered at the Los Angeles Whole Life Expo, Pasadena, California, February 8, 1987. It is published in *Pearls of Wisdom,* vol. 30, no. 7, February 15, 1987.

Chapter 21 – I Stand By You: Champion the Cause of the Child!

1. The Fourteen Stations in the Aquarian Age. The four cardinal points of God are Father, Son, Holy Spirit and Mother. In each age, one of these cardinal points passes through the crucifixion. Since God is one, all of these elements are present in any manifestation of God, but the emphasis today is the crucifixion of Mother. It is the Divine Mother and her children on planet Earth today who are being crucified. It is woman and it is the life force and the sacred fire, the Kundalini itself, that is being assaulted, condemned and crucified. And it is the body of the Mother—the body of man and woman.

    In the Piscean dispensation, Jesus walked these stations for the initiation of the Christ and of the masculine ray. In the age of Aquarius, it is the Mother and her children who walk the fourteen stations. This was why Jesus said, when he came to the eighth station, "Weep not for me, ye daughters of Jerusalem, but weep for yourselves and for your children" (Luke 23:28). He knew that the mothers and their children would reincarnate to see the day when they themselves would be walking through these fourteen stations.

    Thus it says in the twelfth chapter of the Book of Revelation that when the dragon was cast down into the earth, he attacked the woman who was coming to give birth to the Manchild. And so the attack against woman, against Mother, against the feminine principle within man and woman is rampant. And today is the day when woman is intended to bear the cross of her own karma and of world karma and to teach her children how to do the same. It is the day when the feminine principle in man rises and challenges his karma of the misuse of the feminine energy.

The Fourteen Stations of the Aquarian Cross: (1) The Woman and her seed are condemned to death; (2) The Woman and her seed are made to bear their cross; (3) The Woman and her seed fall the first time; (4) The Woman and her seed meet their afflicted mother; (5) Simon the Cyrenian helps the Woman and her seed bear their cross; (6) Veronica wipes the face of the Woman and her seed; (7) The Woman and her seed fall the second time; (8) The Woman and her seed console the holy women; (9) The Woman and her seed fall the third time; (10) The Woman and her seed are stripped of their garments; (11) The Woman and her seed are nailed to the cross; (12) The Woman and her seed die on the cross; (13) The Woman and her seed are taken down from the cross, and (14) The Woman and her seed are laid in the tomb. See *The Path of the Universal Christ,* Mark L. and Elizabeth Clare Prophet, pp. 210–12.
2. Exod. 20:5, 6; 34:6, 7; Num. 14:18; Deut. 5:9, 10.
3. For additional ascended master teachings on abortion, see *Wanting to Be Born: The Cry of the Soul,* compiled by Dr. Neroli Duffy. Lectures by the messenger presented during the March 30, 1991, *Life Begets Life* seminar are available on CD-on-Demand.
4. A number of films have been produced showing the life of the newborn in the womb, including *Ultrasound: "Eyewitness to the Earliest Days of Life"* (Educational Center for Life), *The Miracle of Life* (WGBH Educational Foundation) and *The Silent Scream* (American Portrait Films).
5. The ascended master Lanello sponsors the Order of the Holy Child for the defense and protection of the little child. He inaugurated the order in his final embodiment as Mark L. Prophet in 1952 for legislators, rulers, directors of culture and citizens who would promise to be "ever-mindful of the little child of the future." Education of the child and teaching them how to give and receive love is an important focus of the order, as well as giving guidance to the child in the development of

the heart to pursue their goal in life. Membership in the order is open to anyone who chooses to become an advocate for the child by signing a pledge and devoting one minute a day to reading it. See www.holyorders.org.

6. This dictation was delivered during the seminar, *How to Contact Angels*, Chicago, Illinois, February 27, 1993.

Chapter 22 – The Gift of a Mother's Heart: The Mystery of the Fifteenth Rosary

1. This spiritual board dispenses justice to this system of worlds, adjudicating karma, mercy and judgment on behalf of every lifestream. All souls pass before the Karmic Board before and after each incarnation on earth to receive their assignment and karmic allotment for each lifetime beforehand and the review of their performance at its conclusion. These Lords of Karma determine who shall embody, as well as when and where. They assign souls to families and communities, measuring out the weights of karma that must be balanced. The Karmic Board originally consisted of seven ascended beings: the Great Divine Director, the Goddess of Liberty, the Elohim Cyclopea and the ascended lady masters Nada, Pallas Athena, Portia and Kuan Yin. (On December 30, 1993, the Dhyani Buddha Vairochana announced that, by special dispensation, he was accepted as the eighth member of the Karmic Board.) For profiles on each of the Lords of Karma, see *The Masters and Their Retreats*.

2. The ascended masters Jesus and Kuthumi currently hold the office in hierarchy of World Teachers. Serving under Lord Maitreya, they are responsible for setting forth the teachings and sponsor all souls seeking union with God. In every nation on earth, they have inspired teachers, philosophers, scientists, artists, professional and nonprofessional people with the wisdom of the ages as it applies to each particular culture, even as the many cultures of the world serve to bring forth the many facets of the Christ consciousness. For additional teaching on the World Teachers, see *Saint Germain On Alchemy: Formulas for Self-Transformation*, recorded by Mark L. Prophet and

Elizabeth Clare Prophet, pp. 462–63.
3. When the opportunity for the ascension comes to an individual, at the very hour when he has reached the balance of 51 percent of his karma, he is brought (in his etheric body) before the Lords of Karma that he might make the decision to take his ascension or to enter into another round of service.
4. Gen. 18:14; Jer. 32:17, 27.
5. Matt. 17:1–13.
6. *Ishwara:* from the Sanskrit, meaning master or lord.
7. The stations of the cross correspond to the stations of the hierarchies of the sun. Listed in the dictation are the perversions of the God consciousness of the solar hierarchies on each line of the cosmic clock. For further information, see Elizabeth Clare Prophet, *Predict Your Future: Understand the Cycles of the Cosmic Clock.*
8. Matt. 28:18.
9. Matt. 9:37, 38; Luke 10:2.
10. Gen. 22:1–18.
11. Matt. 13:33; 26:26; John 6:35; Rev. 2:17.
12. The ascended lady master Maria Montessori, the Messenger of Education, set forth the fundamentals of ascended master education for the Aquarian age in her final embodiment. She developed what became known as the Montessori Method, inspired upon her by Mother Mary. Mary has explained that she and Elisabeth devised this method for teaching John the Baptist and Jesus when they were children. See *The Masters and Their Retreats,* pp. 209–11.
13. This dictation was delivered on March 19, 1980 in Los Angeles, California. It is published in *Pearls of Wisdom,* vol. 23, no. 27, July 6, 1980.

Chapter 23 – The Hour of the Mother's Crucifixion

1. *Christus:* Latin for "Christ," from Greek *Christos,* literally "anointed." During the Feast of the Resurrection Flame, the messenger read from *Christus: A Mystery,* "The Divine Tragedy," by Henry Wadsworth Longfellow.
2. See chap. 20.
3. Matt. 26:39; Mark 14:36; Luke 22:42.

4. Refers to a mount, or chain of mountains, on which Moses received the Law. The northern part of this chain was called Horeb; the southern, Sinai. See Exod. 19: 1, 2; Num. 1:1; Lev. 7:38.
5. John 9:39.
6. Song of Sol. 2:1.
7. Gal. 4:19.
8. Refers to hunger strikes by imprisoned terrorists in West Germany and Northern Ireland, which resulted in the death of Sigurd Debus. Debus, 38, of West Germany's Red Army Faction, died April 16, 1981, in Hamburg after a twenty-four-month hunger strike which he and twenty-three other convicted terrorists staged to protest solitary confinement and to demand treatment as prisoners of war.
9. Isa. 7:14; Matt. 1:23.
10. Ezek. 34; John 10:1–16.
11. See Rev. 6:1–8 (Four Horsemen of the Apocalypse); Rev. 21:4.
12. John 10:17, 18.
13. Isa. 53:5; Matt. 26:28; Heb. 9:22.
14. I John 4:18.
15. Matt. 16:21; 17:22, 23.
16. According to Luke (23:39–43), one of the malefactors repents and believes, saying unto Jesus, "Lord, remember me when thou comest into thy kingdom." Matthew (27:39–44) states, however, that while "they that passed by reviled him,... likewise also the chief priests mocking him,... the thieves also, which were crucified with him, cast the same in his teeth." The archives of the Brotherhood reveal that some of the accounts set forth in the Book of Luke are unreliable. See also Mark 15:30.
17. Rev. 12:7–12.
18. Rev. 13:8.
19. Matt. 25:6.
20. John 6:29.
21. Col. 2:9.
22. The Deathless Solar Body is the ascended master light body. It is also the wedding garment that the soul must weave through

devotion to God if she is to enter into the alchemical marriage (the soul's permanent bonding to the Holy Christ Self) and the ritual of the ascension.

23. "In the beginning was Brahman with whom was the Word. And the Word is Brahman." The *Vedas*. See also John 1:1.

24. This dictation was delivered on April 17, 1981, in Los Angeles County, California. It is published in *Pearls of Wisdom*, vol. 24, no. 17, April 26, 1981.

Picture Credits

Cover: *Madonna of the Chair,* by Raphael, Galleria Palatina, Palazzo Pitti, Florence, Italy, Alinari / Art Resource, NY.

p. 9 *The Virgin and Child with Saint John and an Angel* (a detail from), by Sandro Botticelli, © National Gallery, London.

p. 11 *Madonna and Child with Two Angels* (detail), by Fra Filippo Lippi, Uffizi, Florence, Italy, Erich Lessing / Art Resource, NY.

p. 155 *The Madonna Standing Holding the Child Who Imparts His Blessing,* by Giovanni Francesco Guercino, Galleria Sabauda, Turin, Italy, Alinari / Art Resource, NY.

p. 204 *Madonna of the Veil,* by Carlo Dolci, Palazzo Corsini, Rome, Italy, Alinari / Art Resource, NY.

p. 226 *Mother of the World,* by Nicholas Roerich, Nicholas Roerich Museum, New York.

p. 253 *Seated Guanyin Bodhisattva,* Chinese, Liao Dynasty (907-1125). Wood with paint, 95 x 65 inches (241.3 x 165.1 cm). The Nelson-Atkins Museum of Art, Kansas City, Missouri. Purchase: Nelson Trust, 34–10. Photograph by Robert Newcombe.

Other Titles from
SUMMIT UNIVERSITY ☙ PRESS

Maitreya on Initiation

Fallen Angels and the Origins of Evil

Mary Magdalene and the Divine Feminine

Saint Germain's Prophecy for the New Millennium

The Lost Years of Jesus

The Lost Teachings of Jesus (4 vols.)

Inner Perspectives

Keys to the Kingdom

The Human Aura

Saint Germain On Alchemy

The Science of the Spoken Word

Kabbalah: Key to Your Inner Power

Reincarnation: The Missing Link in Christianity

Quietly Comes the Buddha

Lords of the Seven Rays

Prayer and Meditation

Corona Class Lessons

The Chela and the Path

Mysteries of the Holy Grail

Dossier on the Ascension

The Path to Your Ascension

Understanding Yourself

Secrets of Prosperity

The Opening of the Temple Doors

The Soulless One

The Sacred Adventure

Nurturing Your Baby's Soul

Sacred Psychology of Love

Sacred Psychology of Change

Dreams: Exploring the Secrets of Your Soul

Emotions: Transforming Anger, Fear and Pain

Soul Reflections: Many Lives, Many Journeys

A Spiritual Approach to Parenting

CLIMB THE HIGHEST MOUNTAIN® SERIES:

The Path of the Higher Self

The Path of Self-Transformation

The Masters and the Spiritual Path

The Path of Brotherhood

The Path of the Universal Christ

Paths of Light and Darkness

The Path to Immortality

The Masters and Their Retreats

*Predict Your Future:
Understand the Cycles of the Cosmic Clock*

POCKET GUIDES
TO PRACTICAL SPIRITUALITY:

Alchemy of the Heart

Your Seven Energy Centers

Soul Mates and Twin Flames

How to Work with Angels

Creative Abundance

Violet Flame to Heal Body, Mind and Soul

The Creative Power of Sound

Access the Power of Your Higher Self

The Art of Practical Spirituality

Karma and Reincarnation

THE SUMMIT LIGHTHOUSE LIBRARY®:

The Opening of the Seventh Seal

Community

Morya I

Walking with the Master: Answering the Call of Jesus

Strategies of Light and Darkness

The Enemy Within

Wanting to Be Born

Wanting to Live

Afra: Brother of Light

Saint Germain: Master Alchemist

Hilarion the Healer

Publications of Summit University Press that display this crest are the authentic Teachings of the Ascended Masters as given to the world by Mark L. Prophet and Elizabeth Clare Prophet.

For More Information

Summit University Press books are available at fine bookstores worldwide and at your favorite online bookseller.

For a free catalog of our books and products or to learn more about the spiritual techniques featured in this book, please contact:

Summit University Press
PO Box 5000, Gardiner, MT 59030-5000 USA
Telephone: 1-800-245-5445 or 406-848-9500
Fax: 1-800-221-8307 or 406-848-9555
www.summituniversitypress.com
info@summituniversitypress.com

ELIZABETH CLARE PROPHET is a world-renowned author. Among her best sellers are *Fallen Angels and the Origins of Evil, Saint Germain's Prophecy for the New Millennium,* her 10-book series Pocket Guides to Practical Spirituality including *How to Work with Angels, Soul Mates and Twin Flames,* and *Alchemy of the Heart;* and *The Lost Years of Jesus: Documentary Evidence of Jesus' 17-Year Journey to the East.* She has pioneered techniques in practical spirituality, including the use of the creative power of sound for personal growth and world transformation. Her books have been translated into more than twenty languages.

Printed in the United States
65452LVS00003B/178-192